Religion and the South
JOHN B. BOLES, SERIES EDITOR

God's Rascal

J. Frank Norris & the Beginnings of Southern Fundamentalism

BARRY HANKINS

THE UNIVERSITY PRESS OF KENTUCKY

Scholarly publisher for the Commonwealth,
serving Bellarmine College, Berea College, Centre
College of Kentucky, Eastern Kentucky University,
The Filson Club, Georgetown College, Kentucky
Historical Society, Kentucky State University, Morehead
State University, Murray State University, Northern
Kentucky University, Transylvania University,
University of Kentucky, University of Louisville,
and Western Kentucky University.

Editorial and Sales Offices: The University Press of Kentucky
663 South Limestone Street, Lexington, Kentucky 40508-4008

Library of Congress Cataloging-in-Publication Data

Hankins, Barry, 1956-
 God's rascal : J. Frank Norris and the Beginnings of Southern
fundamentalism / Barry Hankins.
     p.   cm. — (Religion and the South ; 2)
 Includes bibliographical references and index.
 ISBN 0-8131-1985-5 (alk. paper)
 1. Norris, J. Frank (John Frank), 1877-1952.   2. Baptists—United
States—Clergy—Biography.   3. Fundamentalism—Biography.
I. Title.   II. Series.
BX6495.N59H36   1996
286'.1'092—dc20
[B]   96-6117

Manufactured in the United States of America

Contents

Acknowledgments ‖

Citing individuals and groups that have been influential in the writing of this book is certainly not to suggest that the work's shortcomings can be attributed to anyone but me. Rather, such is merely an acknowledgment of the debt I owe to so many. Without the input and encouragement of those cited below, this book would never have seen the light of day.

While not meaning to list a rank order of contributors, I do need to cite first Robert Linder, who served as my "critic and guide" while I was working on a Ph.D. degree at Kansas State University. Kansas Bob was my major professor throughout my doctoral program, which included the period when I first began research on Norris. While there are certainly universities whose names carry more prestige, I am convinced there is no place where I could have received better scholarly training than in the history department at K-State under Bob Linder. (He also plays a mean second base.)

Before entering doctoral work I was helped along considerably at Baylor University, especially by James Wood, director of the J.M. Dawson Institute of Church-State Studies, where I did my masters degree work. As an undergraduate I had been what is called, euphemistically, a student-athlete, usually more the latter than the former, and it was in my master's work that I first aspired to high academic achievement. During my studies under Professor Wood I saw for the first time how a true scholar works and lives. It was also at Baylor, in a seminar with Rufus Spain, that I began to learn the difference between everyday writing and scholarly writing. In the past decade Rufus has been a mentor-friend to me, and according to what I am told at Louisiana College, he writes good recommendation letters. Some of my former colleagues have been so blunt as to suggest that without his letter in 1990, I would never have gotten my first college position.

Several individuals read parts of the manuscript and rendered advice of various kinds. Among these are Bill Leonard, Morgan Patterson, and the series editor John Boles. The latter was gracious enough to ask to see the manuscript while on the campus at Louisiana College in 1994 for a lecture. Boles's recommendation that I pay more attention to Norris's racial views was critical and greatly appreciated. Also, C. Allyn Russell, after serving anonymously as a referee for an article I wrote, was kind enough to write a letter encouraging me to pursue a full biography of Norris.

In terms of research assistance, I owe a public thanks to Kent Keeth and Ellen Brown at the Baylor University Texas Collection. Both were extremely helpful and supportive. For several consecutive summers I felt as though I worked at the Texas Collection full-time with them, and they never once complained about the clacking of my typewriter as I pounded out note after note while reading Norris's newspaper. They also led me to sources that I might not have found if left to my own devices.

While at Louisiana College I received a summer sabbatical from the Walker Endowment as well as the encouragement and interest of several of my colleagues in the history department and in other departments of the college as well. So, thanks to "da group."

It has been a pleasure working with the folks at the University Press of Kentucky. Thanks to all of them, and to freelance copy-editor Elaine Otto. I feel as though I know you all, virtually at least.

Finally, and most important, I acknowledge my dept of gratitude to my parents and family. Bob and Shirley Hankins always took seriously the dreams and aspirations of their children and never once laughed when told their son was going to be a professor. Jennifer, D.J., and JoJo, my own family now, always help me remember what is most important in life. The latter two keep me humble by reminding me that in college their mom was a better student than I was and that, so far, they are too. I owe a huge debt to Jennifer, who has delayed her terminal degree far too long so that I could get a career started. It is to these three, the dearest in all my life, that this book is dedicated.

Introduction ‖

J.Frank Norris was one of the most controversial figures in the history of Christianity in America. Loved by most fundamentalists and very nearly hated by mainline Southern Baptists, he was hardly ever ignored. Such controversial individuals and movements are always difficult to interpret. With regard to Norris, this difficulty has been compounded by recent developments in the Southern Baptist Convention. As the conservative wing of the SBC has come to dominate the denomination, Norris has become even more important. He was in a very real sense the SBC's first fundamentalist, yet Norris was so extreme in many of his views and actions that the new fundamentalists in the SBC are not quick to claim him.[1] Moderates, on the other hand, often consider him father of the more recent movement.

While this book is not about the SBC controversy, it would benefit no one to pretend that I could analyze Norris's life without some reference to the current state of affairs in the SBC or that I have not been influenced by recent developments in the Southern Baptist subculture. It would be a simple matter for someone to check my educational credentials and learn that I have two of my three degrees from Baylor University. While completing this book I held a position at a Baptist college (Louisiana College); I am now back at Baylor. Such would perhaps lead one to presume that I am a lifelong Southern Baptist who came to an interest in Norris because of my own moderate leanings—in other words, because I wanted to study the other side. This is not the case. I grew up neither southern nor Baptist and in fact went all the way through my student years without ever joining a Baptist church or attending one regularly. It was not until my doctoral work in the mid-eighties at a state university that I came to understand the history of the Baptist movement. Nearly every Baptist historian has emphasized as the distinctives of Baptist history some combination of the following elements: the authority of the

1

Bible, believers baptism, religious liberty, the priesthood of believers, congregational autonomy, and opposition to creedalism.

By the time I was thrust into the SBC by virtue of accepting a position at a Baptist college, I was already well into my academic work on Norris. My interest in him was primarily an extension of my interest in fundamentalism and American culture and the interplay between religion and politics. Little did I know at the time I started to do research on Norris that I would wind up teaching at a Baptist institution caught in the middle of a battle between moderates and conservatives, the latter often referred to by historians as fundamentalists. When I began to study fundamentalism seriously, I had very little knowledge of Norris. My first real introduction to him came when I began to search for a dissertation topic in the area of fundamentalism and politics. I read C. Allyn Russell's *Voices of Fundamentalism,* in which Norris is the first of Russell's seven biographical subjects.[2] Russell placed Norris in the context of national fundamentalism. The other scholarly works on Norris had been, for the most part, dissertations at Baptist institutions in which Norris was interpreted primarily as a Southern Baptist schismatic or as a Texas fundamentalist.[3] It appeared that Norris was a figure who, while well known in Southern Baptist circles, had not been given his due with regard to southern religion in general and American fundamentalism in particular. Russell himself believes that Norris warrants more attention than he has received thus far.[4]

The principal argument of this book is that Norris introduced fundamentalism in the South and thereby helped shape both the religion of his region and the fundamentalist movement nationwide. There is another important undercurrent in the work that needs to be stated explicitly. Norris was not a typical Southern Baptist. In fact, I have wondered whether he should be considered a Baptist at all.[5] Where Southern Baptists have been traditionally anticreedal, Norris was constantly attempting to force a creed on SBC institutions. Rather than church-state separation, which has been so vital to Baptist history, Norris preferred a government that officially encouraged evangelical Protestantism. In church polity, the historic Baptist distinctive has been that local congregations should be both autonomous and democratically organized. While Norris was often vigilant on the first of these, arguing that it was a violation of autonomy for the SBC to even ask his church to join a denominational effort, he ran his own congregations in the most undemocratic way imaginable. Finally, Norris showed little affinity for the Baptist principles of the priesthood of the believer and soul liberty. In his churches, seminary,

and missionary organization, teachers either taught his interpretation of the Bible or they left.

Southern Baptists have been conservative, biblicist, and revivalist since the formation of the Convention in 1845, but they have
not been, for the most part, militant defenders of theological orthodoxy or theological rationalists. Until recently, the denomination
had been controlled by moderates who focused on evangelism and
missions. They were willing to tolerate a certain amount of theological diversity, within conservative bounds to be sure, for the sake of
the great mission efforts of the denomination. Furthermore, they
feared the schismatic tendencies Norris exhibited and determined
not to allow the rightwing to capture the convention. Although the
threats were rarely from the left, it has been argued that these moderates also resisted any efforts on the part of the liberal minority to
control the denomination. For better or worse, depending on one's
point of view, moderates controlled the convention and refused to let
theological issues become divisive and thereby hinder the missionary enterprise.[6]

Since 1979, the conservatives in the Southern Baptist Convention have taken control away from the moderates. Where the moderates sought compromise, the conservatives seek theological renewal,
which has entailed the shoring up of doctrine and a drive to bring
about greater conformity. The rallying cry has been the "inerrancy of
Scripture," which has been combined with a conservative social and
political agenda. Where moderates sought unity for missions and tol-
erated diversity theologically, conservatives seek unity in theology
with inerrancy as the baseline. Clearly, Norris would have felt much
more at home with the conservatives who have taken control of the
SBC since 1979 than he did with those who led the denomination in
his own day and for another quarter century after his death. As cited
above, however, all this is not to say that the leaders of the recent
conservative resurgency in the SBC have been willing to claim him.
No movement seeking legitimacy with a large mass of people can
afford to claim a rabble-rouser like Norris as its forefather.

What should be clear, therefore, is that Norris was not prin-
cipally a Baptist schismatic. He really fits into the broader history
of American fundamentalism. His status as a Southern Baptist was
incidental and a product of geography more than theology. Only by
accident of birth in the South did he become a Southern Baptist.
It is important to note here, even though this will be stressed in
chapter 2, that Norris was a Southern Baptist almost precisely until
the advent of fundamentalism. He then became immediately part of

that first generation of religious figures for whom particular denominational labels were secondary to the name fundamentalist. The term *Southern Fundamentalist* fits Norris much more accurately than *Southern Baptist*. This is not meant to suggest, however, that he was merely a regional figure. As will be argued below, for most of his career Norris attempted to carry out a national agenda to a national audience, but he always did this with a pronounced southern accent. That is, he recognized himself as being in charge of the southern theater in a national war on modernism (liberalism) even as he attempted to take the presumably purer southern theology and mores northward in an effort to stem the tide of modernism before it reached the Mason-Dixon line.

In addition to the problem of interpreting Norris in the midst of the recent Southern Baptist controversy, there are yet other ways in which Norris is a difficult historical case. It is extremely hard to reconstruct his private and personal side. There are few sources from his childhood, and he was not a reflective person. His extant personal papers go back only to the late twenties, and he almost always dealt with public issues in his letters. There are some fragmentary glimpses here and there of Norris the family man, but even those who worked with him and knew his family seem to have little to offer us with regard to the private Norris. The paucity of sources related to his personal life may be no accident of history. For Norris, his work was his play. He was constantly plotting his next theological or political battle.

Even where Norris's adult public personality can be pieced together, he presents the historian with another peculiar problem—specifically, how to be fair to Norris. For a long time while researching and writing this work I tried to balance Norris's positive contributions and commendable efforts with his moral lapses and ethical blind spots. I finally concluded that such a balanced Norris was inaccurate. Sadly, in this book one will find an important American religious figure who often exhibited an almost complete disregard for basic standards of civility and honesty—so much so that even other fundamentalists who agreed with Norris on virtually all issues could not long tolerate his antics. Nearly every important fundamentalist with whom Norris aligned himself eventually broke ranks and denounced him. At the same time, however, he was an exciting leader who appeared to many common people as someone who spoke up for them against all kinds of entrenched elites. For this reason, he was taken seriously by thousands of followers and a host of adversaries. For the former, Norris was the hero they loved, for the latter, the villain they dared not dismiss lightly. The impact he had within American Fundamentalism makes him a figure worthy of scholarly attention, and I have attempted to take his ideas and actions seriously wherever that is possible. While I deal with the question of character specifically in chapter 6, Norris's paranoia and moral blindness always loom in the background. Unfortunately for fundamentalists of his own time, Norris helped shape the movement during its darkest years, from the Scopes trial of 1925 until the advent of the neo-evangelical movement in the forties and fifties.[7] Not coincidently, during this period the balance of power in fundamentalism shifted from the North to the South. Norris was one of the reasons for this shift.[8]

This assessment of Norris is certainly not intended to be an indictment of fundamentalism as a whole. It is never fair to evaluate a movement on the basis of its worst members, and Norris was about as bad as fundamentalists got. He was a classic case of Richard Hofstadter's "paranoid style" in politics and religion. His was a world of swirling conspiracies of leftists who intended to subvert both evangelical religion and American culture. These sinister forces were especially virile in the North, but there was still a chance to save southern culture from demise. There were times, however, when Norris's own ego loomed so large that he seemed less interested in the threat these alleged conspiracies posed than in the mileage he could get out of them in his never-ending quest to make himself famous. He relished a good fight, but it is sometimes hard to tell whether he was fighting for a higher cause or simply for the sake of publicity. Either way he seems often to have cared less about winning these battles than about keeping them going until another issue arose. In the process of hopping from one issue to another he displayed a perceptive understanding of the public's short attention span. This was especially true in his newspaper, where certain issues appeared, disappeared, and reappeared with almost seasonal regularity, as if to ensure that his readers never lost interest in an issue because of overexposure.

Throughout the many issues Norris addressed, he exhibited tremendous consistency. When fundamentalism emerged as a viable and militant movement (roughly 1920), Norris was in his early forties. In most respects, from that time forward, he displayed very little development in his thought and style. One can read his sermons from the 1920s attacking Roman Catholics and those from the 1940s attacking communists and find him saying nearly the same things about both groups. In a few areas he showed genuine development over the years—for example, on the issue of dispensationalism covered in chapter 4. Most of the changes in Norris's public theology, however, were the result of changes in circumstances and not a result of inner reflection. Even on the issue of Roman Catholicism, where Norris's attitude underwent a complete reversal, one looks in vain for a theological shift that required Norris to stop hating Catholics. Rather, he ceased his anti-Catholicism because by the 1940s he found himself and the Church on the same side of what he perceived to be the most important world issue, namely communism. It was as if Norris had two or three guns, all of the same make and model, which he used from the early twenties until his death in 1952. He could aim these at different targets, but he never contemplated changing guns or trading the guns for construction equipment. In the few areas where he attempted to be constructive, in the building of his empire including his seminary, he did so to equip others with the same weapons he possessed. The whole point was to widen the war against modernism in order to save at least the South and perhaps all of America. In the process, Norris drew heavily on the southern populist dissenter tradition and joined it with the more recent tradition of militant fundamentalism. This was a very natural combination, and Norris made it work quite well as he introduced fundamentalism in the South and brought some southernness to fundamentalism.

1

The Making of a
Populist Preacher

J.Frank Norris's career as a Baptist and fundamentalist preacher, newspaper publisher, political activist, and general controversialist spanned roughly the first half of the twentieth century. During this period he pastored simultaneously two of the largest churches in America, traveled the world, corresponded with congressmen, and attended a presidential inauguration at the invitation of a newly elected chief executive. He once shot and killed a man in his own church office and was subsequently tried for murder. On other occasions he was indicted and tried for arson and perjury in connection with the burning of his own church. Everywhere he went, controversy was sure to follow. During his lifetime, he was one of the most hated men in Southern Baptist circles and one of the most admired among fundamentalists.

Norris fits well into the tradition of populist preachers in America identified in Nathan Hatch's 1989 book, *The Democratization of American Christianity*. Hatch has argued persuasively that the populist, democratic impulse has been one of the most powerfully defining influences in the history of religion in America from the Revolutionary period to the present. Furthermore, Norris was one of the individuals who made the fundamentalist movement possible. As Hatch writes, "Had not dominant personalities sounded an alarm and begun their own popular constituencies, these movements [fundamentalism, pentecostalism, and holiness] would not have come into existence."[1]

Norris was easily one of the most influential religious personalities in America during the first half of the twentieth century. In addition to the parishioners at his Fort Worth and Detroit churches, thousands of others heard him preach as he traveled the nation holding revival services. In many of the cities he visited, he received prominent newspaper coverage, and radio listeners could hear Norris via WJR in Detroit, the city's most powerful station, as well as over a whole network of Texas radio stations that carried his impassioned messages. Norris's newspaper, the *Fundamentalist*, had subscribers across the South and in the Detroit area, and its circulation in the thirties and forties was estimated to be around forty thousand.[2] Norris also headed, or "owned" as he once put it, a seminary with about five hundred students, and he helped found and lead a fundamentalist denomination.

By the forties, Norris was a nationally known religious figure with a following quite possibly the largest of any preacher in America, and his influence extended well beyond fundamentalism. During his years in Detroit from 1935 to 1950, he became friends with various presidents and vice presidents of the three major automobile companies—General Motors, Chrysler, and Ford. His personal papers are replete with correspondence to and from them, and they sometimes supplied him with loaner cars as he traveled on crusades.

Even more important, Norris was on a first-name basis with some of the leading politicians of his era. He left behind in his files nearly one hundred pieces of correspondence between himself and Senator Tom Connally of Texas, a powerful member of the Committee on Foreign Relations. He almost always referred to Connally as Tom, and Connally usually headed his letters "Dear Frank."[3] Norris's letters to the Speaker of the House of Representatives, Sam Rayburn, were far less frequent but just as cordial as those to Connally. He also corresponded with all of the presidents from 1929 to 1952 and many of the unsuccessful presidential candidates. On one occasion he traveled to Europe bearing letters of introduction from two of President Franklin D. Roosevelt's cabinet members, one other administration official, other politicians, and public figures.

That Norris could rub shoulders with the rich and powerful without losing his place as leader of a popular movement attests to the complexity of his personality and his power of persuasion. He portrayed himself successfully as a champion of the righteous and orthodox masses of commoners against the establishment types whom he perceived to be subversive of religion, politics, and culture. In doing so, he became influential in places both high and low and was equally at home preaching in a state capitol or a tent revival. Arguably, no other fundamentalist of Norris's era had anything that even resembled his power base and influence. Although Norris's empire continued for a brief period after his death in 1952, a schism in his ranks in 1950 had already resulted in the establishment of Baptist Bible College of Springfield, Missouri, and the Baptist Bible Fellowship, both of which remain to this day as bulwarks of American fundamentalism. The most visible fundamentalist of the 1980s, Jerry Falwell, is an alumnus of the college and a product of the fellowship. The Texas wing of Norris's movement that did not join the Baptist Bible Fellowship has also survived, albeit through several more divisions, and it could be argued plausibly that the independent Baptist-fundamentalist movement in Texas and across the South can still be traced to its Norrisite origins.[4]

Up from the Frontier

Norris was born on September 18, 1877, in Dadeville, Alabama. His father, James Warner Norris, and his mother, Mary Davis Norris, maintained a marital relationship that was certainly not unique but was nearly unbearable. Mary was a devout Christian who dreamed of having a preacher son, whereas James was a hopeless alcoholic. With few prospects for success in Alabama, the family tried living in Arkansas briefly before moving to Columbiana, Alabama. In the late 1880s, the Norrises moved west to Hill County of Texas and settled in Hubbard City, a small town in the central part of the state, about thirty miles from Waco. There they purchased land and began a farm. Norris spent his teen years in Hill County before leaving for college in 1898.[5]

Norris's boyhood was brutal in many respects. Later in life, he would relate to his associates the harsh treatment he endured from his alcoholic father. Norris claimed that he was once whipped repeatedly for emptying his father's liquor bottles and that as a result he spent Christmas Day severely injured.[6] Without a doubt, the worst episode in Norris's boyhood took place in the early 1890s. Texas at this time was still a rough section of the country with gangs of horse and cattle thieves who often terrorized the populace. In 1891, Warner Norris was shot by John Shaw. Frank was working in a nearby garden when he heard the gunshots and saw his father fall to the ground. As he ran to the scene, the gunman shot Frank several times. Shaw would claim in court documents that Warner had intended to kill him, but Frank told associates throughout his life that his father had come forward with evidence against Shaw's gang and thereby earned Shaw's enmity. Shaw also claimed that at the moment he shot the boy, Frank was charging him with a knife, evidently in defense of Warner. Whatever the truth of the circumstances, Shaw was eventually sentenced to three years in prison for shooting Warner, while the charges for shooting Frank were dismissed. Warner's injuries seem to have been minor, and he recovered quickly. Frank, however, was in critical condition for a number of days and later experienced gangrene and inflammatory rheumatism. By his own recollection, Norris did not recuperate fully for three years.[7]

From time to time in history, seemingly normal circumstances produce truly extraordinary individuals. Norris's case, however, is perhaps more understandable in that he became an extraordinary personality as a result of a very atypical childhood. After all, how many young people, even on the American frontier of the 1880s and 1890s, were shot and nearly killed by outlaws? Still, nothing in Norris's childhood would have led one to predict that he would become a famous preacher and leader of a popular movement. The best explanation of Norris is that the circumstances of his childhood produced an individual determined not only to live but to succeed, and his conversion determined that he would choose the ministry as his profession.

Norris experienced an evangelical conversion at a Baptist revival meeting in the early nineties and concluded shortly thereafter that God had called him to be a preacher. He took his first pastorate at Mount Antioch Baptist Church in 1897, when he was about twenty, then the following year he entered Baylor University in Waco to begin formal training for the ministry. J.S. Tanner, a professor of biblical languages there, had served for a time as interim pastor of Norris's Hubbard City church. While Baylor was a natural choice for Norris, it may have been Tanner who convinced him to attend college at all in a day when higher education was hardly a prerequisite for aspiring Baptist pastors. At Baylor, Norris lived in a boardinghouse run by the Tanner family. Also residing there was future Texas Baptist leader Joseph Martin Dawson. Dawson and Norris would collaborate briefly on a journalistic endeavor in 1907-1908 before becoming lifelong enemies within the ranks of the Southern Baptist Convention. As pastors of two of the more influential churches in Texas, Norris and Dawson would be on opposite sides of several theological and political issues.[8]

Also, while at Baylor, Norris was involved in an event that, although comical, revealed early his penchant for controversy. During chapel time some students smuggled a dog onto the second floor of the building where the service was taking place. University president Oscar H. Cooper became so enraged when the dog would not stop howling that he seized the animal and threw it out of a window. He later apologized, but Norris refused to drop this dog defenestration incident. Instead, he led a student uprising, informing the local Society for the Prevention of Cruelty to Animals and the university trustees. Incredibly, Cooper was forced eventually to resign.[9] Throughout his career, Norris would delight in going one on one with powerful people, especially when it meant his own notoriety would be enhanced.

Perhaps more important than any other event during Norris's Baylor years was his courtship of Lillian Gaddy, the daughter of a Baptist preacher. Norris first met her when he was a sophomore and she was a senior. They were married in 1903, just prior to Norris's graduation. Lillian would remain Norris's constant companion and confidante for the rest of his life, and together they would rear four children.

Norris took another part-time pastorate during his college years. This time the location was Mount Calm Baptist Church, where Norris served as weekend pastor from 1899 to 1903. The Mount Calm church was dominated by a Southern Baptist splinter group known as the Haydenites. They were named for Samuel Hayden, who in the 1880s had led a revolt against the Baptist General Convention of Texas, alleging fraud and liberalism. Many Southern Baptists viewed the Haydenites as a serious threat to Baptist work. Catlow Smith, for example, the pastor under whom Norris was converted, refused to attend Norris's ordination service largely because of Norris's affinity for Hayden's views. It appears, however, that Norris's attraction to Haydenite ideas helped him land the Mount Calm position, and in light of the rest of Norris's career one can surmise that Hayden's influence was a significant factor in his development as a fundamentalist.[10]

Norris graduated from Baylor in 1903 and promptly enrolled at Southern Baptist Seminary in Louisville, Kentucky. He completed his master's degree in theology in two years and graduated at the top of his class in 1905. His valedictory address was on the topic "International Justification of Japan in Its War with Russia." Norris would later remark that the speech, which was reprinted by the Louisville *Courier-Journal*, was a "humdinger."[11] Throughout his life he would show a keen interest in international affairs.

Formal training now behind him, Norris was ready for his first full-time pastorate. He accepted a call by the McKinney Avenue Baptist Church in Dallas. Other than its location in Norris's home state of Texas, it appears that the church had little to commend it.

Norris preached his first sermon at the church in June 1905 in a dilapidated building with thirteen people in attendance. Fresh from the intellectual sophistication of Southern Baptist Seminary, he prepared a manuscript sermon that he intended to deliver in "Declaration of Independence style." Looking out over his little flock he put the sermon draft in his coat pocket and preached extemporaneously.[12] Believing that the situation at McKinney demanded something other than polished sermons, he worked diligently to increase the church's size and stature. According to his own account, the church grew to about five hundred parishioners after one year and a thousand after two, by which time the congregation had a new building.[13]

Having worked himself nearly to exhaustion, Norris was sick and frail by the end of his second year at McKinney Avenue, carrying only about 130 pounds on his more than six-foot frame. He would remain at the church only until 1908, by which time he had accepted the editorship of the *Baptist Standard*, the leading Texas Baptist newspaper. He bought controlling interest in the paper and embarked on a short career as full-time religious journalist. He would leave in 1909, but this brief period was significant for at least two reasons. One, it reunited him with his college rival, Dawson, whom Norris hired as editor of the *Standard*. The relationship lasted only a year before Dawson resigned. Later, Dawson said that he resigned because of continual interference from Norris that restricted his prerogative as editor. This episode completed the alienation between Norris and Dawson that seems to have begun during their college years.[14]

A second significant aspect of Norris's foray into journalism was that during his tenure at the *Standard* he thrust himself into Texas politics for the first time. The issue was racetrack gambling, and Norris devoted large portions of several 1909 issues of the *Standard* to the subject. He eventually went to the capital himself and lobbied for a bill outlawing the amusement. When the measure passed, the governor of Texas presented Norris with several pens used to sign the bill into law. Significantly, it was Norris's political activity, not his preaching, that put him in the public eye of Texans for the first time. Later, Norris would refer to this episode as his "first big fight," and he reported that by the end of it his health was broken.[15] However, he had also won his first taste of statewide notoriety, and if the rest of his life is any indication, he liked it.

Early in his career, Norris exhibited all the attributes of a driven man. At first, he attempted to succeed through rather normal

Baptist avenues: he took a struggling church and turned it into a success, then did the same with a fledgling newspaper. That he worked himself to exhaustion in the process suggests either a fear of failure or a dogged determination to continue enjoying the fruits of victory. More than likely, some combination of these two forces kept him reaching for still greater results. By the time he was thirty he had achieved modest success that when measured against the backdrop of his early life of deprivation would have been enough to satisfy many individuals. Norris, however, was a restless sort, with great ambition, an almost insatiable desire for recognition, and the boundless energy required to reach greater goals than he had thus far attained. In striving to succeed in the work of God, he had moved within the well-worn traditions of Southern Baptist life. He would stay within those confines for a short time before beginning to make his own tracks.

Populist Preacher

In October 1909, Norris took a brief sabbatical from his work and stayed at the home of J.H. Wayland of Plainview, Texas. Wayland, who was organizing Wayland Baptist College, reportedly offered Norris the presidency of the new school, but Norris declined. While deciding what his next career move would be, he was invited to preach at First Baptist Church in Fort Worth. The pastor there had recently resigned, and the church was making do with guest preachers. Unbeknownst to Norris at the time, the search committee considered him the church's prime candidate. Shortly, the congregation issued a call for him to become head pastor. Norris accepted in the fall of 1909 and embarked on a forty-three-year career as pastor of First Baptist Fort Worth.[16]

The church was in many ways typical of large urban Baptist churches at that time. Fort Worth was a growing city of about 100,000. It was a western cow town, and First Baptist had been known as the "church of the cattle kings," at one time boasting thirteen millionaires among its several hundred members.[17] When Norris came to Fort Worth he believed he had arrived as a prominent Baptist preacher, and he could easily have settled into a comfortable life as pastor of a large church with all the advantages and bonuses that came with the job. He remembered later that for two years he tried to fit the mold of a big-city preacher who ministered to the establishment without ruffling the feathers of the affluent and influential members of his flock.[18] He was restless, however, and eventually had to break out of the strictures of southern genteel respectability.

The turning point for Norris came in 1911 at a time when he was so frustrated that he was contemplating leaving the ministry. First Baptist had a large membership and strong Sunday morning attendance, but most members, Norris would recall later, viewed the church as a comfortable club. After a Sunday night sermon to about one hundred people in the First Baptist auditorium, which seated six hundred, he told his wife that he was going to quit the ministry. "I was drawing a big salary," he wrote a decade later, "wearing tailored, Prince Albert suits, preaching in the midst of a city of over a hundred thousand people, none of them paying any attention to me. The whole city [was] given over to idolatry and wickedness. And I was not causing a ripple. . . . Something had to happen."[19] That summer, Norris preached a revival in Kentucky in which many people either converted for the first time or rededicated themselves to a deeper Christian commitment. He caught a vision of success and dedicated himself to a ministry to the masses. Norris would later say that he came to understand that God intended for people to hear the old gospel message in plain language that they could understand. Like the apostle Paul, who had become "all things to all men," Norris decided that he would have to make adjustments to reach a wider segment of the population of Fort Worth. He therefore made a deliberate shift to sensationalized sermons. Before returning home, he wired a Fort Worth newspaper to place an advertisement for his upcoming Sunday night sermon: "If Jim Jeffries, the Chicago Cubs, and Theodore Roosevelt Can't Come Back, Who Can?" The church was packed when he entered the pulpit that Sunday night, and Norris had launched his method of sensationalism, which would continue for the rest of his life. Years later, Norris recalled that he switched to this extraordinary style of preaching because he had noticed that those preachers who engaged in it were the ones most successful in winning converts.[20]

A Fort Worth resident named Harry Keeton once told a story that illustrates Norris's use of advertising gimmicks to build his crowds. It seems there was a fierce rivalry between the baseball teams of Dallas and Fort Worth, and the Fort Worth team was the better of the two. In an upset, however, the Dallas team beat Fort Worth, much to the dismay of Keeton and other avid fans. Keeton reported that as he walked dejectedly down the streets of Fort Worth following the game, he saw Norris place a huge banner outside the First Baptist Church announcing his sermon topic for the following evening: "Why Dallas Beat Fort Worth in Baseball." Keeton, like many others in town, attended the meeting to hear why their team had lost the game, but Norris made only one reference to the athletic contest when he said that the Dallas team won because it was better prepared. He used this to launch into an evangelistic sermon urging people to prepare themselves to meet Christ, concluding with an appeal for those present to "knock a home run for Jesus" by coming forward to be saved. Others would recall Norris's preaching style by saying that he would "raise hell" for the first twenty minutes or so to get the attention of the people, then settle in and preach the old-time gospel.[21]

While many in Fort Worth were flocking to hear Norris, however, many of the established members of First Baptist were growing disgruntled with this unorthodox approach to preaching. The affluent parishioners seemed to care little for the incoming commoners. When told by a powerful member that he was ruining the church by bringing in lower-class people, Norris allegedly responded, "I would rather have my church filled with the poor, the halt, the lame, the sinning . . . than to have it filled and run by a high-browed bunch."[22] That Norris would recall this in such a way shows the extent to which he came to view himself as a minister to the masses. Eventually, the church split over Norris, and six hundred members departed. Norris, however, was able to replace them with new parishioners as quickly as old ones bolted.[23]

As the socioeconomic makeup of the church began to change, the turnover satisfied Norris immensely. He fashioned himself a religious populist and loved to recount how he had enraged the wealthy women of the Ladies Aid by inviting poor people to the church for entertainment and ice cream. According to Norris, one of the women remarked in dismay that he was changing the church into a Salvation Army.[24] In 1911, nothing could have pleased Norris more because he believed that the simple folk were in fact more virtuous than the high and mighty of society. Norris liked to say that he would rather have poor people in his church than the rich crowd that drank Budweiser at the lake on Saturday night and then returned to church to take the Lord's Supper on Sunday morning. The implication was clear. Common people were more susceptible to righteousness. He also wanted to pastor a church that was well known to the masses. By his own characterization, First Baptist Church before 1911 was so exclusive that many in downtown Fort Worth did not know exactly where the church was located. In 1922, by contrast, if one asked directions to the church, the answer might well be "Just follow the crowd." Indeed, the streetcar operators, according to Norris, shouted, "First Baptist Church stop," when letting people off in the vicinity of the church.[25]

Norris's First Brush with the Law

Norris's populist stand against the establishment quickly ran over into politics, putting him afoul of the city fathers of Fort Worth. His first clash with the mayor came as a result of a crusade aimed at vice and liquor traffic in a section of Fort Worth notorious for its crime and corruption. "Hell's Half Acre," as this section of town was called, was filled with saloons and houses of prostitution. As part of his crusade, Norris held a tent meeting in which he preached against the lax enforcement of laws in the city. The mayor, Bill Davis, citing a violation of city regulations governing outdoor meetings, ordered Norris to remove the tent. When the preacher refused, the fire department, acting on the mayor's orders, disassembled the meeting place. This crusade was the beginning of a chain of events that would result in Norris's indictment for perjury and arson.[26]

By January 1912, Norris had accused Mayor Davis of misappropriating city funds. Davis responded with accusations and veiled threats. Then, on February 5, First Baptist Church was destroyed by fire and someone attempted to torch the Norris home. This was actually the second fire at the church. The first had occurred on January 11 and had done only minor damage. Norris accused his opponents, now a fairly large number of city leaders, of setting the fires in an effort to intimidate him into leaving town. The mayor hired a New York private detective agency to investigate what clearly had been arson, but the investigation centered on Norris himself. To convince the public that he was the object of a conspiracy, Norris produced threatening letters he claimed to have received before the fires. Going public with the conspiracy theory backfired, however, and on March 1 a grand jury indicted Norris for perjury in connection with his statement that he did not know who had sent him the threatening letters. The indictment was based on the belief that Norris had written the letters to himself.[27]

On March 2, there was a second fire at Norris's home, this time serious. Norris and his family had to escape through a second-floor window. The Fort Worth *Record* reported, "The mystery of the war against Reverend J. Frank Norris, if there be such a war, was elevated to the highest pitch this morning when his home was burned." The paper also suggested skeptically, "How the residence was set afire without arousing any of the family or awakening the night watchman is the question that thousands of citizens are asking one another."[28] The city attorney believed he had the answer, and on March 28, Norris was indicted for arson in the burning of his own church and home.[29]

In the midst of this controversy, Norris tendered his resignation from First Baptist. As he probably expected, the congregation rejected it unanimously. Then, with his parishioners in full support, he endured a three-week trial in April in which a jury acquitted him of perjury. When the court read the verdict, his supporters broke into song and tears as they mobbed their preacher. Norris himself spoke tearfully of the ordeal.[30]

Norris was not tried for arson until January 1914, and he was acquitted of that charge as well. The prosecutor in that trial alleged that the judge on four occasions before the actual trial had expressed his opinion that Norris was innocent. The judge, however, refused to recuse himself. The prosecution's fears of a biased judge seemed well founded when during the trial the judge did what he could to sway the jury in Norris's favor. When asked by the press if he would order a retrial in case of conviction, the judge responded, "That matter will not come up. There will not be a conviction."[31] Then, to ensure that his prediction came true, the judge informed the jurors during their deliberations that, in the event of a hung jury, he would give preemptory instructions for a verdict of not guilty. Within a few minutes the jury returned with the acquittal. More than two hundred people, most of them women, mobbed the judge, after which he said the indictment against Norris was the weakest he had ever seen.[32] It does appear quite likely that Norris was framed for the crime. His trial, however, became something of a circus attesting to his growing popularity. It also showed that he had a growing number of enemies. Throughout his life, few would be neutral in their attitudes toward Norris.

If the indictments and trial had been an attempt to scare Norris into silence, as he would allege for years thereafter, they seemed to have done just the opposite. By this time, Norris was proving that he thrived on controversy of any kind, especially if it pitted him against powerful forces of the religious or political establishments. Following the trial and throughout the second decade of the century, Norris turned First Baptist into a southwestern religious empire. By 1920, the main auditorium could accommodate five thousand people, and the physical plant included a recreation center complete with gymnasium and pool. Norris continued to increase his congregation through the use of his sensational sermons. For example, he alleged that prominent Baptists were secretly involved in "liquor traffic." Weekly attendance at First Baptist climbed from about four hundred in 1911 to over three thousand in the early 1920s.

Norris had crossed a divide during his first few years at First Baptist. Whereas he at first attempted to play by the unwritten rules that seemed to be set for public figures, he would now play against those who made the rules. Whether or not he was guilty of setting the fires, and it is almost impossible to tell by studying the extant evidence, he had beaten the system by going outside acceptable procedures and coming out on top. This style would mark him for the rest of his life. He would be unpredictable simply because most Baptist preachers were predictable. He would align himself with whomever he pleased whenever he pleased. He had committed himself to outsider status, and he would be a populist preacher.

2

From Populism to
Southern Fundamentalism

The development of Norris's populism prepared him well for the coming of fundamentalism after World War I. Having pitted himself first against the leaders of First Baptist, then against the political fathers of Fort Worth, Norris was ready by 1920 to go head to head with the Southern Baptist Convention and the Baptist General Convention of Texas. Just as Nathan Hatch has counted fundamentalism as part of the recurring populist impulse in American Christianity, so fundamentalism became for Norris a vehicle for the acceleration of populist tendencies he had developed during his first few years in Fort Worth.[1] Norris's move into fundamentalism closely patterned the development of the movement itself. This is not surprising inasmuch as Norris was a classic fundamentalist and not merely a Southern Baptist schismatic. Norris's importance for the national fundamentalist movement was twofold. First, he brought fundamentalism to the South. Second, he brought the South to fundamentalism—that is, he gave a unique southern accent to a movement that was largely northern.

Briefly defined, in the words of George Marsden, fundamentalism is "militantly anti-modernist Protestant evangelicalism."[2] Marsden has identified several roots of fundamentalism, including revivalism, the holiness movement of the nineteenth century, millenarianism, conservative evangelical theology generally, and a Baconian scientific outlook. The sum total of these roots did not equal fundamentalism. They comprised merely various aspects of American evangelical Protestantism at the turn of the century. For these ingredients to coalesce into a movement there would have to be a common denominator—in this instance a common enemy, theological modernism. Modernism can be defined briefly as the attempt to harmonize Christian theology with modern ways of thought, especially Darwinism and higher criticism of the Bible.[3] Various conservative evangelicals came to understand that they operated under a different set of philosophical and scientific assumptions than did the modernists. As modernism moved to the forefront of American Protestantism, therefore, those who would emerge as the leaders of fundamentalism rallied to defend their own views. It is important to note that while the fundamentalists viewed modernism as the most diabolical attack ever on orthodox Christianity, modernists believed they were saving Protestantism from becoming the ideological laughingstock of the modern world.[4]

Two major intellectual issues confronted Protestantism in the late nineteenth century. Both would be important for the fundamentalist-modernist split and the development of the militant defense of orthodoxy that would become part of fundamentalism. The first issue was evolution. After the appearance of Charles Darwin's *Origin of Species* in 1859, Protestants had to deal with this threat to biblical literalism. Sometimes forgotten in the caricature of the brilliant scientist debating the idiot preacher is the fact that in the late nineteenth century many scientists rejected evolution and some ministers accepted it. David N. Livingstone's work shows clearly that from early on there were serious evangelicals who wrestled with the issue of evolution and sought to harmonize it with biblical authority.[5] Certainly it is safe to say, however, that as time went on most conservative evangelicals who tended toward a literal interpretation of Scripture found it nearly impossible to reconcile evolution with the Genesis account of creation. Although the full flowering of fundamentalism was still two decades away, evolution would serve as an issue that immediately divided the most conservative Protestants from the modernists. Modernists attempted to reconcile biblical interpretation with the new science, while most conservatives rejected out of hand what they viewed as a serious attack on the Bible. It was not until the 1920s, however, that evolution would serve as the focal point of the controversy. In the meantime, higher criticism was an even more serious threat.

Higher criticism of Scripture stemmed largely from German philosophy and theology. Scholars who appropriated higher criticism believed that the Bible should be subjected to the same historical and scientific analyses as all other literary works. The most significant and enduring conservative reaction to higher criticism came from Princeton Seminary, the citadel of Protestant orthodoxy. Here Scottish Common Sense Realism and the philosophy of Francis Bacon had been dominant since the early nineteenth century. While Princeton scholars acknowleged that there may be minor errors and inconsistencies in the extant biblical manuscripts, they insisted that the original autographs were inerrant in all respects. This intellectual and scholarly defense of the conservative approach to Scripture survived to become an important part of fundamentalism in the early twentieth century.[6]

The Princeton view contained what was and is known as verbal inspiration—the idea that the Holy Spirit inspired not just the ideas of Scripture but the words themselves. When one considers the Baconianism of the conservative evangelicals and the doctrine of inerrancy, which included verbal inspiration, it is understandable why the fundamentalists would find no common ground for compromise with the modernists. If the Holy Spirit inspired the words of Scripture, and if those words were therefore without error, one need only properly classify biblical knowledge to come to a commonsense understanding of the truth. To go further than this in biblical exegesis was to question inspiration and undermine the authority of Scripture.

There are several outstanding examples of how the issue of modernism in general and higher criticism in particular became divisive in major Protestant denominations. Although most took place in the North, even the Southern Baptist Convention, with no hierarchy or established creed, experienced division over modernism. In this case the controversy revolved around Crawford H. Toy, a professor at Southern Baptist Seminary in Louisville. As a result of his graduate theological training in Germany, Toy concluded that in studying Scripture one must "take the kernel of truth from its outer covering of myth."[7] For Toy, biblical views of science were part of the husk he could leave behind in his search for the truths of Scripture. He reminded his Baptist opponents that the Bible itself said nothing about the way in which the Holy Spirit inspired the authors. With no creed to impose on Toy, the seminary board could only conclude that the professor's views diverged from the generally accepted views of Southern Baptists. Toy graciously resigned and left Southern for a career at Harvard.

While the Toy case was rather isolated in the South, in the late nineteenth and early twentieth centuries the conservatives battled the modernists within most Protestant denominations in the North, usually on the issues of the authority of Scripture, its scientific accuracy, and the supernatural element in Christianity. The disputes were contained within particular denominations at first, but over time the conservatives, put on the defensive by modernism, began to rally across denominational lines. This was the beginning of interdenominational fundamentalism—the coming together of the various roots into a coherent movement.

By the second decade of the twentieth century there was clearly a movement, though it was still incipient and without its firm identity. The publication of *The Fundamentals* from 1910 to 1915 was strong evidence that the conservatives were coming together. Conceived and financed by California laymen and millionaires Lyman and Milton Stewart, and edited by Bible teachers, seminary professors, and evangelists, *The Fundamentals* consisted of twelve paperback volumes of theology intended to be the movement's tour de force. Marsden writes that the real significance of these volumes, more than either their short- or long-term impact, is that they offer "a symbolic point of reference for identifying a 'fundamentalist' movement." These volumes represented the movement's less contentious and less militant beginnings. In fact, the many authors hardly discussed dispensationalism and premillennialism, and some of them after 1920 would cease to be identified with fundamentalism. The emphasis was the defense of the faith against modernism.[8]

Although most of the theological issues were met head on in *The Fundamentals*, the tone was balanced. While the conservative evangelicals certainly opposed the modernists, it was not yet a war as it would become in the 1920s. There were still mediating positions represented by the likes of Southern Baptist Seminary president E.Y. Mullins, who would be unable to support fundamentalism in its fully developed form.[9]

Before World War I, therefore, conservative evangelicals had united in an antimodernist movement that can be interpreted now as early, proto, or incipient fundamentalism. They were not yet called fundamentalists, however, and they did not use the term themselves. The final ingredient that would make this conservative movement into fully developed fundamentalism has to do with the relationship of Christianity to American culture. Before 1917, the theological conservatives, premillennialists, and revivalists warned against modernism, but all these groups still operated together with the modernists in the various denominations and interdenominational agencies. As a result of the American social experience that accompanied World War I, however, the right wing of evangelical Protestantism became strident fundamentalists. As Marsden puts it, "After 1920 conservative evangelical councils were dominated by 'fundamentalists' engaged in holy warfare to drive the scourge of modernism out of the church and culture."[10]

While the war heightened premillennialist theorizing about the signs of the end times, the fundamentalists also began to identify German militarism with German rationalism. They reasoned that German rationalism had taken evolution and fashioned a might-makes-right, superman philosophy that had resulted in militarism. German rationalism had also produced higher criticism of Scripture. The fight against German militarism and the fight against modernism and higher criticism were part of the same battle. After the war, the battle continued against modern philosophy and science, including the theory of evolution, as these were also products of German rationalism. If they did not defeat these, the fundamentalists believed America could end up like Germany.[11]

In the 1920s, therefore, fundamentalists argued that their battle was more than a theological debate. The whole course of civilization was at stake. This helps explain why fundamentalism became a widespread, populist movement after the war. Had the issues remained merely theological, the average American would have been uninterested and the debate would have been confined to the theologians and preachers. Lay people were more likely to join the fray when convinced that the whole American way of life was threatened. This was especially the case as the leaders of the movement began to argue that they were defending not just narrow points of theological doctrine but the whole civilization.[12] After 1920, fundamentalists fought to maintain a nineteenth-century evangelical consensus that had already been gone, unbeknownst to them, for a generation. They began a crusade to save Protestant orthodoxy and thereby save civilization, which had already undergone changes far more profound than they could possibly have recognized at that time.[13]

Curtis Lee Laws, the editor of the Baptist *Watchman-Examiner*, coined the term *fundamentalist* in 1920 and defined an *adherent* as one who was ready "to do battle royal for the Fundamentals."[14] There were many Protestants who answered this call to arms, and Norris was certainly to be counted among that number. By the summer of 1925, fundamentalism was at its height of popularity and power. Then the movement began to break apart, partly as a result of the Scopes trial. One of the most famous trials in American history, it pitted fundamentalists and others who wished to ban the teaching of evolution against modernizing forces at work in American culture. In the end, William Jennings Bryan, and by extension all fundamentalists, were humiliated by the brilliant defense attorney and well-known agnostic Clarence Darrow.[15] Although Bryan and the fundamentalists won the narrow legal question, the circus atmosphere and behavior of some of the principal actors, as interpreted by a hostile media, gave some weight to the extreme view that the fundamentalists were a bunch of rural lunatics bent on depriving the young of an honest education. After the trial, Norris's own murder trial in 1926 seemed to confirm this bizarre caricature. Consequently, whereas the movement had commanded a degree of respect before Scopes, after the trial even many conservative evangelicals shied away from fundamentalism to escape being embarrassed by association. Fundamentalist influence within the Northern Baptist Convention and the (northern) Presbyterian Church U.S.A. declined precipitously, and any chance of victory by fundamentalists within those denominations was gone forever.[16]

Throughout the thirties and forties, when Norris was at the height of his popularity and influence, fundamentalism seemed moribund, but it was actually undergoing a realignment as many in the movement pitched to and fro in search of an identifiable center. Those who remained within the major denominations had abandoned hope of excluding modernists. The more ardent fundamentalists formed independent churches, new fundamentalist associations, denomi-nations, colleges, and seminaries. A network of fundamentalist churches, schools, and associations developed. At the same time, fundamentalists were viewed by the opinion makers in the larger culture as the lunatic fringe, even though many who had taken the antimodernist side were actually educated and rather sophisticated in their approach to religion. Eventually, many within the latter group who had remained within major denominations and were not a part of the independent fundamentalist movement, stopped using the term *fundamentalist* to describe themselves. As a result, by 1960 or so, only the most extreme and separatist fundamentalists, almost all of them dispensationalists, clung to the term. Most of these independent fundamentalist churches since 1960 have also been Baptist, at least in name.[17] Individuals from several, mostly northern denominations, who had been influenced by the fundamentalist movement in the 1920s but were uncomfortable with the militancy and schismatic nature of fundamentalism, formed a "postfundamentalist coalition" and chose the more acceptable name *evangelical* or *neo-evangelical*.[18] Perhaps the overriding reason that many within the early fundamentalist coalition became uncomfortable with the movement was because of the activities and actions of leaders like Norris. He was probably the most bizarre fundamentalist in America in the 1930s and 1940s when the movement was realigning in the wake of its many defeats.

It is understandable that historians have paid much more attention to northern fundamentalists than to Norris. The movement was more virulent in the North than in the South. This was because modernism was stronger in the North, and fundamentalism arose in response to the threat that modernism posed to Protestant orthodoxy. When Minnesota fundamentalist William Bell Riley warned his followers of the threat of modernism in the Northern Baptist Convention, he could point to real modernists as the malefactors.[19] Norris, by contrast, faced a peculiar problem not encountered by his northern brethren. Namely, how can one attack modernism when little of it exists in one's culture? Indeed, James Thompson, in his book on Southern Baptists in the 1920s, argues that the Southern Baptist Convention was a "bastion of orthodoxy," making the development of fundamentalism in the South a "superfluous act."[20]

While the development of southern Fundamentalism may have seemed superfluous to most historians, it was an absolute necessity by Norris's way of reckoning. As his successor at First Baptist, Homer Ritchie, confirmed in a recent interview, Norris saw as the most important aspect of his ministry his opposition to liberalism in the Southern and Northern Baptist Conventions and in other bodies worldwide.[21] Norris admitted that the North had gone over to modernism far more than the South, but his job was to ready the defenses of the faith before the onslaught of modernism reached the Mason-Dixon line. He conceded that southerners often viewed fundamentalists as being overly alarmed without sufficient cause, but he argued that in war the foot soldiers must be ever reminded of the gravity of the situation lest they lose the will to fight. Noah, John Chrysostom, Savonarola, Luther, Calvin, Whitefield, and Wesley all had their detractors, Norris argued, but they all did great work for the kingdom. So it was with the fundamentalist leaders of the twentieth century, who in extreme language warned against the threat of modernism. With little real heterodoxy to attack in the South, Norris in effect created his own enemies by portraying himself as the defender of orthodoxy and everyone who opposed him personally as an enemy of the faith. To audiences that may have wondered where the modernists were in the Southern Baptist Convention, Norris could conjure up images of nameless heretics, or he could single out those on the opposite sides of various issues and portray them as modernists, often obscuring facts and creating evidence to do so. Furthermore, Norris spoke often of the conspiracy of Northern Baptist modernists to liberalize all Baptist denominations, in effect saying that the defense lines had to be drawn before modernism moved southward to invade the Baptist zion.[22] Ever optimistic, he saw his role as that of leader in a holy war in which fundamentalists were "militant and conquering and certain to win."[23]

What was lost in Norris's battle was the tolerance for diversity that Baptists had always maintained. As historian William Estep has argued in the context of the more recent fundamentalist insurgency movement in the SBC, "In the absence of any binding authority to hold Baptists together, a certain degree of diversity within biblical parameters is as necessary as it is inevitable."[24] Norris found such diversity dangerous because it left the door ajar for the winds of modernism. Ritchie remembers that if Norris opposed someone, he would "cut them to pieces." He might even hire a detective to investigate his enemies, then publish the findings in his newspaper. Although he might resort to such measures in a few cases, he regularly used violent and extreme language in attacking his opponents.[25] Looking at the situation from another perspective, it is clear why Norris became, in the words of the *Christian Century*, "probably the most belligerent fundamentalist now abroad in the land."[26] He believed his southern culture was threatened by modernism. While fundamentalists everywhere felt acutely the loss of the dominant evangelical consensus of the nineteenth century, Southern Baptists had even farther to fall than their northern brethren because of the near establishment status of their own denomination. Norris may simply have been ahead of his time in detecting the threat of pluralism to the hegemony of southern Protestant orthodoxy. In keeping with his populist approach to religion, therefore, he began in the teens and twenties to fashion for himself and his followers a simple fundamentalist theology. Just as his populist orientation pitted him against a Southern Baptist leadership that he perceived and portrayed as more bourbon than himself, so too did it make him wary of a movement like modernism that was a product of elite intellectual centers of higher education and that was led by the established leaders of various Protestant denominations.[27]

Norris's Move toward Fundamentalism

From 1917 to 1921, Norris began to align himself with the leadership of the fundamentalist movement in the North. In 1917, for example, James Gray, William Bell Riley, and A.C. Dixon all spoke at First Baptist Fort Worth. Gray came from Moody Bible Institute in

Chicago, one of the early bastions of fundamentalism. Riley was developing a powerful fundamentalist enterprise in Minneapolis, and Dixon was a Southern Baptist who had pastored the Moody church before Gray's arrival as well as the prestigious Spurgeon's Tabernacle in London. Norris held a revival meeting at Moody in December 1917, and in 1920 First Baptist Fort Worth hosted a Bible conference that became an annual affair for American fundamentalism.[28]

During the first two years of the 1920s, as Norris was becoming increasingly involved with northern fundamentalists, he began to rebel against the Baptist General Convention of Texas. One of the issues that led to a breach between Norris and other Texas Baptists was a fund-raising effort of the Southern Baptist Convention called the Seventy-five Million Campaign. This operation grew out of a postwar religious optimism that saw Southern Baptists determined to reach the world with the gospel. For Norris, however, the campaign came at a time when First Baptist was strapped for money. The church had just finished expanding its auditorium, and the postwar economic recession had not yet abated. Norris rebelled against the campaign in the name of Baptist principle, the autonomy of the local church. He interpreted the enterprise as an attempt by the leadership to usurp the prerogative of local congregations. Making matters worse was the fact that in Texas the three leaders of the Seventy-five Million Campaign were old rivals of Norris's—his long-time nemesis Joseph Martin Dawson; George Truett, pastor of First Baptist Dallas; and, L.R. Scarborough, president of Southwestern Baptist Seminary in Fort Worth, who along with Dawson and Truett was locked in combat with Norris in an evolution controversy at Baylor. Norris lashed out at the Seventy-five Million Campaign in much the same fashion that he had attacked vice and corruption in Fort Worth in 1911 and 1912. In the end, the Seventy-five Million Campaign was an inglorious flop—but for reasons that had little to do with Norris. The effort was overly ambitious in a denomination that was overwhelmingly rural during a period when agriculture was fairing poorly.[29]

Norris's fight with the Seventy-five Million Campaign soon blended into charges against Baylor University that one of the professors there allegedly was teaching evolution. Norris also went after the president of the university, Samuel P. Brooks, for tolerating the teaching of what fundamentalists considered a major heresy. Dawson, Scarborough, and many others rallied to Baylor's defense, believing Norris's attacks completely unjustified and based on spurious evidence at best. Scarborough led an effort that resulted in "A Statement and a Pledge" against the Norris movement. This document accused Norris of being "divisive, self-centered, auto-cratic, hypercritical and non-cooperative." Thirty-three of the most prominent and influential Baptists in Texas signed the statement, registering "[our] emphatic disapproval upon, and our most earnest condemnation on the method and spirit of this destructive reaction-ary movement . . . ruthlessly carried on by the *Searchlight* of Fort Worth [Norris's newspaper]."[30] This further alienated Norris from Texas Baptist leadership.

As a result of the Baylor evolution controversy and the fight over the Seventy-five Million Campaign, Norris was in effect censured by the Baptist General Convention of Texas in 1922. The charges, among other things, centered on Norris's lack of cooperation and his attacks on Baptist institutions. Norris was not mentioned by name, but it ap-peared obvious that he was the target. Although Norris was cited for his viciousness, the BGCT agreed that evolution had no place in Christian higher education, and it denounced the teaching of the theory in Texas Baptist schools.[31] On that score Norris could console himself that he had snatched victory from the jaws of defeat. Norris was also pleased when a Baylor professor, Grove Samuel Dow, re-signed after the administration determined that sections of the soci-ology textbook he had authored diverged from orthodoxy. In his book, Dow stated clearly that all attempts to bridge the evolutionary gap from anthropoid ape to humans had proven unsatisfactory, but he also wrote that the Bible was unclear as to the origins of humankind. In an atmosphere charged with suspicion generated by Norris's charges, Baylor president Brooks was unwilling to defend the pro-fessor's work and accepted his resignation instead.[32]

The following year, the BGCT cited Norris for his role in the formation of the independent fundamentalist association, the Baptist Bible Union. The BBU, like many of the northern fundamentalist en-deavors, resulted from the efforts of Riley. Fundamentalists intended it to be an organizational alternative to the major Baptist groups in the United States and Canada, which in the view of Norris, Riley, and others were all infected by modernism to one degree or another. In the view of Texas Baptist leaders, however, the BBU was a pseudo-Baptist organization. The BGCT charged correctly that Norris was attempting to take Texas Baptists into this interdenominational so-ciety and that he was leading people into pedo-Baptist movements. Because of Norris's involvement in the BBU and his attacks on the Seventy-five Million Campaign and other Southern Baptist endeav-ors, the BGCT refused to seat messengers from Norris's church. The stated charge was that First Baptist had already been expelled from the Tarrant County Baptist Association and therefore lacked good standing with a county association, which was a prerequisite for membership in the Baptist General Convention of Texas.[33]

In 1924, the battle intensified between Norris and the BGCT. Norris continued his attacks on Baylor when he learned that a student there, Dale Crowley, had accused a history professor of supporting the theory of evolution. Once again, Norris assailed the university and its president. In his report to the BGCT, Brooks responded with a ringing declaration in favor of academic freedom and the university's responsibility to "acquaint" students with all theories of man's origins. In a thinly veiled reference to Crowley, the Baylor president lashed out at students who came to the university not to learn but to straighten out their professors on doctrinal matters. Then, clearly referring to Norris, he charged, "The refined cruelty and pitiless newspaper criticisms with which Christian college teachers of today are subjected in Texas are calculated to deter any man or woman from entering the profession." Moreover, in a bid to be rid of Norris permanently, the BGCT amended its constitution to require a majority vote to readmit congregations that had been expelled. This meant that Norris's church would remain outside the BGCT until a majority of the Convention's messengers wanted him back in, which never happened.[34]

During the early twenties, as Norris became estranged from Baptist life in Texas, he associated himself more and more with northern fundamentalists. In helping to form the aforementioned Baptist Bible Union, Norris joined ranks with both Riley and T.T. Shields, a fundamentalist leader from Toronto. Norris also joined with Riley and a host of other northern fundamentalists to become a charter member of the World's Christian Fundamentals Association, which was intended to unite dispensational premillennial fundamentalists from various denominational backgrounds into a worldwide antimodernist fellowship.[35]

Norris's association with national fundamentalist leaders also resulted in pulpit exchanges that took him into the leading fundamentalist churches in the nation and brought most of these other leaders to Texas. For example, Norris preached in the nation's largest fundamentalist churches in Boston, New York, Minneapolis, and Chicago. He addressed the 1922 meeting of the World's Christian Fundamentals Association and served as guest pastor and lecturer that year at the Church of the Open Door in Los Angeles, which was pastored by Reuben A. Torrey. In 1926, he brought Shields to Houston for a tent revival meeting intended to compete directly with the

Southern Baptist Convention's meeting there. Norris also merged Riley's *Baptist Beacon* with his own *Searchlight* in 1926, which resulted in Riley becoming a frequent contributor to the Fort Worth paper.[36]

Norris endeavored to forge a close relationship with America's most famous fundamentalist, William Jennings Bryan. The "great commoner" came to First Baptist Fort Worth to speak in 1924, and at the 1925 meeting of the World's Christian Fundamentals Association Norris shared the platform with Bryan and others. Norris claimed to have received a letter from Bryan inviting him to the Scopes trial that summer. Like almost all the leaders of the fundamentalist movement, Norris failed to attend the trial, but he gave it wide publicity and sent his own stenographer to Dayton to record the proceedings. When Bryan died six days after the trial, Norris attempted to cash in on the publicity by printing in his newspaper what he claimed was the last letter Bryan ever wrote. The letter, addressed to Norris, said in part, "Much obliged to you [Norris] for your part in getting me in the case."[37] Bryan also expressed his regret that Norris had been unable to attend the trial. Bryan asked that he be allowed to correct his part in the stenographic record of the trial before Norris published it, but since his death precluded this, Norris put the trial record into booklet form and began to sell copies of the "Only Authentic Book on the Dayton Trial."[38]

As Norris took his place alongside the other fundamentalist leaders of the nation, he began to envision his own fundamentalist training school. He first mentioned this idea in print in 1923 and later formed the Fundamental Bible Institute. Eventually he changed the name to the Bible Baptist Institute, and finally the school evolved into the Bible Baptist Seminary.[39] By the end of the twenties, therefore, Norris was publishing a newspaper, serving as a leader in most of the national fundamentalist organizations, and administering his own fundamentalist school. He was a frequent companion of the other recognized leaders of the movement and was without rival as the leading fundamentalist in the South. He often seemed acutely aware of his responsibility as chief opponent of modernism for his whole region.

The Attack on Modernism

World War I was a turning point for fundamentalist opposition to modernism. During the war, conservative evangelicals made an intellectual connection between German philosophy, which had spawned higher criticism of the Bible, and German militarism, against which the United States was engaged in mortal combat on the battlefields of Europe. By the early twenties, for example, Norris had begun to argue that the threat of German rationalism was even worse than German militarism. "We have conquered Germany with arms," he liked to remind his listeners, "and now it remains to be seen whether German rationalism shall conquer our schools, state and denominational [sic]." Three years later, he stated flatly that German rationalism had captured America. Whereas northern fundamentalists had warned implicitly and explicitly that if rationalism took root, America could end up like Germany, Norris merely regionalized that message to argue that what was happening in the North in the 1920s—the inroads of German rationalism—could happen also in the South if fundamentalists failed to do something about it.[40] Perhaps realizing the difficulty of finding true modernists in the South, he lashed out at the so-called northern modernist juggernaut, which was fueled by Rockefeller money and led by Harry Emerson Fosdick and the faculty of the University of Chicago.[41] While Norris never said that Rockefeller money was the root of all evil, it certainly symbolized for him the corrupting influence of elitism and intellectual sophistication.

The battle lines were drawn along the Mason-Dixon line, and Norris called southerners to holy war against northern infidelity. Having published in his newspaper several articles by Riley and Shields documenting the devolution of the Northern Baptist Convention, Norris himself wrote, "That everybody in the South will be compelled to take sides in the present war to a finish between Fundamentalists and Modernists of the Northern Convention, goes without saying." Southern Baptists could join the fight by praying for the fundamentalists in the NBC, using newspapers to build a wall of fundamentalist sentiment around the modernists, having no fellowship with modernists, and, perhaps most important, by sending missionaries from the "orthodox South to the modernist camp in the North."[42]

While Norris spoke of modernism as an alien force from Germany and the North, he also inveighed against the insidious doctrines he believed had begun to seep into Southern Baptist life. Making such charges plausible was difficult, but Norris gave his best effort. His favorite target was his longtime rival, Dawson.[43] Although Dawson was more liberal than most Southern Baptist theologians and leaders, it still took some ingenuity to argue that he was comparable to Shailer Matthews of the University of Chicago. When

Dawson explained that the fire that had destroyed Sodom and Gomorrah was perhaps much like an oil-well fire, Norris detected immediately the attempt to explain in natural terms a biblical event that was supernatural in its origins. In the same address, Dawson had speculated that Lot's wife had perhaps been covered with molten lava, hence the biblical reference to her having turned into a pillar of salt. For Norris, even the slightest intimation that God had worked through nature was tantamount to arguing that God had not worked at all. This was but another example of the modernism of the Northern Baptist Convention moving southward. In Norris's view, Dawson was just like Matthews, the SBC was becoming like the Northern Baptist Convention, and Baylor looked suspiciously like the University of Chicago.[44]

Norris's attacks on Dawson were not merely specious, but often deceitful and willfully misleading as well. On one occasion Dawson wrote a review of a modernist work of scholarship, John Erskine's *Human Life of Jesus*. Like many liberal works on the life of Jesus, Erskine's attempted to strip away the religious myths that modernists believed encapsulated the real Jesus. For example, Erskine argued that the resurrection was merely the remembrance of Jesus in the minds of his followers. The author also speculated that Jesus had problems with a woman in his early adult life, may have had a family prior to his public ministry, and had suffered possibly from certain psychological maladies. Norris reasoned that since Dawson had not explicitly repudiated the book but had instead given it a fair hearing, Dawson must agree with it. Norris could not accept that Dawson had taken the work seriously and criticized it fairly rather than merely trashing it. Where Dawson wrote, "Erskine has probably taken the track that leads to the view of Jesus that may dominate the future judgment of mankind," Norris tried to make it appear that Dawson was writing prescriptively, when in fact Dawson was speaking only predictively. Furthermore, Norris did not complete the above quotation from Dawson's review, which read, "but he [Erskine] has not shown more acuteness in defining the person of Jesus than those who formulated the historic creed at the Council of Nicea, and not as much comprehension as the modern orthodox scholar who accepts the supernatural."[45] Dawson stated explicitly that Erskine's book was not only theologically liberal but probably diverged more from orthodoxy than previous works of its genre. Clearly, Dawson himself preferred the interpretation of the Council of Nicea over that of Erskine. Norris, however, deliberately distorted Dawson's words in order to charge that the Texas Baptist leader was in the same league with modernists.

There is no doubt that Dawson's theology did indeed diverge from Norris's on several points—the verbal inspiration of Scripture being the primary example. Still his views were a far cry from real theological modernism of the University of Chicago type. The extent to which Norris could go to identify Southern Baptist modernism was most evident in his attack on J.R. Sampey of the Southern Baptist Theological Seminary in Louisville. The leading Old Testament scholar among Southern Baptists, Sampey was conservative to the core, affirming both that Moses wrote the Pentateuch and that Isaiah wrote all of the book bearing his name.[46] These were direct challenges to the higher criticism of Scripture common among modernists. Having sat under Sampey while a student at the seminary, Norris, as late as 1922, had touted the eminent scholar as one of the four great influences on his life while he had been a student. In 1925, however, he charged that the professor had employed higher criticism of Scripture, affirmed theistic evolution, and questioned the scientific accuracy of the Bible. Furthermore, Norris revealed the often mean-spirited nature of his attacks when he told with obvious delight how Canadian fundamentalist T.T. Shields had "trimmed [Sampey] up" at a Baptist Bible Union meeting in Lexington, Kentucky.[47] In between Dawson on the left and Sampey on the right were a host of Baptists like S.P. Brooks and L.R. Scarborough, presidents of Baylor University and Southwestern Baptist Theological Seminary, respectively, who could scarcely have professed their own orthodoxy and conservatism more adamantly. Norris, however, tended to lump all his adversaries together as modernists.[48]

While the terms *modernism* and *liberalism* are not very precise, in Norris's hands they became slippery. Not only could he employ them to assail a variety of conservative theologians, but he could also use the words to identify a host of evils such as evolution, rationalism, atheism, communism, and even loose morals in general. In 1925, while in New York, command central for the Rockefeller-Fosdick conspiracy, Norris wrote, "Liberalism in doctrine and liberalism in conduct are Siamese twins." The occasion of this observation was his visit to Park Avenue Baptist, Fosdick's church, which contained a ballroom built by Rockefeller. Expanding his terminological umbrella, he continued, "Evolution and the dance are to each other as cause and effect."[49] In Norris's mind, everything he believed was subversive to American culture either resulted from or was connected to modernism.[50] In addition to the appeal to the moral conservatism of his readers, Norris was in essence making a connection between northern theological liberalism and moral decline, in keeping with the southern sense of moral purity.

At other times, especially later in his career, Norris could be eloquent in his defense of orthodox Christian doctrines. In a Christmas Eve sermon in 1944 he articulated the importance of the deity of Christ for the Christian message of redemption. "Our Lord's divinity is not the mere crown and beauty of His manhood," he contended affably. "The Godhead of Jesus is not a metaphor, it is a great and solemn fact, the confession of which is for us Christians no lifeless formula or dead dogma. . . . It is a living, an intense conviction resting at once upon authority and upon conscience. . . . Deny the Godhead of Jesus, and you forfeit the essence of Christianity." J. Greshem Machen could hardly have said it better. In this same sermon, Norris criticized true liberals like Strauss and Renan, whose conclusions had diverged rather dramatically from premodernist orthodoxy concerning the person of Christ.[51] Such calm and felicitous analyses were far from the norm for Norris, however, as he was much more comfortable with bald attacks on his opponents. Such assaults were justified, he believed, because modernism undercut faith in the Bible.

The Bible

The importance of the Bible for fundamentalism could hardly be overstated. The reason fundamentalists like Norris peppered their opponents with such a vengeance was because they were convinced that modernism was undermining faith in Scripture. The subtle and sophisticated ways of the modernists could not be allowed to obscure the pervasive injuries that their conclusions inflicted on biblical Christianity.[52] While there is little in Norris's approach to the Bible that is unique, his views are nevertheless important for a full understanding of how and why he carried his theology into practice.

Addressing the convention of the World's Christian Fundamentals Association in the summer of 1922, Norris outlined briefly what he perceived to be the two kinds of heresy regarding the Bible. Religious traditions like Judaism, Roman Catholicism, and Christian Science added to the Bible, whereas rationalism took from the Bible. Although either form of apostasy was bad, clearly the more immediate threat was rationalism, which Norris was here using as a synonym for modernism.[53] Before leaving for this convention, Norris had appealed to Baptist history for justification of his attendance at such a conference. "If there is any one thing above every-

thing else that Baptists have stood for throughout the ages," he announced to his readers, "it is the Word of God, and that is the one
and only issue in the World's fundamental Convention."[54] Norris
was clearly sensitive to the interdenominationalism that fundamentalism required of him. Joining together in transdenominational
movements was something from which Southern Baptists had his-
torically shied. In this article Norris therefore justified his actions
no less than five times in the space of two columns of print. The jus-
tifications hinged on the perceived necessity that fundamentalists
band together across denominational lines to defend the Bible more
effectively. Clearly, in his mind, the situation was so dire that extreme measures were necessary. Still in the period of his career
before he had made a clean break with his Baptist heritage, he recognized that his actions might be interpreted by some of his followers
as being unbaptistic, so he pitted one facet of Baptist history, the importance of Scripture, against a strictly Southern Baptist trait, resistance to interdenominational movements. The Bible won.

Exhibiting the strong commonsense philosophy of the fundamentalist movement, Norris in the mid-twenties stated flatly, "The
word of Scripture is very plain. We need no one to interpret it for us.
Every man with common sense can understand the plain, written
page of God's sacred word."[55] On this occasion and many others,
Norris, was engaging in what historian Timothy Weber has called
the overselling of the perspicuity of the Bible.[56] Similarly, at the
WCFA meeting in 1922 Norris had claimed as his motto "that the
open Bible, in the open hand, with an open mind, with an open
heart, will do the work God wants done." He told the pastors present
at the convention that the way to avoid problems with deacons was
to have them read the Bible.[57] In the best commonsense tradition,
Norris believed that the message of Scripture was plain to all reasonable people of goodwill. That tradition had not prepared Norris or
other fundamentalists for the collapse of the evangelical consensus
of the nineteenth century. In other words, he could not accept that
two people could have an honest disagreement over the teachings of
the Bible. There had to be something wrong with one of them.[58]

Norris believed so strongly in the perspicuity of the Bible that
he junked all Southern Baptist Sunday school literature and boasted
thereafter that his church used only the Bible. In reality, however,
First Baptist had merely replaced convention literature with the biblical views of Norris himself. He explained that he and his staff had
organized a four-year course of study paced to get the people through
the entire Bible. Every week Norris would meet with the 250 or so

Sunday school teachers to teach them what they would in turn teach to the 4,000 or so parishioners on Sunday. That way, he said, "Next Sunday morning I know what 4,000 men, women, boys and girls are studying."[59] So much for people interpreting Scripture for themselves in commonsense fashion.

Although Norris believed that the Bible was clear and unequivocal and that reasonable people of good intent would agree on its meaning, the above method of study clearly shows that he also believed that people needed Bible teachers like himself to help them. Like most other fundamentalist leaders, he could advocate that people study the Bible by themselves, but he was very reluctant to let them.[60] Norris not only controlled the Bible teaching at his church but at his seminary as well. Norris spent a good deal of his time lecturing to the seminary students. In addition to adding geographical and historical context to various biblical events, Norris would also uncover hidden meanings. For example, the words of Genesis 12:3, "In thee shall all families of the earth be blessed," were not just for Abraham and his offspring. Rather, in Norris's exegesis, they pointed also to the first and second comings of Christ.[61]

Occasionally, in sermons or lectures, Norris would incorporate the Greek language, sometimes erroneously. In preaching on Matthew 24:21, which he quoted as "Then shall be the great tribulation," he assured his listeners that although the word *the* did not appear in their English Bibles, it was in the Greek text.[62] In this particular instance Norris was in error, but the point was important for him because he was preaching on *the* tribulation that plays such a prominent role in dispensational theology. Norris explained that the writer of Matthew was not referring to just any period of difficulty like the Black Death or the Thirty Years' War but to the seven-year period that would come after Christians had been taken up in the rapture. Aside from his inaccurate translation of this passage of Scripture, the irony of Norris's use of biblical languages was that he boasted that his seminary was the only one in America that based all its theological degrees on the whole English Bible, requiring no Greek or Hebrew nor "a lot of other outmoded and out-of-date—just dead courses."[63] His exegesis in this instance, however, was consistent with his view that in some passages of Scripture every word was extremely important, while in others individual words were not so critical.[64]

For all practical purposes, the Bible Baptist Seminary was simply a place where students could come to hear Norris and his subordinates recite fundamentalist interpretations of the Bible. Norris once outlined several approaches to the study of Scripture, including J.M.

Gray's synthetic method, so popular on the Bible conference circuit, then concluded that Bible Baptist used the best of all of them. He then put in a plug for the populist approach to learning by telling of a converted policeman who had no formal theological training but preached one of the greatest sermons Norris had ever heard.[65] Norris's own courses ranged from various books of the Bible to "The Life of Christ" to "The Whole of Human History."[66] In advertising a course entitled "The Holy Roman Empire and History Beginning with Christian to Present," Norris listed 224 items he intended to cover, many of which revealed his own rather detailed knowledge of historical events.[67] The items listed, if actually covered, would have constituted a good college-level Western Civilization course. That Norris could slide around the curriculum with no apparent specialty, and that the faculty as a whole was less educated than Norris, makes the probability of sound academic training seem rather low. However rigorous the student workload, there was simply little advanced study taking place at Bible Baptist. This was in keeping with the Bible institute tradition that put a premium on the quick training of lay people for work as evangelists and missionaries. Students emerged from Bible Baptist well acquainted with the King James translation of the Bible and thoroughly indoctrinated with fundamentalist interpretations of it.

Since the Bible was so clear and understandable, all that was really necessary was that people follow its teachings strictly. Norris could argue, consequently, that the Bible was like a medical prescription. If a druggist changed just a few words on the label, the medicine that was supposed to cure the patient might be lethal instead. Scripture could also be compared to mathematics. If one changed the multiplication tables, the whole world could be thrown into confusion. Likewise were the dangers presented by those who denied verbal inspiration—the theory that the very words of the Bible were inspired, not merely the ideas. Each word was a product of God's special revelation—not a general inspiration like that of William Jennings Bryan when he gave the "Cross of Gold" speech, or the way that one would speak of William Shakespeare as being inspired. It was specific inspiration, every word exactly as God would have written it himself.[68] To tinker with God's words was a perilous endeavor.

Aside from true modernists, not even all Southern Baptists of Norris's day could accept a view that on its face seemed to be nothing other than a dictation theory of inspiration. While holding to the special revelation of the Bible, for example, Joseph Dawson argued that biblical inspiration was not uniformly verbal. "It was not merely dictation as to a stenographer," he wrote. Furthermore, Dawson asked a very simple question with which Norris was unprepared to deal: If God dictated the very words of Scripture, why did the four Gospels contain different words and styles to describe the same events?[69] This was to say nothing of the more serious problems arising from the fact that Norris and other fundamentalists referred almost exclusively to the King James Version of the Bible and not to the original manuscripts, which were written in Greek and Hebrew and no longer existed.[70] That some Southern Baptist leaders openly repudiated verbal inspiration as defined by Norris made his job easier. He could now point to something specific when he charged that they were modernists. In his strict allegiance to the fundamentalist view of Scripture, Norris, in fact, devised implicitly and perhaps unintentionally one of his many definitions for modernism. Quite simply, in this context, a modernist was anyone who denied the verbal inspiration of Scripture. This definition is nearly identical to more recent use of the word *liberal* emanating from fundamentalist leaders in the SBC, except that the words *verbal inspiration* have been replaced by the word *inerrancy*.

Naturally, verbal inspiration meant that the Bible was infallible—"truth without any mixture of error for its matter," as Norris liked to quote the confession adopted by the Southern Baptist Convention of 1925. That confession did not claim verbal inspiration, nor did it affirm Norris's view that the books of the Bible in their original form "do not contain the word of God, but are the word of God." All these issues became intertwined in Norris's mind, however, including the issue of the authority of the Bible. Norris identified three views of religious authority: the Roman Catholic position, which held that the pope was infallible and therefore authoritative; the rationalist notion, which held that human reason was the highest form of authority; and the belief that only Scripture was authoritative, which amounted to the historic Baptist position.[71] It was inconceivable to Norris that someone could hold the third view without believing also in the verbal inspiration and the infallibility of the Bible. To deny any of these was to reject them all. Denial of verbal inspiration equaled a rejection of infallibility and was therefore a repudiation of the Bible as the sole authority in matters of faith. This was a slide into the modernist negation of Scripture.

Evolution as a Form of Modernism

Norris's biblicism drove him inexorably to the issue of evolution. His view of verbal inspiration left no room for compromise or equivocation with regard to the literal interpretation of the Genesis account of creation. As discussed earlier in this chapter, the evolution controversy at Baylor and Norris's role in it proved to be critical in his alienation from Texas Baptist leaders. Norris was as militant against evolution as he was against modernism, largely because he saw very little difference between the two. Both were products of the rationalistic way of thinking that destroyed the Bible. It made no difference whether evolution came in its theistic or atheistic forms because "if you deny the Genesis account of creation, you had just as well throw the Bible in the fire." The literal creation story was the cornerstone of faith in the Bible, the foundation. If it were undermined the whole edifice of Christianity was in jeopardy as was civilization itself.[72] Those who supported evolution in any form, therefore, were enemies of the faith who nailed Christ to the cross again. Put simply, evolution was the "worst and most insidious form of modernism of today, the most destructive." Norris stated flatly that any question as to the Bible's accuracy on scientific matters amounted to the most serious attack ever on the fundamentals of the faith.[73]

As Norris battled to have the evolutionists rooted out of Baylor University, he also lent his support to a bill before the Texas legislature outlawing the teaching of evolution in public universities and schools. Echoing the ideas of fellow Southern Baptist evangelist T.T. Martin in his just published book, *Hell and the High Schools*, Norris traveled to Austin in 1923 and told the legislators that the bill was necessary to end the teaching of sectarian dogma in the schools. Like Martin, he reasoned that evolution was not true science because it violated commonsense philosophy. Since it was not true science, it was a form of sectarian belief, the teaching of which was forbidden in public schools by the state constitution. Furthermore, evolution destroyed religion, and the state had an interest in protecting all religions equally. The fallacy in Norris's reasoning was that if evolution were a form of religious belief, it should have warranted the same protection as other forms of faith. He sought to bridge this logical gap by arguing that the bill did not outlaw the teaching of evolution in private schools and institutions but only in tax-supported public facilities. In other words, one could teach evolution privately just as one could further Baptist sectarian thought. The teaching of evolution in the public schools, however, was no different than teaching particular points of doctrine from the Baptist, Methodist, Presbyterian, or Catholic faiths.[74]

This still left a problem, however, for if evolution were too sectarian for the schools, what about the Genesis account of creation?

Should it be barred as well? Obviously, Norris did not think so. Not only did he believe that the Genesis account of creation was better science than evolution, which was just a bunch of absurd guesses strung together, but he also believed that the Genesis account was acceptable in public schools because the people agreed with it. Norris concurred heartily with William Jennings Bryan's dictum, "The hand that writes the check rules the school." Stated in raw populist form, the people did not have to support with their taxes theories with which they disagreed. Did that mean that if someday the people came to support evolution that it should then be taught in tax-supported schools? Norris would say only that he would cross that bridge when he came to it.[75]

In his address to the Texas legislature, Norris left few stones unturned. If charged that he was leaving science to the vote of the popular majority, he could retort that this was not the case because evolution was not science. If charged that banning evolution would be tantamount to state support for a sectarian account of creation, he could argue that the Genesis account was so widely accepted that it was not sectarian in the least. Conversely, only a minority of elites believed in evolution and, since it was not really science, the state had an interest in seeing that the minority did not foist their sectarian views on the majority. Finally, Norris maintained that the state should outlaw the teaching of evolution in the public schools because the theory destroyed morality. Evolution meant naturalism, which precluded belief in a transcendent source of morality. "Evolution denies the ten commandments [because it] says nothing came from above." It would lead to a might-makes-right philosophy like that found in Germany during World War I. As he often argued with regard to modernism, "Evolution was 'made in Germany.' " These two isms were part of the same package. Evolution showed that "German rationalism like poison gas of the German armies, is sweeping through our schools."[76]

As the Baylor fight showed, the battle against evolution raged on two fronts, both in the public schools and in various Protestant denominations. The Southern Baptist Convention was divided over what to do about the issue. Although there were a few theistic evolutionists, most people in the convention, even the educated elites, held tenaciously to the creation story. A report adopted by the SBC at the 1922 convention even advocated that scientific teaching in Baptist schools be held up to the scrutiny of the Bible. Furthermore, the report stated, "It is our profound conviction that no man can rightly understand evolution's claims as set forth in the textbooks of today and at the same time understand the Bible and believe both the Bible and the accepted theory of evolution as set out in the textbooks."[77] Still, some questioned whether evolution was the proper subject for a confession of faith. Fundamentalists supported an effort to include an antievolution statement in the SBC's 1925 confession. Seeing the danger of making the Bible the final arbiter in matters of science, however, preeminent Southern Baptist theologian E.Y. Mullins spearheaded the opposition to such a statement. Along with Mullins there were other thinkers in the SBC who by the mid-twenties had ceased to see all forms of evolution as necessarily antithetical to creation.[78] Norris, not surprisingly, trained his sights on Mullins, accusing him of waffling on the issue. Mullins refused to be pinned down and seemed to Norris to be indecisive. Norris could not appreciate that someone might accept parts of evolutionary theory while still maintaining that human beings had not evolved from lower species of life. Neither could he abide the notion that God's creation was a slow process that may have included the evolution of certain life forms. When Mullins and others accepted facets of evolution while still maintaining that they believed in creation, Norris saw only vacillation. Referring to Mullins in a 1925 headline, Norris wrote, "On Again Off Again and Gone Again."[79] The following year, he accused Mullins of attempting to turn in two directions—toward the evolutionists and toward the antievolutionists. By that time, the *Baptist Faith and Message*, as the 1925 confession was called, was complete and the fundamentalists had failed in their attempt to include in it a specific reference to evolution, just as they had failed to pass an antievolution law in Texas.[80]

Church Polity

A final aspect of Norris's fundamentalist theology that would become increasingly important in his career was his church polity. Nathan Hatch has argued that while mainline denominations in the early twentieth century became more centralized and bureaucratic, fundamentalist, holiness, and pentecostal movements reacted strongly against this trend. They were democratic, upholding the congregational autonomy of local churches. Even Presbyterian churches in the fundamentalist camp tended toward congregational autonomy.[81] With the possible exception of adult believers baptism, congregational autonomy was the most consistently defended Baptist distinctive among Baptists who became fundamentalists. Although Norris in his creedalism usually moved in the opposite direction as Baptist history, in this instance he attempted to out-Baptist his opponents in the Southern Baptist Convention.

In 1922, Norris stated unequivocally that congregational autonomy was "the greatest jewel among us Baptists. . . . God forbid that Baptists should ever be guilty of building overhead, top-heavy, ecclesiastical, dominating, tyrannical conscienceless machines over the church of Jesus Christ."[82] Norris made this statement in the context of the Seventy-five Million Campaign, which he characterized as a centralizing, ecclesiasticizing endeavor. Nearly a quarter century later, after Norris had founded his own fundamentalist denomination and seminary, both of which he controlled to a large degree, he was still extolling the virtues of congregational autonomy but arguing that a local church had to be grafted into a wider movement even to be a true church. "But one thing is certain," he wrote, possibly to discourage the splintering of his own movement, "no 'church' can call itself a 'church' unless it has a worldwide fellowship, or has a definite missionary program." Churches that had no association with such a fellowship were "twentieth century small editions of the Ishmaelites."[83] Norris's perspective on the absolute autonomy of the local congregation had changed once he, rather than his enemies, led the association.

Although fundamentalism and Baptist history intersected on the issue of the autonomy of local churches, they often diverged with regard to how those local congregations should be administered. Norris did not practice the democratic polity of the individual church. At First Baptist Church Fort Worth, after Norris's arrival, power fell into the hands of an increasingly small number of men until finally Norris controlled the church virtually by himself. He occasionally made references to the fact that he ran the church with an iron hand.[84] When asked what changes Norris would have made had he been able to control the Baptist General Convention of Texas, Luther Peak, one of Norris's former associates, responded that Norris would have eliminated deacons or would have had a deacon board with no power or authority. Norris "would have deacons, but he might as well not have," Peak recalled. First Baptist Fort Worth, in fact, did not even have regular business meetings, and by the end of Norris's life, according to his successor, Homer Ritchie, there were no deacons at First Baptist. There was only a finance committee.[85]

Possibly to justify this set of affairs, Norris, in 1945, published in his newspaper an article arguing that the ordination of deacons was unscriptural. The author, Ohio fundamentalist B.H. Hilliard, elevated pastoral authority by portraying deacons as merely the pastor's allies. "Truly this type of man is like Aaron and Hur," Hilliard wrote, "who uphold the hands of their pastor, who defend his honor when unjustly attacked . . . and who prays while he preaches, and who defends the faith for which he [the pastor] stands."[86] Even in the early 1920s, long before Norris had eliminated the historic role of deacons, Norris's church had been criticized by his adversaries for its undemocratic and unbaptistic practices.[87] In 1922, F.S. Groner, the executive secretary of the Baptist General Convention of Texas, predicted that because Norris's methods differed so markedly from those of other Baptists he would undoubtedly drift away from the organized work of Baptists in Texas. While Groner was correct in that prediction, he also asserted that Norris "has practically no following in the state." That would not be true for long.[88]

In the twenties, Norris would appeal occasionally to Baptist polity. Understandably, however, such appeals appeared only when they fit into his fundamentalist agenda. One such example came in 1926 when he published an article by J.B. Rounds entitled "Northern Baptists No Longer Baptists." Rounds criticized Northern Baptist churches that allowed people who had not been immersed as believers to become members, something Norris himself had done on at least one occasion. This article was spliced into Norris's own appeal for Southern Baptists to join the fight against modernism in the Northern Baptist Convention. It was entitled "What Attitude Will Southern Baptists Now Have toward the Northern Baptist Convention?" The allegation that the northern churches were adding members without baptism was but an adjunct to Norris's larger point that the NBC was infected by modernism. He was not appealing to Southern Baptists to defend the distinctives of Baptist church polity as much as he was calling for a war against modernism. Furthermore, in addition to the issue of baptism, Rounds alleged that in the West many NBC churches did not even choose their own pastors, a practice every bit as unbaptistic as accepting members who had not been baptized.[89] Significantly, by the 1940s, First Baptist, under Norris's leadership, had joined the ranks of congregations that did not choose their own pastors. Essentially, he had the power to name his own successor and did so on at least three occasions.[90]

Conclusion

In Norris's scheme of things, the defense of the fundamentals of the faith against modernism overrode all other considerations. Fundamentalist firebrand John R. Rice preached a historic sermon at First Baptist Fort Worth in 1928 entitled "Why I Am a Big F. Fundamentalist." In it he said, "Fundamentalism is not only what you believe but how strong you believe it. . . . In my case Fundamentalism means more than believing the Bible. . . . It means, if necessary, speaking against men I love and who love me, for it. It means, if necessary, offending and grieving people and institutions that have meant a great deal in my life."[91] When Norris published this sermon in his newspaper, he prefaced it by explaining that, although Rice had once opposed him, this sermon was a testimonial to the fact that the positions of First Baptist Church and its pastor had been right all along. Superfluously, Norris was saying that he was in hearty agreement with Rice as to the nature of fundamentalism. Clearly, for Norris, as well as for Rice, fundamentalism meant speaking out against former associates and offending and grieving institutions that had once been important in one's life.

Many, probably most, fundamentalists would have agreed with Rice's argument. Militancy was the indispensable characteristic of fundamentalism—the one trait that distinguished fundamentalists from other conservative evangelicals. While Norris may have been more militant than most, he certainly did not invent this ingredient nor any of the other distinctives of fundamentalism. Neither was Norris's contribution in the realm of ideas. Rather, it was in the regionalization of fundamentalist concepts that had been articulated first by northerners. Every theological distinctive Norris fought for had been delineated first by northern fundamentalists. Norris attempted merely to import those ideas into the Southern Baptist Convention in much the same way that Riley had in the Northern Baptist Convention. Norris's was the only voice in the South on a par with Riley and the other northern fundamentalists. In military parlance, of which Norris was so fond, he was one of the generals in the fundamentalist army.[92] His assignment was the Southern theater of the war on modernism.

3

American Nativist

Events from the preceding chapter show the extent to which Norris could be ruthless in dealing with his theological adversaries. Likewise, in his political life, he spared no enemy his wrath, especially when he perceived his enemies as subversive of America. In the twenties, he counted as subversives Catholics and immigrants especially. The result was an extreme form of American nativism that has been a recurring theme in American cultural history. This was especially evident in his effort to help defeat Al Smith for the presidency in 1928, but the starting place for this story is prohibition.

This issue was as divisive religiously as it was politically. The movement began in the early nineteenth century, when preachers and other religious workers began to recognize the debilitating effects of alcohol. Prior to the late nineteenth century, few in America espoused teetotalism. American Protestants during colonial times had imbibed spirits, and more than a few early-nineteenth-century revivalists carried flasks in their saddle bags. There was cause for concern, however, as America advanced across the frontier. When the father of a family became addicted to alcohol, as Norris's own father had, the entire family could face extreme deprivation.[1]

In light of this growing social problem, voluntary organizations came into existence. The Women's Christian Temperance Union was organized in 1874 with Frances Willard as its head. Then, in 1893, Methodist minister Alpha J. Kynett formed the Anti-Saloon League. Two years later, a former Republican congressman from Iowa, Hiram Price, became president of the League. Soon, this organization had representatives in every state and some very wealthy benefactors. The goal was to bring about dry laws and eventually a prohibition amendment to the United States Constitution. Its single-minded approach to the problem of alcohol made the League the leading proponent of reform as it drove other organizations like the WCTU virtually to the sidelines. By 1916, three-fourths of the American population lived under some kind of state or local dry law.[2]

The concerted campaign for a constitutional amendment began in 1913, gained momentum with America's entry into World War I, and secured the necessary two-thirds support in Congress in December 1917. Quickly, states began to ratify the Eighteenth Amendment (only Connecticut and Rhode Island failed to ratify), and it went into effect in January 1919. Its success was largely the result of the Methodists, Baptists, and Presbyterians. These groups not only supplied most of the leadership for the Anti-Saloon League but became directly involved as denominations as well. Although evangelists and pastors from Billy Sunday on down supported prohibition, the most visible leader was Presbyterian layman and three-time presidential candidate William Jennings Bryan, who called the effort "a veritable religious crusade." When the amendment took effect, Bryan exclaimed, "Let the world rejoice. . . . The greatest moral reform of the generation has been accomplished."[3]

Once thought to be a victory for the rural South and West against the urban North and East, it appears now that support for Prohibition cut across geographic lines. Rather, the division was between middle-class Protestants mostly of British extraction and Roman Catholic, Jewish, and Lutheran immigrants. Throughout the twenties, the old-stock Protestants battled against repeal of the Eighteenth Amendment, especially in 1928 when Roman Catholic wet Alfred E. Smith ran for president on the Democratic ticket. Although Smith probably would have lost the election even had he been Protestant, the campaign did arouse an ugly strain of American nativism and anti-Catholicism that fueled the already potent prohibition forces that opposed Smith. Following Smith's defeat, the clamor for repeal of the Eighteenth Amendment only grew, however, and prohibition came to be viewed increasingly as a remnant of bygone days. Finally, in 1933, prohibitionists lost the battle for maintenance as the Twenty-first Amendment made the Eighteenth null and void.

Prohibition in Texas

In Texas, prohibition has been called a surrogate for the social gospel. While most social reform movements dealing with the problems of working-class urban dwellers and rural farmers never gained wide support from religious denominations and institutions, prohibition was the one reform around which Protestant religious leaders rallied. Furthermore, prohibition was easily the most popular issue for progressive Democrats in Texas, and it dominated state politics during the teens and twenties. The prohibition movement in Texas, and possibly nationwide, was not merely a remnant of a bygone era. It was in a real sense a progressive reform, offered plausibly as the key to cleansing politics and society. The brewing industry had been a force for corruption in politics, and no one would have disputed the ill effects of alcohol consumption for many families both urban and rural.[4] Logically, Norris and many others who were consumed by the prohibition issue believed they were saving America from destruction.

Norris's involvement in prohibition was intense during the twenties. Although it is difficult to discern to what extent he was involved before that time, he appears not to have seen the issue as important until after passage and ratification of the Eighteenth Amendment.[5] When he began his newspaper in 1917, he made only passing references to the prohibition cause. For example, in the very first issue Norris informed the president of Texas Christian University that he would not help raise money for the school because the fund-raising campaign was being led by a person who was a notorious ally of the liquor interests.[6] In August, Norris issued a headline, "Why vote the saloons out of Fort Worth." Then, in October, he announced a "Big Prohibition Convention" of representatives from Oklahoma and Texas, the purpose of which was to petition President Woodrow Wilson to proclaim dry zones around military bases.[7] Norris hardly mentioned the issue again until after the Eighteenth Amendment took effect.

In 1919, a traveling Norris reported back to First Baptist Fort Worth that he had met with Texas senator Morris Sheppard and presented him with a silver set engraved with the words, "Presented to Senator Morris Sheppard by the largest Sunday School in America, The First Baptist, Fort Worth, Texas as an appreciation of his successful work in securing constitutional prohibition."[8] Sheppard had been one of the most active senators in the prohibition movement and had introduced in the Senate the resolution calling for a constitutional amendment. Some have even called him the father of constitutional prohibition.[9]

In the 1920s, Norris's involvement in prohibition became not only a regular part of his activity but the dominant political issue for him, eclipsing in importance even the crusade to ban the teaching of evolution. He expended a great deal of time and energy badgering local officials into more stringent enforcement of prohibition laws. He got into a particularly intense controversy with a federal judge,

James C. Wilson. The issue began in the fall of 1921, when another
judge named R. Walker Hall from Amarillo, while teaching a Sunday
school class there, accused Wilson of lax enforcement of dry laws
against bootleggers. Norris got wind of the accusation and published
it in the *Searchlight*. Although Judge Hall cautioned Norris to investigate the charges before publishing them, Norris published what
he had and challenged Wilson to come forth with evidence refuting
the story. Norris said he would resign and never preach again if
the charges proved false. He in turn called on Wilson to resign if the
charges proved to be true.[10] Evidently, Judge Wilson had rendered a
judgment unfavorable to the local Ku Klux Klan, which led Norris to
pit the Klan against the Knights of Columbus, the liquor interests,
and Wilson. Norris wrote, "I hold no brief for the Ku Klux Klan. . . .
But I am unwilling to take a verdict of Federal Judge Wilson against
the Ku Klux Klan when he is the known representative friend and
companion of boot-leggers."[11]

Norris used the dispute with Judge Wilson to launch into a dia-
tribe against the power of federal judges that was not unlike the criticisms leveled by the modern Religious Right against the United
States Supreme Court. Because appointed judges with life tenure
held such power, argued Norris, it was extremely important that
they be above reproach. Norris listed several transgressions committed by the judge, some of which went back to when Wilson had
served as a U.S. district attorney and then a U.S. congressman. What
seems to have been most serious for Norris was Wilson's alleged association with bootleggers, his dismissal of cases against them, and
the low fines and short jail sentences rendered for alcohol-related
convictions. Norris also claimed that he had an eyewitness who had
seen the judge drunk on several occasions. Norris knew that the real
power and effectiveness of prohibition rested with local law enforcement officials and federal judges, and he believed it was his duty to
keep these people vigilant.[12]

In June 1922, Norris, thinking aloud during a sermon, entertained the idea of purposely breaking a law so he could go on trial
before the judge. He then told his parishioners that one could not be
held in contempt of court when the court itself had become con-
temptible, and he also accused Wilson of wrecking the lives of young
people by allowing bootleggers to continue their operations in Fort
Worth.[13] The following week Norris must have issued even more serious charges against Wilson because the printer of the *Searchlight*,
on the advice of his attorney, refused to publish the sermon. To
Norris, this attempt to silence the opposition was part of the con-

spiracy of the bootleggers and their friends to render constitutional prohibition ineffectual.[14]

Norris continued the assault against Judge Wilson, however. In June, he preached a two-hour sermon to a congregation that included members of the media and some of Wilson's supporters. Throughout the sermon Norris bantered back and forth with them. In this circus atmosphere Norris called a deputy sheriff to the platform who told the audience of the many arrests he and other officers had made that had strangely yielded no convictions. Then, to give an air of officiality to the proceedings, Norris called a notary public forward and had the deputy swear to the notary that he was telling the truth.[15]

Eventually, the county bar association began a probe into the Norris-Wilson controversy, but the investigation was interrupted by Wilson's threat to sue Norris for libel and to have him held in contempt of court. Norris at first welcomed the probe, but he seems to have backed off after Wilson threatened retaliatory action. Possibly to save face, he wrote in the July 21 issue of the *Searchlight* that Wilson had mended his ways by giving stiffer fines to bootleggers. Wilson may indeed have succumbed somewhat to the pressure—at least that is what Norris wanted his readers to believe. Two years after the controversy, and again in 1926, Norris had occasion to praise the fine work of Judge Wilson in enforcing prohibition, and it appears that by that time Norris was convinced that Wilson had indeed changed.[16]

Throughout the controversy with Judge Wilson, Norris tried to show that enforcement of prohibition was an effective means of reforming lives. He sprinkled his sermons with stories of people ruined by alcohol. He told of one man who had stayed sober for several months after prohibition went into effect but who had succumbed once again to alcohol when the bootleggers got to him. In an analogy appealing to Texas racism, Norris charged that the bootlegger was just as bad as a black rapist who raped and murdered white women, and he reasoned that the bootleggers could only operate effectively in the absence of rigorous enforcement of prohibition. The solution, therefore, was to get people elected to office who would enforce prohibition laws vigorously. In the early twenties, Norris was still confident that prohibition was permanent, and he believed that lax enforcement was the strategy chosen by his opponents for effectively circumventing prohibition without issuing a futile frontal attack on the Eighteenth Amendment. He warned, "I want to service [sic] notice on the whole bootleg gang and all of their officials, you just as well to get ready to fold your tent, for America is going to be as dry as the Sahara."[17]

When Norris began to campaign actively for public officials who were staunchly in favor of prohibition, he quickly recognized that the issue often pitted Protestants against Catholics. In the summer of 1922, he endorsed Earle B. Mayfield for the U.S. Senate against former governor James E. Ferguson and urged all Protestant ministers to endorse Mayfield. Ferguson, alleged Norris, opposed prohibition.[18] Norris then plunged headlong into the governor's race two years later when Ferguson's wife, affectionately known as Ma, was running for the Democratic nomination against Felix D. Robertson, the Klan's choice for the office. James Ferguson, before running for the Senate, had been impeached as governor of Texas, and he was therefore prohibited by law from seeking election again. Norris and other Ferguson opponents assumed naturally that the former governor wanted his wife to win the office so he could run the state over her shoulder for another term. In announcing his avid support for fellow Baptist Robertson, Norris claimed that every "black-bosomed celibate Roman Catholic from El Paso to Texarkana and from the Red River to Galveston is fighting him tooth and nail."[19] Norris reasoned that Robertson must be a good candidate since Catholics were opposing him.

Robertson obviously relished Norris's endorsement, as he cited it in some of his paid political advertisements in the *Searchlight*. He also appeared at Norris's church during the summer campaign and spoke a few words to the congregation. Norris said he had invited both candidates, but clearly, if the articles Norris had been running in the *Searchlight* were any indication, Ferguson would not have felt welcome at First Baptist.[20] Norris continued with a barrage of anti-Ferguson articles throughout July and August, issuing such headlines as "Robertson vs. Jim Ferguson; Rum, Romanism, Russianism, the Issue," "Is Liquor Coming Back?" and "Can You Vote with the Bootlegger?"[21] He accused Ferguson of a variety of improprieties, but the primary issue was always prohibition. Despite Norris's best efforts and predictions, Ma Ferguson won the Democratic nomination, which assured her she would be the next governor of Texas. Norris took the defeat graciously, saying that the women voters had had their way, and he consoled his readers with the fact that at least Ferguson was opposed to the black-market sale of liquor in drugstores. Significantly, however, advertisements for George C. Butte, the Republican candidate, appeared that fall in the *Searchlight*. Butte urged people to forget he was a Republican and to cross party lines just as many Republicans in other states had crossed over in voting for Woodrow Wilson when he had run for president in 1912 and 1916.[22]

While Norris was heavily involved in the governor's race of 1924, he virtually ignored the presidential campaigns. At this time he was just beginning to pay close attention to national politics, and he evidently did not believe that the contest between incumbent Calvin Coolidge and Democratic candidate John W. Davis was very important. He may have discerned correctly that Davis had little chance of unseating Coolidge, and in light of the fact that Davis was nearly as conservative as the Republican incumbent, Norris probably would not have been too dismayed had Coolidge lost. The stakes were obviously much higher in the Texas governor's race. During the off-year election season of 1926, Norris issued a warning that candidates should stay away from him. It was at this time that he was under indictment for murder (to be discussed in chapter 6), and he seems to have wanted to stay out of the political spotlight as much as possible. He therefore made it clear that he would not be endorsing individuals. He did instruct his congregation, however, that the litmus test by which candidates should be judged was whether or not they supported prohibition.[23]

Anti-Catholicism

Throughout the political battles over prohibition during the first half of the twenties, Norris exhibited strong anti-Catholicism. Although the two issues were always related, the latter transcended prohibition. During the battle with Judge Wilson, Norris spoke of a cardinal from Boston who had opposed prohibition, and he accused the prelate of giving comfort to those who would violate the constitution. He warned that if the cardinal fought Prohibition, he would find himself opposed by 90 percent of the American population. Norris also feared that Roman Catholics would gain control of the district attorney's office in Fort Worth and other political offices, and this led him into a discussion of the fitness of Catholics for political office in America.[24] Claiming that "many of my warmest personal friends are Catholic," he launched into his argument on why they should not be allowed to gain power. "It knows allegiance only to the Pope," he wrote of the Roman Catholic faith. "They would behead every Protestant preacher and disembowel every Protestant mother. They would burn to ashes every Protestant Church and dynamite every Protestant school. They would destroy the public schools and annihilate every one of our institutions."[25] In listening to Norris, one would have thought he was speaking as a French Huguenot in the late sixteenth century, and, incredibly, Norris referred periodically to the Saint Bartholomew's Day Massacre of 1572. In one sermon he went into vivid detail concerning that slaughter, telling his congregation of the Catholic atrocities perpetrated against Protestant children. He concluded, "This same bloody beast now undertakes to control the politics of this country."[26] In discussing the alleged Roman Catholic effort to take over public education, he said, "When the time comes that they seek to dominate and control the free institutions of this country, then it's high time that every man speak out as a true red-blooded American citizen."[27]

Norris reasoned that any candidate opposed by Roman Catholics was probably worthy of election. " I am for the candidate they oppose," he said. "I need no further or higher recommendation for any man who is running for office than that the Roman Catholic machine opposes him. . . . If Roman Catholicism opposes him I know that he is a friend of our institutions and therefore, shall vote for him." Norris urged his followers to do the same, and he even argued that Fort Worth should oust all Roman Catholics from positions in city government. Claiming that this had already been done in El Paso and Birmingham, Alabama, he said, "The American people, the real white folks, the Protestant population rose up and put the Catholic machine out of business, and a Roman Catholic is not even allowed to clean spittoons in the Court House of City Hall in Birmingham."[28] In 1922, Norris instructed Protestants of mixed marriages to rear their children in a Protestant church so they could grow up to be "real Americans." Furthermore, he urged Protestants not to marry Catholics because such unions made it difficult for the Protestant member to be "true to the ideals of the American nation and the Protestant religion."[29]

By 1924, Norris was saying regularly that Roman Catholics could not be real Americans. He called the Catholic faith "anti-American and unconstitutional" because the pope claimed temporal as well as religious authority over members. Quoting extensively from Roman Catholic documents going all the way back to Augustine in the fifth century, he reasoned that since the church did not tolerate heresy, it was opposed to the American ideal of free speech. Norris liked to portray as mutually exclusive strict obedience to the pope and loyalty to the American nation, arguing that American Catholics could not be faithful in both realms. This being the case, he reasoned, no Catholic could ever take the oath of office for the presidency. The offensiveness of Norris's words was made apparent when he encountered vocal opposition in some of his meetings. When he claimed in 1924 that a Catholic could never be qualified for the presidency, a woman in the audience cried out, "You're a liar! It's a damn lie! It's a goddamn lie!" The police were summoned to remove the woman and some other hecklers so that Norris could continue.[30]

Norris showed more tolerance for Muslims, Confucianists, atheists, and one presumes others of non-Christian faiths than for Roman Catholics. He said that while people of all faiths should be allowed to live in America, Roman Catholics should be required to renounce their allegiance to the papacy.[31] In 1927, he stated his views plainly when he said, "No true, consistent Roman Catholic, my friends, who actually believes in the doctrine of papal infallibility, can be true to any other government in the world." Citing the apostle Paul's admonition on the Christian's responsibility to the state, he then went so far as to say that an American's first allegiance, above everything else, should be to the government.[32] In discussing the political situation in Mexico the year before, he had applauded Mexican efforts to escape the domination of the Catholic Church, and he even advocated keeping priests from entering the United States to ensure that such domination never reached this country.[33]

It was a short step for Norris from anti-Catholicism to expressions of American nativism and Anglo-Saxon superiority. Having argued previously that only Protestants could be patriots, he quickly added Anglo-Saxon ethnic origin to his list of criteria for being a genuine American. In the 1920s, as many immigrants arrived from non–Anglo-Saxon countries in eastern and southern Europe, Norris saw them as a threat because he was sure that the vast majority of them would oppose the Eighteenth Amendment.[34] Moreover, he saw these new ethnic additions to America—Russian Jews, Mexicans, and others—as "low-browed foreigners." "Let others do as they may," he said. "As far as we are concerned [in Texas] . . . we stand for 100 per cent Americanism; for the Bible; for the home, and against every evil and against every foreign influence that seeks to corrupt and undermine our cherished and Christian institutions."[35]

Fearing Bolshevism, as well as the overturning of the Eighteenth Amendment, he believed that immigrants should have to live in America for twenty-one years before attaining citizenship, figuring that his own children would have to wait until they were twenty-one before exercising full citizenship rights.[36] Working himself into hyperbole, he once claimed that the government should investigate all foreigners, deporting the ones who were anarchists. They should be herded onto ships filled with bombs and sent out to sea to be blown up, he said.[37] He specifically named Catholic cardinals in America, none of whom were Anglo-Saxon. "Most of them are Italians, some of them are Irish, some are Hungarian, some are Austrian, some Bavarian—and most of them barbarians," he exclaimed. Norris added that the Latin or Italian mind was incapable of understanding the Anglo-Saxon mind and that the former was certainly unfit to rule the latter.[38]

New York City represented to Norris in microcosm the threat to America. Claiming the city was only one-third Protestant in 1926, Norris lamented, "New York is the world's largest Jewish city. New York is the world's largest negro city. New York is the world's largest Italian city. New York is the world's largest Irish city."[39] Two years earlier, he had preached a sermon outlining how New York's Tammany Hall political machine was a Catholic organization that dominated city politics.[40] Little wonder, then, that when Al Smith, an Irish Catholic from New York who was connected to Tammany Hall, ran for president, Norris entered into the most intense period of political involvement in his entire career.

The Campaign Against Al Smith

The portent of Al Smith's nomination for the presidency allowed Norris to combine more tightly than ever before the two issues of Prohibition and anti-Catholicism. He wasted little time, beginning his campaign against the possible nomination of Smith in 1926. Reiterating his belief that Catholics were second-class citizens, Norris listed three reasons why a Roman Catholic could not be president: One, the Church for Catholics was supreme in all things. Two, the Church claimed to be infallible. Three, it claimed to be unalterable. Norris asked, "Are we ready to permit a man to occupy the highest office, the chief magistracy over this Government, who owes his first allegiance to a foreign power which claims these three things?"[41] If the Democrats nominated a Catholic or a wet, Norris stated, he would campaign the South for the Republicans because they were the ones attempting to enforce prohibition.

Norris considered advocating that southern Democrats nominate Sheppard if the northern Democrats nominated Smith. This would possibly have split the party, allowing the Republicans to retain the White House. The likelihood of this plan succeeding, however, was very low because southern Democrats were too loyal. Norris castigated his fellow southerners for "playing kite-tail to Tammany Hall and the other strong Catholic centers of the North."[42]

In the spring of 1926, Norris issued the headline "Roman Catholics Plan Huge Broadcasting Scheme to Make 'The United States a Catholic Country,'" and when he planned a rally in Lexington, Kentucky, he was refused use of a city auditorium because his sermon topic was "The Conspiracy of Rum and Romanism to Elect a Wet Roman Catholic President of the United States." When the First Baptist Church of Lexington began construction of a temporary tabernacle to house the Norris meetings, the city threatened to issue an injunction against the building. Norris wrote a stinging letter to the city leaders, saying that they ought to be ashamed that the state that had produced Abraham Lincoln and Henry Clay now had Catholic bosses running its political parties. He also said that he intended to ignore the injunction if it were indeed issued.[43]

As would often be the case, Norris had hit on an issue that was of real concern for many Americans, especially those like himself who saw it as their duty to save America. The problem for Norris was that his sensational style of preaching and writing precluded him from ever offering a calm appraisal of the facts. In the spring of 1927, however, he did reprint an article, written by a jurist from New York named Charles C. Marshall, that reasonably analyzed the issues at stake. Marshall simply asked for a clear exposition from Smith on how he would resolve the tension between his allegiance to the pope and his oath of office should he be elected president. He also addressed the doctrine of separation of church and state, which Pope Leo XIII had denounced in his 1885 encyclical *Immortale Dei.* These were important issues, and Marshall requested that Smith clarify them for those who would be unable to endorse him until the religious questions had been answered.[44]

Rather than printing Smith's answer to Marshall, Norris went on the attack again himself one month later. He explained that having a Catholic president was different from having a Baptist or Methodist in the office because only the Catholics believed that "if you don't belong to us you are just as certain for hell as you are living." Norris asked his congregation, "Do you want a man to be president of the United States who says that he believes that?" It was surely a great irony for Norris, who was so often intolerant of anyone whose views diverged from his own, to attempt to portray Catholics as unfit for public life because of their theological intolerance. Furthermore, in addition to the weightier matters, he also asked in mock seriousness on what Bible a Catholic president would swear when taking the oath of office, since Catholics do not believe in the Protestant Bible. Norris then rehashed his arguments from the year before on the infallibility of the pope and the Catholics' allegiance to him. Norris did, however, bring up the important issue of separation of church and state, as had Marshall. He juxtaposed the view of Pope Leo XIII, who said that a state should not be indifferent to matters of religion, with that of the Supreme Court, which had said that the "law knows no heresy and is committed to the support of no dogma, and the establishment of no sect."[45] Smith's famous answer to questions concerning Leo's encyclical—"Will somebody please tell me what in hell an encyclical is?"[46]—was not nearly enough to satisfy Norris. Nothing Smith could have said would have dissuaded Norris from the belief that a Catholic president would use his office to further the Church's influence over American culture and politics.

Norris, of course, attacked Smith for being wet as well as Catholic. He charged that as governor of New York Smith had tried to secure state nullification of the Eighteenth Amendment, and he said that if each state attempted to take out of the constitution what it did not like, there would soon be anarchy. Norris compared Smith with William Jennings Bryan, who in Norris's view could have had the nomination in 1920 had he been willing to remove the "bone dry" plank from his platform. When Bryan had died in 1925, Norris had cited in eulogy Bryan's greatest achievement—prohibition. In a comparison that must have seemed absurd to many, he compared Bryan to Lincoln, saying that one had freed the slaves while the other had freed people from liquor.[47] The obvious implication was that Smith would enslave the people once again.

Norris began working privately in the spring of 1927 with Republican National Committee member R.B. Creager of Brownsville, Texas. Writing to Creager, he said that the "wire-pulling" Democrats of Texas had sold out to Smith, and he feared that if he did not arouse the Protestants and prohibitionists, Smith would be elected. With Hoover not yet a candidate, he planned to oppose Smith's nomination in an effort to crystallize support for Coolidge.[48] By summer, Norris had published a booklet on why Smith should not be president, and by the end of 1927 he was prepared for an extensive campaign against the New York governor.

Norris devoted 1928 to helping the Republicans defeat Smith. For him, the campaign was nothing short of a crusade to save America. Norris pulled out every device he could think of to rally opposition. He rehashed the Saint Bartholomew's Day Massacre in an effort to scare people into opposing Smith. He said that if Catholics had enough political power their intolerance would lead to persecution of Protestants. The campaign also provided Norris with another classic opportunity to address prohibition along with the Roman Catholic issue. He did so by portraying Smith as an alcoholic who had been drunk in public several times. On at least one occasion, Norris even said that something positive could come from Smith's nomination because two questions could be solved at once—prohibition and Roman Catholic control of the government.[49]

Realizing that many Texans would be reluctant to support a Republican for president, Norris toyed with the idea of supporting a third-party movement. When contacted by a member of the executive committee of the California State Democratic Party about such a move, Norris was at first agreeable. He told the Californian, "If you will put out a high class man for president you will at least defeat Al Smith and thereby save the nation from the domination of Rum and Romanism."[50] Norris clearly had in mind splitting the Democratic vote to afford the Republicans a victory in November. A week after writing this, however, he backed off. Having been asked to help launch a third-party movement in Fort Worth, Norris responded that he preferred to wait until after the Democratic convention in Houston to be sure that Smith would indeed get the nomination.[51] In reality, it seems that Norris may have shied away from supporting a third-party candidate because he believed it more effective to simply campaign hard for the Republicans.

Throughout the spring, Norris ran at least one anti-Catholic article in the *Fundamentalist* nearly every week. He showed little reluctance to twist facts and statements in order to show that anti-Catholicism was among the best traditions of American history. For example, he wrote of Lincoln's fear that Roman Catholicism would sweep the country, and he quoted Thomas Jefferson's opposition to domination by "kings, priests, and nobles" to allege that he too was anti-Catholic.[52] Norris found it more difficult, however, to enlist living politicians in the anti-Smith campaign—especially if they were Democrats. He wrote to Rep. Tom Connally, who was starting his own campaign for the U.S. Senate, informing him that there was only one issue in Texas at that time—"Al Smith, Tammany Hall, the liquor question and all that goes with it."[53] The candidate who fought the hardest against these would be the candidate who would win the Senate seat, suggested Norris, as he also offered free radio time to whichever candidate opposed Smith the best. Connally, however, would not be intimidated by Norris. He replied, "I am a Democrat and expect to support the nominee." Furthermore, Connally resented that his entire record as a member of the House of Representatives should be judged on whether or not he supported or opposed Smith. "I can see no reason why my candidacy should be judged by the presidential campaign," he retorted. "I am running on my own record. The record of no other man can change or modify my record in the least respect."[54]

Norris had much better success finding anti-Smith allies among his former enemies in the Southern Baptist Convention. L.R. Scarborough, president of Southwestern Baptist Theological Seminary, whom Norris had opposed during the Seventy-five Million Campaign several years earlier, opposed Smith on church-state grounds and on prohibition. Norris published in the *Fundamentalist* an article by Scarborough in which the seminary president dealt thoughtfully with the Roman Catholic position on church-state questions and marriage, before allowing his discussion to degenerate into the same charges of alcoholism that Norris had been issuing. Scarborough concluded that he was voting for the good Christian candidate, Hoover.[55]

Both the Baptist General Convention of Texas and the Southern Baptist Convention passed resolutions opposing any candidate who was not in favor of prohibition. George Truett of First Baptist Dallas, also a Norris enemy during the Seventy-five Million Campaign, was less direct than Scarborough, saying only that he supported the resolutions but that he did not intend to engage in partisan politics from the pulpit. He refused to sign any petition or statement attesting to his support for Hoover, which left doubt as to whether he would indeed support Hoover or sit out the election. For Norris, such lukewarm opposition to Smith was not enough, and he alleged that Truett was actually a Smith supporter. Truett's brother, an attorney from McKinney, Texas, was a known Smith ally, and Norris capitalized on this in an effort to bring Truett out in the open on whether he planned to vote for Hoover.[56]

Norris challenged other Baptists to speak out during the campaign. To the editor of the *Baptist Standard* he issued the headline "Your Attitude Is Distinctly Cowardly," and he asked, "Will the Baptists of Texas Submit to the Compromise of Their Paper on Al Smith and Tammany Hall?"[57] The *Standard*, like Truett, had not taken a hard enough line against Smith. In fact, it had said that it would not become overtly involved in the campaign but would urge good citizenship on the part of all regardless of party label.[58] Norris also went after Baylor University for harboring an Al Smith club on its campus, saying, "They Have Defiled the Oldest and Greatest Baptist University."[59]

Encouraging to Norris was the position of E.Y. Mullins, the eminent Baptist scholar from Southern Baptist Theological Seminary in Louisville. Although he had lambasted Mullins on the evolution issue just three years earlier, Norris now published Mullins's statement outlining his opposition to Smith. Mullins spoke first of prohibition, saying that he would oppose the wet Smith even if the candidate were Baptist or Methodist. Then, in a trenchant analysis of regional politics and the urban-rural split in America, Mullins classified Smith plausibly as a representative of the wet, urban East whose interests were opposed to those of the dry, rural and agrarian South. Furthermore, argued Mullins, the Democratic platform in its stated support for the Eighteenth Amendment was inconsistent with the candidate who believed that prohibition was unenforceable. Mullins concluded that while an expression of partisanship was a departure from his usual approach to political questions, in this election he was voting for Hoover. Mullins's involvement in the election of 1928 was an anomaly for him, and it shows the degree to which prohibition and the Smith candidacy affected even the most thoughtful southern Protestants.[60]

As was Norris's practice, he aligned himself with any group or individual who was on the same side of an issue as he was. In late summer, he received a form letter from the *Fellowship Forum*, a newspaper that purported to support "Patriotic Americanism," that read in part, "Without in any way intending to unduly disturb your peace of mind . . . , we are compelled . . . to warn you that, unless the Protestant forces of the United States get busy AT ONCE our country is doomed to fall into the hands of the Pope." The rest of the letter appealed for support through the purchase of subscriptions. It concluded: "If Smith wins, Rome and whiskey Rule. If Hoover wins, America is saved for Americans."[61] Nothing could have summed up Norris's own sentiments any better than those few words, and it is of little surprise that he responded by purchasing several subscriptions to the newspaper.[62]

Believing this was the opportunity for Republicans to break the Democratic stronghold over Texas, Norris aligned himself with the Republican Party itself, as well as the various anti-Smith factions. He believed that there were many Texas Democrats who wanted an excuse to support a Republican candidate, and Hoover was the best one available in his view. He told Creager of the Republican

National Committee that northern Republicans opposing Hoover for the nomination needed to be informed that in Texas there existed a multitude of Democrats who would cross party lines if Hoover were indeed nominated. Norris himself said that he had been convinced for years that the Republicans were better equipped than the Democrats to run the government, but he recognized that it would take the right combination of events to convince many stalwart Texas Democrats to vote Republican.[63] After Hoover had secured the nomination, Norris urged the chairman of the Republican Party to send several well-known Republicans to Texas to stump for Hoover. "While this is the largest Democratic state," he wrote, "yet I would remind you that over half the voters of Texas never vote, and multiplied thousand [*sic*], like myself, welcome the opportunity to break from the old traditional party and this is our opportunity."[64]

Recognizing, however, that most of his followers would not slide as easily into the Republican camp as he had, Norris worked diligently to defeat Smith's nomination. He urged his congregation and readers of the *Fundamentalist* to vote against Smith in local conventions, and he even instructed his parishioners on how to vote in precinct elections. Envisioning a repeat of 1912, when Texas Democrats helped nominate Wilson, he hoped there would be enough anti-Smith Texas delegates at the national convention in Houston to turn the party toward another candidate. Even though he knew a Smith defeat was unlikely, he nevertheless persisted, believing that the sooner he and others could mobilize public opinion against Smith, the better chance there would be to defeat him in the general election if he did get the nomination.[65] Clearly, he hoped that Democrats who could be persuaded to oppose Smith in the spring might be willing to vote for a Republican in the fall.

Warning his readers that he was not going to involve himself in local politics, Norris launched full force into his anti-Smith crusade during the summer of 1928. "As far as the political arena is concerned," he wrote, "[the editor] is interested only in the presidential election, and is wholly indifferent to local issues, persons and controversies."[66] As he had the previous year, he spoke again of the recent assassination of the president of Mexico, accusing Roman Catholics of assassinating the president. Norris told his listeners that the Roman Catholic faith had produced this assassin just as it had produced Leon Czolgocz, the man who had murdered President William McKinley in 1901. "Do the American people want that system in the White House, which resorts to the assassin's bullet or the bloody dagger?" he asked.[67]

Considering charges such as this, it is little wonder that on a few occasions Norris met with hostile opposition just as he had the year before. At a rally in Dallas a woman stood to take issue with Norris's remarks, and according to the stenographer, she used profanity as she approached the platform. She was stopped by ushers and escorted from the premises by police. Norris responded with what was probably his bitterest anti-Catholic invective of the entire campaign:

> Now, we are prepared to have order here tonight. We are not surprised at the lowdown whiskey-soaked imps of Hell. The toe-kissing Tammanyites are here for the purpose of creating a disturbance, and I will serve notice on you now that this is Texas and not Mexico. Now, you who are here to disturb this meeting, get up on your hind feet and stand where we can see you. . . . Now, we will proceed and I call upon all red-blooded white folks here tonight, who love God, who love the flag, and who love order, to exercise your rights as American citizens and see to it that none of this ring-kissing Tammany Hall gang cause any more interference or disturbance.[68]

For Norris this was holy war. He expressed to fellow evangelist and pastor Mordecai Ham his hope that Al Smith would come to Texas to campaign, saying, "[We'll] get on his tail light and stay on it until he leaves. We will hang on to him like Wellington did Napoleon and Waterloo's inevitable."[69]

In June, after Hoover had secured the Republican nomination, Norris broadened his anti-Smith campaign into support for Hoover. To Texas Democrats worried about bolting their own party, Norris attempted to portray Hoover as a Democrat in Republican clothing. In jubilation at the nomination, he issued the headline "The Republicans Nominate a Democrat," citing as evidence that Hoover had worked in the Wilson administration. It mattered little that for most of the twenties Hoover had been employed in the Harding and Coolidge administrations. Norris supported Hoover because he was in favor of prohibition and he was running against a Roman Catholic. Norris envisioned a holy crusade to save America that would proceed under the Stars and Stripes and the "white flag of Prohibition." The theme song would be "Onward Christian Soldiers," and the campaign would be the start of a great spiritual awakening for America.[70]

Having exposed Smith's religious position for more than a year, it was now time to delve into Hoover's Quaker background. Norris pronounced Hoover orthodox in matters of the trinity, deity of Christ, new birth for the believer, and the work of the Holy Spirit. He went into an extended discussion of George Fox, the founder of the Quakers, emphasizing that the Society of Friends had always stood for justice for all men. Norris found evidence of the same conviction in the Belgian relief effort Hoover headed during World War I. Norris wrote: "It is not far to see the religious influences that have entered the life of Herbert Hoover. One of the outstanding characteristics of Quakerism is justice for all men. And it is not difficult to understand how the call of Belgian's [sic] millions of suffering human beings made an appeal to him whose practical application of Christianity is 'to visit the fatherless, the widows, and the strangers.'"[71] Understandably, Norris made no mention of the Quaker doctrine of the inner light, which could be interpreted to mean that believers sometimes received direct, extrabiblical revelation from God, nor did the militant Norris discuss the central Quaker doctrine of pacifism. It would have been difficult indeed to square such beliefs with fundamentalist theology.

Norris clearly revealed his enthusiasm for this campaign in a letter he wrote to Creager. He told the Republican Committee member that the Hoover supporters needed to do more. He suggested that the party send an appeal for support to every Protestant minister in the state, that it create a press bureau to answer pro-Smith newspaper propaganda and to send pro-Hoover material to the small county newspapers, and that it set up a separate women's brigade to support Hoover. Bewildered, Creager responded that these were all worthy ideas but that the party could only do so much because of limited resources.[72]

Norris was virtually indefatigable as he barnstormed Texas. For the week of September 10, he scheduled speeches in nine cities, and at the end of the week he estimated that he had spoken to thirty thousand people.[73] The harder he campaigned, the more optimistic he became about Hoover's chances to take Texas and win the election. He wrote privately in late August, "I am speaking every day and night against [Smith], and speaking to crowds of from five to ten thousand," and he estimated that at best Smith would take only a few southern states.[74] In September issues of the *Fundamentalist* Norris published results of straw polls that showed Hoover gaining strength. Upon receiving a request from a Baptist pastor in Indiana for materials to be used in the anti-Smith campaign there, Norris replied that victory for Hoover in Indiana appeared certain.[75] The September 28 issue of the *Fundamentalist* included a front-page headline that referred to New York fundamentalist John Roach Straton,

"Dr. Straton versus Governor Smith." That same page was plastered with headlines reading, "Plains Going for Hoover in Landslide" and "Eight Thousand Hear J. Frank Norris at Lubbock."

On a few occasions Norris appealed for support for Hoover on issues other than Prohibition and Roman Catholicism. In August, he had said that even if the primary issues were economic, he would still back Hoover because the Republican had the most far-reaching program for industrial development of any candidate who had ever run for the presidency. Norris also discussed immigration, warning people that Smith's open policy would threaten Americans' jobs.[76] As the campaign entered its final month, Norris emphasized the issue of immigration again and also began saying he supported the Immigration Act of 1924 because it virtually ended immigration of southern Europeans. The massive influx of southern Europeans provided foot soldiers for corrupt political machines like Tammany Hall, he said.[77]

In addition to the immigration of non-Anglos, Norris also dealt with the question of race and segregation during the anti-Smith campaign. While this story is covered in chapter 8, suffice it to say here that Norris went into some detail attempting to show that the election of Smith would be a threat to southern segregation and white supremacy. The race issue came up at the end of the campaign season and marked the end of Norris's anti-Smith efforts. Hoover went on to win a resounding victory much to the delight of the "Hoover Democrats" in Texas. Texas electoral votes went to a Republican candidate for the first time since Reconstruction, and anti-Smith headquarters recognized Norris accordingly. At a celebration at Norris's church, the chairman of the Texas anti-Smith forces presented Norris with an engraved watch and thanked the fundamentalist preacher for having done more than anyone else to swing Texas into the Republican column.[78] Norris was also invited to Washington, D.C., for the inauguration in March. He accepted and attended.

The Meaning of the Election of 1928

On the Sunday following the election, Norris reflected on its meaning. He outlined five important points. One, it was a referendum on prohibition. Two, it proved that Tammany Hall could not intimidate the American people. Three, it showed that the alien crowd of immigrants with "un-American" ideals could not take charge of the White House. On this point, Norris remarked that southern European immigrant groups in New York who voted for Smith would have to go to school some more in the "university of one-hundred percent Americanism." Four, the election showed that the Roman Catholic hierarchy could not control the American government. This was the primary issue of the campaign according to Norris. Finally, the election reaffirmed religious liberty. Norris believed, ironically, that Protestant ministers, like himself, were the ones who had been under attack during the campaign.[79]

Sensing a possible backlash from his intense involvement in politics, Norris vigorously defended the preacher's place in the political arena. He named political preachers throughout history from the prophets to the Protestant reformers of the sixteenth century who had been involved in the burning issues of their day. Calling for renewed involvement in a variety of political issues, including, of course, prohibition, Norris remarked that Christianity needed "political preachers" more than ever and that their churches would be the ones to grow.[80] That such a defense was necessary became evident when the Baptist General Convention of Texas adopted a "Report on Laymen's Work" that lamented the divisive partisanship that had infected Baptist churches during the campaign of 1928. Norris simply attributed the resolution to Democrats who were bitter about defeat.[81]

Norris also proved to be a rather ungracious winner when he sent the following message to John Jacob Raskob, the head of the Democratic National Committee: "As one of the tens of thousands of ministers that you and the Roman Catholic Hierarchy, plus the liquor crowd, failed to intimidate, I hope you will understand the meaning of the handwriting on the wall, the unmistakable verdict of the American people against you and all others who called prohibition a damnable affliction, and who made the un-American and unfair threat against the ministry of America." Scheduled to preach the following week in New York City, Norris challenged Raskob to be present. To Norris's way of thinking, he was emulating Elijah when the Old Testament prophet challenged the false prophets of Baal.[82]

In the months following the election, Norris carried on his anti-Smith, anti–Roman Catholic campaign. At the end of November, he issued the headline "The Final Dual Alliance of the Beast or Anti-Christ and the False Prophet, the Papacy."[83] The following week he charged that a prominent Baptist who supported Smith had engineered a huge embezzlement scam at a local hospital. The next week, he announced in the *Fundamentalist* that "Anger and Despair Mark Reaction in Vatican at News of Smith's Defeat." Then, in February, came the headline "Rome Defies Protestant America."[84]

Norris recognized that, having helped persuade a solidly Democratic state to go Republican, he now had a stake in the performance of the man he had worked so hard to help elect. He wasted no time, therefore, in propagandizing for Hoover. Using his newspaper, he portrayed the president-elect as "An Inspiration to Every American Boy" for having risen from poor orphan to president. As he had done during the campaign, he emphasized Hoover's strong religious background. Upon returning from the inauguration festivities in Washington, Norris told how heartened he had been when he saw a Bible on the desk of the new president. This occasioned Norris to comment on the history of the presidency itself. "Of the 30 Presidents this country has had," he opined wistfully, "it is worth while to say, not one of them has ever been an infidel. I know it was said one or two were, but it was not so. . . . And I don't ever expect to see an infidel or a Roman Catholic in the White House."[85] In a letter to Mordecai Ham, Norris gloried in the memories of the inauguration just passed, saying, "Indeed it was like an old-fashioned revival. A new era has come for America." He told the fellow evangelist that Hoover was "a strong believer in the fundamentals of the Christian faith."[86]

On practical political matters, Norris tried to capitalize on his influence within the Republican Party. He wrote several letters to R.B. Creager of the Republican Party in Texas suggesting various individuals for appointive office within the Hoover administration. That Norris indeed carried some influence at this time was evidenced by his being called to testify before the Brookhart Committee, which was investigating some of the activities of the Republican Party in Texas during the election. Creager thanked Norris for his defense of the party and assured him that the Republicans would go forward with plans to build a strong organization in Texas.[87]

The End of Prohibition

The euphoria of victory did not last long for Norris, however. He realized that prohibition was coming under increasing attack. In the spring of 1929, he began a new round of sermons and articles on the issue, even warning during a postinauguration sermon entitled "A New Era for America" that opposition to prohibition was mounting and that the battle would continue.[88] When the president of the Catholic University of America criticized prohibition, Norris used the occasion to keep the issues of liquor and Roman Catholicism tightly intertwined. He argued that such criticism was really an attack on the constitution, and he charged that the papacy had al-

ready entered into an alliance with the Soviet Union, Italy, and
Mexico and would seek to rule America, too. Norris reiterated his
belief that one's allegiance went first to the nation. He quoted ap-
provingly a Texas friend who had told Norris he was a loyal Catholic
but that he would choose his nation over his church if ever faced
with a decision of that kind.[89]

By the summer of 1929, Norris exhibited an almost pathologi-
cal anger in the face of the continued attacks on prohibition. Although defeated in the election of 1928, the wet Roman Catholic
forces refused to surrender on the liquor issue. When a former
Roman Catholic, Barry Miller, was rumored for the governorship of
Texas, Norris launched once again into the sort of rhetoric that had
been so prevalent during the anti-Smith campaign. He accused
Miller of an insincere conversion to Protestantism, since the
candidate's wife and family were still of the Roman Catholic faith.
Miller opposed prohibition, which also proved to Norris that the potential candidate had not really forsworn his allegiance to the
Catholic Church. Miller's candidacy gave Norris a new opportunity
to address issues from the 1928 campaign, and he attacked the perceived conspiracy anew, saying: "I am trying to show you people
here, God's own white men and women, thoroughbred Americans,
who love your flag and native land, who love home and children, I
am trying to show you tonight the deepest laid scheme ever born in
hell now that this crowd from John Jacob Raskob on down through
the Texas Senate to Barry Miller—that alien, liquor, Roman Catholic, negro crowd are trying to undermine everything we hold dear!
But they are not going to do it." Norris's venom was unmatched
even by the 1928 campaign when he said, "I think it is high time
that the Texas Senate was passing a resolution, that the Pope of
Rome and John Jacob Raskob leave the Democratic party and go to
hell where they belong." Expressing a desire that the Roman Catholics sue him for libel, he spewed, "I wish they would—if I could ever
get one of those black bosoms on the witness stand I would twist
that bosom back behind where it belongs before I got through with
him."[90]

In 1930, after Miller had officially entered the race for the
Democratic nomination for governor, Norris continued to pursue
him. Norris ran a picture in the *Fundamentalist* showing the candidate with a priest on the steps of a Roman Catholic college in
Austin. The caption alleged that if Miller were elected, the new governor would replace the Protestant Bible with a Catholic one in the
governor's mansion.[91] Norris endorsed Earle B. Mayfield for gov-

ernor and alleged that Roman Catholics were planning to spend a million dollars to defeat this Protestant candidate. Norris cited as evidence a deceased state senator who had revealed this Catholic plot to Norris personally while on his death bed. Norris also refuted rumors that Mayfield himself was secretly wet, saying these charges were based on hearsay, but they were precisely the kinds of charges that Norris always accepted as true when leveled against his opponents. Several candidates were vying for the nomination, and Mayfield did not make the runoff. Norris was only slightly disappointed, however, because the two who did, Ross Sterling and Ma Ferguson, were also in favor of prohibition. (Much to Norris's surprise, Ferguson, unlike her husband, had favored prohibition while governor in the twenties.) Sterling eventually beat Ferguson for the nomination and thereby the governorship of Texas.[92] Norris expressed his approval of Sterling's nomination with the headline "Texas Elects Life-Long Prohibitionist and Hoover Democrat as Governor."[93]

Norris supported several other prohibition candidates during the summer of 1930. He issued a strong plea for Bob Stuart's reelection to the district attorney's office of Fort Worth, alleging that Stuart's opponent was a bootlegger. Norris lauded Stuart for his strict enforcement of prohibition.[94] Throughout the summer, Norris argued that prohibition was working, as he urged his listeners and readers to make it the primary issue in politics. He also reminisced about the campaign of 1928, and he once again defended his intense involvement in politics.[95]

Interspersed throughout the articles and sermons on the specific political races of 1930 were Norris's general comments on the broad conspiracy of the wet Roman Catholic forces. He sought to keep the various elections always in this context. For example, in August he charged that Raskob, the Roman Catholics, and the liquor forces were spending huge sums of money to malign President Hoover. With Smith temporarily in the background, Norris identified Raskob, the Democratic Party chairman, as the primary conspirator. Now the issue was "Raskob, Rum, and Romanism." Norris believed it was time to put party affiliation aside in an effort to save America from this "triple conspiracy." Rome, he charged, had seized absolute control of the Democratic Party, while Hoover and his attorney general fought vigorously to enforce prohibition laws.[96]

In the spring of 1931, Norris predicted that Smith would be nominated by the Democrats for a second time in 1932, and he charged that the Roman Catholic forces were capitalizing on the depressed economy to criticize Hoover. Norris had so convinced himself of the Roman Catholic conspiracy within the Democratic party that he could not anticipate the nomination of anyone other than the Catholic Smith.[97] He wasted no time in gearing up for another crusade to save the nation. In the classic paranoid style of politics identified by historian Richard Hofstadter, Norris began with the plausible and factual argument that the Catholics desired to overturn the Eighteenth Amendment, then proceeded to the implausible and irrational belief that they were out to overthrow the country. "The very ecclesiastical power I have been talking about is doing its level best, in league with all hell, to overthrow the Constitution," he wrote in March 1931. "You say, 'why do they want to do it?' Here is why—if they could break down our educational system, do away with our public schools, if they could destroy free speech, then Rome could hold high carnival in the greatest land on the earth today! That's what they want. That's their purpose."[98]

To make his appeal to Texas Democrats, Norris once again had to emphasize that the issues were too great to let party affiliation or anything else stand in the way of saving America. He told how he had supported Bryan in 1896 and had in fact been a Democrat right up until Smith became a candidate. To soften the perception that he had turned against his southern Democratic heritage, he defended himself to the applause of his congregation by saying, "Listen, friends, my grandfather was a Democrat, my father was a Democrat, and I am a Democrat, but I don't care if the whole South, the whole state, my church, and everybody else shall vote with John Jacob Raskob, I will be one man that will vote against it [the anti-prohibition conspiracy], so help me God!"[99] When Roosevelt got the nomination instead of Smith, Norris's agenda was reduced to one issue—prohibition. He worried that neither party had come out in favor of national prohibition and that the Democrats had even begun to advocate repeal of the Eighteenth Amendment. Rather than being downcast, however, he believed that this might rally the churches to war once again. Clearly, he was relieved that Smith had not gotten the nomination, writing, "Thank God he never will get in the White House."[100]

Norris called prohibitionist Protestants to war in 1932 by arguing that God may have permitted the scourge of anti-prohibition to come over America because the churches needed to be called to militancy. Privately, however, he feared apathy might be the biggest opponent that year now that the threat of Roman Catholicism had been diminished. He wrote to fundamentalist Presbyterian pastor Mark Matthews in Seattle, saying, "The South went for Hoover four years ago not on account of Al Smith's liquor, but because of his Roman Catholicism."[101] The keys to keeping the country dry were enforcement of the statutes already in force and the maintenance of a dry Congress. Enforcement required the election of dry local officials, and a dry Congress would head off any attempt to repeal the Eighteenth Amendment.[102] Having previously been consistent in his expressed confidence that the amendment would stand, in 1932 he acknowledged for the first time that prohibition might soon become a state issue. He admitted that states such as New York might soon become wet but that Texas could maintain its dry status regardless.[103]

Although the Republican Party was soft on Prohibition in 1932, Norris continued to support Hoover. When Kansas right-winger Gerald Winrod wrote to Norris sounding him out on a possible third party, Norris responded emphatically that this was no time to abandon the president. "He has fought a great battle for prohibition and should not be deserted in this hour of crisis," Norris wrote. "I have absolute unbounded confidence in him and believe that prohibitionists would make the blunder of history to bring about his defeat at this time."[104] Unable to bash Roosevelt on religious grounds, Norris had earlier told the Reverend Matthews that he could scarcely believe the American people would elect Roosevelt because he was "wet and communist." Norris recognized, however, that in the midst of economic depression the people might indeed oust the Republicans.[105]

Surprisingly, Norris did little during the campaign of 1932. After August, he rarely mentioned the election in the *Fundamentalist*, and he seems to have done no serious campaigning himself. He evidently found it much more difficult to support Hoover fervently in the midst of an economic depression than to campaign against Smith when the Roman Catholic issue was burning hotly. In December, with the election completed, the Republicans defeated, and national prohibition in grave danger, Norris was desperate. He urged people to pressure the Texas legislature, which was to consider repeal of the state's main Prohibition enforcement law and whether or not to hold a state constitutional convention. He was angry that this was happening not in Chicago or New York but in Texas. In reference to the temperance agitator of the nineteenth century he said, "I want all the Carrie Nations to get their hatchets out and go to grinding them on the grind-rock before breakfast. You can't win this fight by sprinkling a little Rose water, or reading poetry." Then, speaking more specifically on how to combat the wet forces, he said, "Here is the method, the way to handle them: Publish every last thing you can get on the dirty lowdown liars—go after their skeletons, pull them out—

get a pass key and go into the closet, tear out all the low-down things he had ever done." He warned that if the anti-Prohibition forces succeeded, God would judge America and the nation would be doomed as Babylon had been at the height of its glory.[106]

In January 1933, when Congress repealed the Volstead Act, Norris admitted sadly that the battle to maintain national prohibition was lost. He attributed the defeat to the many churches and ministers who believed that the victory had been won when the Eighteenth Amendment had gone into effect. He did not include himself in this group, and rightfully so, for he had been vigilant throughout prohibition. Norris believed that the impending repeal of the Eighteenth Amendment was the worst tragedy in American history, eclipsing even the Civil War.[107] Clearly, he believed that America's moral foundation, which he equated with maintenance of prohibition, was more important than its constitutional union.

After one more call for a last-ditch effort to save national prohibition, Norris turned his energy toward trying to maintain Prohibition on the state level. He interpreted the demise of prohibition as a sign that American civilization was in decline. To a congregation billed as the largest ever gathered in the First Baptist auditorium, Norris said that former civilizations including Babylon, Phoenicia, ancient Greece, and ancient Rome were all marked by drunkenness in their last days. He was determined to keep as much of the country as dry as possible to avert the decline of America.[108]

The statewide campaign seemed to reenergize Norris, as he campaigned and lobbied with nearly as much zeal as he had displayed against Al Smith in 1928. The *Fundamentalist* was filled nearly every week during the winter and spring of 1933 with articles and sermons on the issue. Norris worked in cooperation with several ministers from various denominations. On March 5, for example, they spoke at the First Christian Church of Fort Worth. They then passed a resolution refuting charges that they were divided on the issue of prohibition. The document read in part, "Be It Resolved, by the Ministerial Association, that on this fight against liquor, gambling, vice and lawlessness, in Fort Worth, Austin and throughout the state and nation—on these particular issues there is no division of opinion."[109] The resolution stated that the ministers present were prepared to fight to "a glorious finish," and Norris, at least, was true to that promise in the following months.

Lamenting that in April fourteen states would reopen legal saloons, Norris attacked the brewing companies, charging that they were bribing state legislatures to repeal dry laws. Clearly more desperate than ever, he interpreted legal advertising campaigns as slush funds. In characteristic Norris fashion, he failed to prove his case, usually saying that if necessary he would reveal all the facts behind his charges. Evidence against brewing companies which he did, in fact, reveal included examples of activities as far back as 1905, but none more recent than 1919 before the Eighteenth Amendment had gone into effect.[110]

Turning the American doctrine of "innocent until proven guilty" on its head, Norris said the burden of proof lay with those who voted in favor of wet laws to show that they had not accepted bribes. Norris called for investigations into the bank accounts of those who had voted in favor of legalized liquor sales. "Watch the bank accounts of every legislator that votes for the beer bill," he wrote. "See if they take long summer excursions."[111] Norris called for the investigation not only of Texas state representatives and senators but of Oklahoma legislators as well. In a move that appears comical today, the beer companies retaliated by accusing Norris of accepting payment from Coca-Cola.[112]

Leading up to the August 26, 1933, vote on whether Texas would remain dry, Norris, by his own count, spoke more than 120 times to audiences ranging from one thousand to ten thousand. The number of speeches eclipsed his record for the 1928 presidential race. In May, he even took his case directly to the Texas Senate, where he outlined the pre-1919 activities of brewing companies. There would be no statewide prohibition in Texas, however. After August, Norris's only hope was to persuade as many counties as possible to pass local dry laws. He attempted to find something positive in the battle itself, which in his view had stirred and unified many Protestants in Texas. In September came the final calamity. Norris's own Tarrant County legalized liquor sales. He maintained adamantly that he would not give up, but he was not specific as to whether he believed Fort Worth could really be dry again or merely that he could persuade people voluntarily to abstain from alcohol.[113]

It was two more years before Norris reconciled himself to the fact that prohibition was gone forever. His campaign was reduced to the county level after August 1933, but he continued to speak frequently on the issue. Whenever a prominent individual or newspaper reported the adverse effects of the repeal of prohibition, Norris was quick to say, "I told you so." In 1935, he all but admitted the improbability of reinstating national or state dry laws when he said that prohibition would triumph again when Christ returned to earth to set up the millennial kingdom.[114]

The End of Norris's Anti-Catholicism

Following the repeal of the Eighteenth Amendment, Norris ceased to be anti-Catholic, at least in the political sense. Over time, he reconciled himself to an America that was religiously diverse. In 1940, when he thought Secretary of State Cordell Hull, a Roman Catholic, might get the Democratic nomination for president, Norris urged that there be no religious prejudice: "The world has lived one hundred years since 1928."[115] In the forties, in fact, Norris viewed the Roman Catholic Church as his ally in the fight against communism, and ironically some other fundamentalists accused him of "selling out to the pope."[116]

Norris was not above using the Catholic issue where it suited his purposes, however. For example, in 1950 when Texas governor Allan Shivers planned to run for the U.S. Senate seat held by Norris's friend Tom Connally, Norris told the senator privately that the governor's wife was an active Catholic, which meant that "the Catholics are in charge of the Shivers family." Norris acknowledged that Connally could not address the issue himself, but told the senator, "Your friends will." Norris planned to say nothing about the Shivers family's affiliation with the Church until late in the campaign. When Connally replied to Norris, he said nothing of the Catholic question—neither endorsing nor vetoing Norris's plan. He said only that he appreciated Norris's support. Curiously, Norris's desire that Connally defeat Shivers was a reversal of the position he had expressed in a letter to General Douglas MacArthur a few months earlier. In that letter he told the general that he hoped Shivers would defeat Connally.[117]

The reason Norris believed that the Catholic issue was viable again in the early fifties was that President Harry Truman had appointed an ambassador to the Vatican. On this particular question, Norris played both sides. When he was lashing out at communism, he often criticized fellow Baptists for being too hard on Roman Catholics on the ambassadorship dispute. Then, when he addressed the ambassador issue itself, he agreed with fellow Baptists that Truman's appointment was a violation of the separation of church and state. As was often the case for Norris, his position on this subject sometimes depended on what point he was attempting to make at the time. For the most part, however, he never publicly displayed the type of rabid anti-Catholicism that had been so much a part of him during the twenties and early thirties. He even received a letter in 1951 criticizing him for his change in attitude. The writer remembered the old anti-Catholic Norris with fondness. Norris refused to even acknowledge that he had changed his views, however, saying only, "My position on Roman Catholicism is unchanged. I do commend the Pope for his anti-Communistic stand and have told him personally."[118]

Norris's disclaimer notwithstanding, his position on Roman Catholicism had changed dramatically. Where once he viewed Catholics as incapable of being real Americans, he now saw them as part of an organization that in its anticommunism was attempting to do the same thing he was—save America. The issues had changed. Norris had once tried to save America from Catholics, but he now stood with them to save America from communism. With regard to prohibition, Norris recognized after 1935 that America's salvation from the evil of alcohol could only succeed through moral persuasion instead of law. The machinery of government had failed to solve that issue, but there were other threats, and Norris would do what he could to influence the political arena to see that these were defeated and America saved. Significantly, whereas Norris changed his position with regard to Catholicism and legal prohibition, he retained one important element of the 1928 campaign against Al Smith—Republicanism. For the rest of his career, there was always at least one major issue that kept Norris in the Republican fold.

4

Dispensational Prophet

While Norris's nativism was driven for the most part by forces other than his fundamentalist theology, he did employ theology in his commentary on many public issues especially in the realm of international affairs. More than any other fundamentalist belief, dispensational premillennialism seems to have affected Norris's views in this and other areas. Whereas fundamentalists like Norris employed the inductive method and literal brand of scriptural exegesis to reject the evolutionary view of the earth's origins, they seem to have abandoned that approach to the Bible to arrive at their preferred theory concerning the other end of the historical spectrum. It seems unlikely that anyone applying merely common sense and the inductive method to the Bible would have arrived at the widely accepted fundamentalist eschatological formulation known as dispensational premillennialism.[1]

This theory, which fundamentalists like to call "rightly dividing the word of truth," divides human history into periods or dispensations, usually seven in number. In each period, God relates differently to humankind. For example, during the dispensation of law the divine demands made on individuals are quite different from those made during the dispensation of grace. Perhaps the most profound practical upshot of dispensationalism is that it divides the Bible, making some passages applicable to one dispensation but not to another. This helped fundamentalists to explain, for example, why some prophecies had not come true, or why they believe it unnecessary to live in accordance with the Sermon on the Mount. In the latter case, they could claim that the Sermon should be taken literally but that it did not apply to the present dispensation. The teachings contained therein were meant only for the dispensation of the kingdom that will come after the end of natural history.

Although church fathers including the great theologian Augustine of the fifth century sometimes divided history into various dispensations, it was left to nineteenth-century British religious leader John Nelson Darby of the Plymouth Brethren to develop dispensationalism in its modern, systematic form. Popularized in America by the Bible conference movement and especially the Scofield *Reference Bible*, which appeared in 1909, dispensationalism, by the 1920s, was well on its way to becoming the dominant eschatological view within Fundamentalism.[2]

Norris's Brand of Dispensational Premillennialism

Norris seems to have been converted gradually to dispensationalism. He began in 1907 to publish in the *Baptist Standard* articles by William Bell Riley, who had become an ardent dispensationalist. The years from 1917 to 1924 also seem important. During this period Norris invited many northern dispensationalists to preach in his Fort Worth church, including James Gray and C.I. Scofield. Norris once cited New York fundamentalist I.M. Haldeman's influence as critical for his own conversion to the theory.[3] In all likelihood a variety of factors contributed to Norris's becoming a dispensationalist, not the least of which was his desire to be a thoroughgoing fundamentalist in contradistinction to Baptist leaders in the South.

Norris would later distinguish himself from most of the leading fundamentalists of the North, however, by junking the sevenfold dispensational system for a simpler three-part doctrine. He specifically repudiated Scofield's formulation in articles entitled "Where the Scofield Bible Is in Gross Error" and "Where Scofield Missed It." In the first he admitted that he still used the Scofield *Reference Bible*, but charged that Scofield had been too much a slave to the number seven, stretching here and shrinking there to find seven of this or seven of that. In the second article, Norris wrote, "There are some people who think more of Scofield et al. than they do of Paul, Peter and James."[4]

As Norris grew old, he became scornful of full-fledged dispensationalism. Preaching in 1951, he charged that "this dispensational business has been the most overdone thing. . . . And they have dispensationed out many of the great truths." He criticized specifically the dispensation of the Holy Spirit, arguing that the Holy Spirit had been present in the Old Testament as well as the New. "I don't any longer believe, and I haven't for years, in the several dispensations." Law, grace, and the millennium were all he accepted. When an ardent dispensationalist charged that Norris's new views were "not according to Scofield," Norris retorted, "Scofield was not Paul and not

Moses." He then joked almost wistfully that rejecting the Scofield system had ruined several good sermons, including some of his own.[5]

In rejecting the more elaborate form of dispensationalism, Norris was being more consistent in his approach to the Bible than many of his brethren. He believed that Scofield had stretched the words of Scripture to say things that a plain, commonsense rendering would never have revealed. Norris was no slave to consistency, however. He junked the seven dispensations because they were not readily apparent in Scripture, but he maintained that premillennialism was absolutely the only correct way to read passages of the Bible referring to the end of time. Premillennialism was more than a doctrine, he argued. It was a way of life. He even argued, rather astoundingly, that premillennialism was as central to Christian orthodoxy as was the crucifixion of Christ. For Norris any other eschatological formulation was rank heresy.[6] Moreover, he retained belief in the pretribulation rapture, the idea that Christians will be spirited out of the world before the great tribulation that many evangelicals believe will erupt just before Christ's return. While held almost universally by fundamentalists, this doctrine is quite possibly as problematic as the seven dispensations. It was perhaps natural that like many twentieth-century evangelicals he would cling to the hope that Christians would not be required to face the great persecution of the tribulation.

Like most twentieth-century premillennialists, and like many Christians throughout history, Norris believed he was living in the end times. The signs were everywhere, and the rapture was quite possibly close at hand.[7] In a 1945 sermon entitled "Is This the Last Generation?" he explicated Matthew 24:34: "Verily, verily, I say unto you, this generation shall not pass till all these things be fulfilled." The word *generation* is the key to interpreting the passage, and Norris said that he had formerly agreed with other premillennialists that the word referred to the Jews. He had changed his mind by 1945, however, and now opted for a more literal reading. The word *generation* meant—the last generation of humankind, during which tremendous signs would appear, all of which were either present or close at hand when Norris preached this sermon. First, there would be a universal war. The second sign was famine, which was likely in the wake of the war. Third, there would ascend to power a worldwide dictator. Josef Stalin was the likely candidate.[8] As was usually the case, Norris hedged just shy of predicting with certainty that God's consummation of history was in progress. However, he kept his listeners in a state of readied expectation. He did this often, usually by applying his dispensational views to world events.

World War I

World War I was a watershed event in American religious history.[9] While most Americans supported U.S. entry into the war in 1917, the level of support varied among conservative evangelicals. William Jennings Bryan and Billy Sunday symbolize the divergence of views within this segment of American Protestantism. Bryan resigned as secretary of state in 1915 because he was convinced that Woodrow Wilson's strong protest to Germany concerning the sinking of the *Lusitania* would lead to war. His effort to keep America from entering the war included a campaign against preparedness and a last-ditch effort to persuade congressmen to put the war issue before their constituents in a referendum before voting for a formal declaration. When these efforts failed, Bryan reluctantly, but dutifully, supported the war effort. He believed that while it was his right to oppose entry into the war, once the nation had entered, it was his duty to support his country.[10]

Billy Sunday became one of America's leading voices in support of the war. For him patriotism and Christianity were synonymous. Shortly after the United States entered the war, Sunday said, "In these days all are patriots or traitors to their country and the cause of Jesus Christ." In a statement that revealed Sunday's own anti-German sentiment and the fundamentalist view that German philosophy was a threat to America, he said, "I tell you it is [Kaiser] Bill against Woodrow, Germany against America, Hell against Heaven." He continued, saying he had no use for "that weazen-eyed, low-lived, bull-neck, low-down gang of cut-throats of the Kaiser."[11]

Sunday was not alone in his pronouncements on the war, and the variations of fervor certainly did not divide along liberal and conservative theological lines. Many other Protestant ministers and theologians, both liberals and conservatives, felt exactly as he did. For example, Professor Ernest DeWitt Burton of the Divinity School at the University of Chicago reasoned that it was in the interest of the German people themselves that the United States defeat their government, since it was based on false ideals. Furthermore, since America was fighting for others and not just itself, the nation was acting in obedience to the Golden Rule. Similarly, W. Douglas MacKenzie of Hartford Seminary argued that America and her allies were exercising the principles of the Sermon on the Mount in opposing Germany and the other Central Powers. Of the even more bizarre variety were statements such as the one by George W. Downs, speaking at Asbury Methodist Episcopal Church in Pittsburgh in November 1917. He said he would have gone over the wall with the other Americans and driven his bayonet into the throat or eye of the Hun without the slightest hesitation of conscience. Similarly, Pastor Herbert Johnson of the Warren Avenue Baptist Church of Boston told his congregation that the bayonet should be driven into the enemy precisely five inches because driving it deeper wasted time that could be used in killing another man.[12]

With support for the war emanating from across the theological spectrum, it is little wonder that dispensationalists came in for some severe criticism at the hands of modernists. If pushed to their logical conclusion, the tenets of dispensational premillennialism precluded the type of enthusiastic support for the war that many Americans exhibited. Beyond merely stemming the German military threat, the war, in the view of many modernists, would bring about positive good. It would, in the words of President Woodrow Wilson, "make the world safe for democracy." Modernist theologians, working from an evolutionary social model, tended to believe that the coming millennial kingdom would result naturally from the progress of modern civilization. In other words, they tended to be postmillennialists who believed that Christ's earthly kingdom was in the process of being built on earth. By contrast, premillennial dispensationalists expected the world to degenerate steadily until Christ's return. Premillennialists' allegiance to earthly powers was always tentative at best. Modernists, therefore, eager for an opening to attack their conservative and premillennial opponents, charged that the views of the premillennialists aided and abetted the Germans. Among several attacks were those by Shirley Jackson Case of the University of Chicago, who even suggested that German money might be fueling the spread of premillennialism. He called for a government investigation of these charges. While premillennialists paid little attention to these specific and spurious accusations, they did prove by the end of the war that they could be as patriotic as anyone else.[13]

Although Norris was neither rabidly anti-German nor consumed with the war, he, like most pastors, supported the war effort. When compared to his extensive coverage of World War II, however, Norris's activity related to the Great War was minimal. Most of his comments on the war came after it was completed and he had had time to reflect on its meaning. During World War I, Norris was busy building his growing church and responding to local issues. He was not well known outside Texas, and he had not yet begun to make world affairs an integral part of his sermons.

Norris started his newspaper the same year that the United States entered World War I. In some of the April and June 1917 issues of this weekly, Norris included anti-German cartoons, a poem about the war, and even a naval chart showing American strength on the seas. In none of these editions, however, was there any other mention of the war. Perhaps most indicative of Norris's attitude toward world events at that time was the June 15 issue of his paper, which included another war cartoon entitled "To France" but carried the headline, "Why Don't They Close the Picture Shows in Dallas?" For Norris, the war was relatively unimportant compared to his role as local social reformer.[14]

In holding "a special service to the soldier boys, their friends and families," Norris recognized and attempted to carry out his pastoral responsibility to those involved directly in the war. He also included in the *Searchlight* a copy of the Fort Worth mayor's proclamation calling for a day of prayer for the war and the young men fighting in it.[15] It was not until after the war that Norris began to acknowledge the political nature of the conflict, and even then he was at first primarily concerned with the theological and prophetic implications of the political changes brought about by the war.

Norris's Zionism

World War I heightened in many conservative evangelicals their sense of the prophetic. This was especially true in 1917 when British forces under General Edmund Allenby wrested Palestine away from the Arabs. Premillennial dispensationalists believe that the dispensation of the church constitutes a historical parentheses or interlude after which God will again work through his chosen people, the Jews. An important part of this end-times scenario was the establishment of the modern nation-state of Israel.[16] Following the war, this is exactly the way in which Norris approached and analyzed the events of 1914 to 1918. He was especially concerned with how this war fulfilled the Old and New Testament prophesies regarding Israel. Accordingly, he announced in 1919 that the cause of the war had not been the actions of the Kaiser, commercial rivalries between Germany and England, nor the ultimatum sent by Austria-Hungary. Rather, God had caused the war to bring Palestine back to the Jews. The nations of the world could not accomplish this alone. Norris went so far as to say that had the nations of the world heeded an earlier appeal to return Palestine to the Jews, they could have averted the war. The war may have left many issues unsettled, and the peace proceedings were yet to be completed when Norris delivered this address, but he was confident that the issue of Palestine was no longer in doubt. It would become a Jewish state.[17]

Norris recognized that the Arabs would not relinquish Palestine without a fight, but he confidently predicted victory for the Jews. As was almost always the case, once Norris chose one group or individual to win, he attempted to convince his readers and listeners that the other side was dastardly and beneath contempt. It was a matter of "survival of the fittest," and the Jew would win because "the Jew is industrious, the Arab lazy; the Jew progressive, the Arab is only half civilized." Considering that Arabs are also Semitic peoples, Norris was anti-Semitic in a way very different from how that term is usually employed. He traveled to Palestine in 1920 and reported that everywhere he went he found "only ignorance, poverty, disease and superstition" among the Arabs. Even a casual glance at the modern Jewish village was enough to convince any person of the superiority of the Jewish way of life over that of the Arab, Norris wrote.[18] Anti-Arab sentiment was the only type of anti-Semitism in which Norris ever engaged.

Because Norris believed the primary significance of World War I would be the ultimate return of Palestine to the Jews, he quite naturally believed that the greatest campaign of the war had been Allenby's defeat of Jerusalem. Norris worked this into biblical prophecy by comparing Allenby's army to the Hebrew followers of Moses who originally settled the promised land. Each "army" had 600,000 people. Futhermore, because Great Britain had rescued Palestine from the Ottoman Turks, they—and indeed the entire Anglo-Saxon race—could claim God's promise, "And I will bless them that bless thee [the Jews], and curse him that curseth thee."[19] These events piqued the interest of many fundamentalists, and Norris was certainly no exception. He viewed the restoration of Israel as a necessary precursor to the second coming of Christ as did most fundamentalists. The Jewish resettlement of Palestine and the advent of the "New Jerusalem" prophesized in the Bible were inextricably related.[20] Norris would periodically return to the prophecy theme and how a restored nation of Israel related to it, and as late as 1933 he reiterated his view that the one significant issue that was settled by World War I was the question of who would rule Palestine.[21]

Norris returned to the issue of Palestine in the late thirties as many fundamentalists engaged in an ugly anti-Semitism. When William Bell Riley began to peddle the famous forgery *Protocols of the Wise Men of Zion*, Norris went on the offensive. The two had already split in 1927 when Norris changed the name of his newspaper to the *Fundamentalist*, convincing Riley that he was trying to make it appear as if the weekly were the official organ of the World's

Christian Fundamentals Association. In 1937, Norris went on the attack against his former associate when he wrote, "I confess my amazement that certain intelligent outstanding Fundamentalist pastors have joined in this age-long and divinely cursed persecution. One of the outstanding Fundamentalists of this hour has published many things that are nothing short of amazing." Norris also published a review of the *Protocols* by "a great jurist" to show how ridiculous the document was.[22] Norris repeated these charges against Riley five months later when he announced, "Dr. W.B. Riley Reverses Himself and Asks for Space in the Fundamentalist."[23] Norris stated clearly why he believed fundamentalists should not persecute Jews: "Of all the peoples on earth that ought not to persecute the Jews or any other race, it is that people called Fundamentalist Baptists. Those who believe in the Premillennial coming of Jesus Christ should certainly do everything in their power to help the Jew because we believe when Christ comes the Jews will be converted, and become the world's greatest evangelists—then why kill them off if they are to be the world's greatest evangelists?"[24] While one might criticize Norris for his overly utilitarian reason for opposing anti-Semitism, he was opposed to anti-Semitism nevertheless, and this set him apart from fundamentalists like Riley, not to mention the likes of Gerald Winrod and Gerald L.K. Smith.[25]

The Norris-Riley debate over the *Protocols* eventually degenerated into a personal battle in which Riley accused Norris of forging material and attributing it to others, and Norris charged that Riley had gone back to the "machine" Baptists he had been opposing for so many years. The battle heated up in the spring of 1938 when Norris wrote his own twenty-five-cent pamphlet refuting the *Protocols*, then published 100,000 copies of a debate between himself and Riley on this matter. Riley finally became so distraught that he claimed he was sorry he had ever taken up with Norris. He was neither the first nor the last who would feel this way.[26]

The debate between Riley and Norris shows the ambivalence that premillennial dispensationalists felt toward Jews. On the one hand, premillennialists believed the Jews were still God's chosen people and were destined to play an important role in end-times prophecy. Conversely, however, Jews were in rebellion against God and as such needed conversion just like other sinners and apostates. Fundamentalists who were premillennialists could not always handle this tension, especially as they became more and more militant after 1920. How could they fight against modernists with such vigor and let Jews, who openly rejected Christ as Messiah, off the hook? Some, like Norris, could do this, while others, like Riley, could not.[27]

The culmination of the Palestine question came, of course, when the modern state of Israel was established in 1948. Understandably, Norris took up the issue again in the late forties, just as he had originally addressed it after World War I. In addition to speaking before a meeting of Jews in Fort Worth, Norris traveled around the country addressing the Palestine question. In Washington, the *Star* announced, "Baptist Official Says Jews Have Just Palestine Claim." The New York *Post* announced, "'Palestine Belongs to Jews by Divine Right': Dr. Norris."[28] Norris also wrote to President Harry Truman outlining the biblical argument in favor of Jewish control of Palestine, and he called for an end to loans to Britain because he believed the Labor government there was controlled by "crackpots" who opposed the formation of Israel.[29] Believing that "the greatest event in 2,000 years is the establishment of the new state of Israel," Norris urged the United States to lift its embargo and supply the Israelis with all the arms they needed. Norris also took another trip to the Holy Land and met with the Grand Mufti, the head of the Arab League, in a futile and perhaps pretentious effort to persuade the Muslim leader to end the opposition to Israel.[30]

Rumors of War

In addition to the question of Palestine, Norris also saw prophetic implications in the League of Nations. He believed the efforts by Wilson and other diplomats to erect the League and eliminate war were commendable but, at the same time, doomed to failure because "the Bible absolutely taught against the possibility of eliminating war from the earth."[31] Furthermore, Norris believed that the only league prophesied in Scripture was one to be headed by the Antichrist. Later in the twenties, when he became concerned about the Roman Catholic Church's influence, he wondered if the pope would rule the League.[32]

Although he opposed Wilson's League, Norris in 1920 praised the president himself. While on a trip to Europe he wrote to his congregation somewhat sarcastically, "The statesmanship of President Wilson is evidenced by the fact that he marvelously succeeded in earning the cordial dislike of all peoples, friend and foe, in Europe." Then, more seriously, he wrote, "Fifty years from now, if the world stands that long, they will be unveiling statues to him as they are now doing to Lincoln."[33] Twenty years later, however, on the eve of America's entry into World War II, Norris's view of Wilson had changed dramatically. At that time, he laid the blame for the second war at the feet of Wilson, whose "untimely" intervention into the first war had brought it to an end before the fighting went into Berlin itself.[34] Norris was referring to Wilson's policy of "peace without victory." He repeated this accusation in 1941. This time he attributed to World War I commander John J. Pershing the advice to carry the war farther and lamented that the Allies had not listened to Pershing.[35] It appears that in addition to the Palestine question, Norris believed that the meaning of World War I was that Germany had been humiliated, but not humiliated enough. Ironically, in 1942 Norris indicated that isolationist senators opposed to Wilson and the League had wrecked the peace and sent the president to an early grave.[36] Norris's ambivalence toward Wilson was tied to the point he wanted to make. When he spoke out against isolationists, as in 1942, Wilson was esteemed for his global-mindedness. When Norris was speaking against Germany, however, as in 1940 and 1941, then Wilson was portrayed as too soft and peace loving for having failed to advocate the total destruction of the Central Powers.

Norris was somewhat ambivalent about Germany itself because Germany did not fit well within dispensational theorizing about the end times. Dispensationalists simply could not identify Germany in the many biblical references to the end of the age. Norris therefore could not work Germany into prophecy to the same extent he would use Russia. Still, the fact that the Allies had failed to thoroughly defeat Germany made the prospects for another world war more likely, and premillennialists were sure there would be another cataclysm. During the twenties and early thirties, there was really only one thing Norris was sure about with regard to the Germans: They would start the next war. His attitude toward Germany and the prospects for another global war changed very little. From Europe in 1920, he wrote, "Germany looks upon war as a business; therefore, the recent war proved a poor business investment and they expect to recoup their losses in the next war. Nobody over here doubts that there will be a 'next war.'"[37] In a letter to the Fort Worth *Tribune* he wrote, "The universal opinion among American and English military men in the occupied portion of Germany is that the war should never have stopped until we went to Berlin. The Germans feel neither repentant nor defeated."[38] He held steadfastly to the view that the militaristic Germans would start another war, and in 1933 he brought together his denunciation of Germany and his ardent Zionism when he claimed, "German militarism ruined the world. German dictatorship is persecuting the Jews, and will plunge the world into another war."[39]

It seems clear that World War I flushed Norris into the open with regard to the prophetic implications of major world events, especially concerning the Jews and the prospects for a new nation of Israel. This was fairly common among premillennialists. Norris was cutting his teeth, so to speak, on the fundamentalist art of fitting the pieces of modern history into the jigsaw puzzle of ancient biblical prophecy. He also came to view Germany negatively, which was hardly unusual in America after the Great War. Furthermore, he made a connection between German militarism and German philosophy and theology from which had come higher criticism and modernism. Norris exhibited this view when he opined nostalgically in 1920, "Ah, if Germany of today were only the land of Luther."[40] This was a typical fundamentalist response following World War I. Clearly, from Norris's perspective, something had gone wrong in Germany. No longer the land of Luther, it was on its way to becoming the land of Friedrich Nietzsche with a might-makes-right, superman philosophy. America's response to such a nation should have been to defeat it totally—the fundamentalist response to modernism—and the failure to do so would bode ill for the world in the future.

Interwar Antichrists

Norris was consistent throughout the twenties and thirties in his effort to place current events into a prophetic framework. Most important, he watched vigilantly for the Antichrist and identified European dictators as possible candidates for that biblical designation. Norris's position regarding the proper responses to these Antichrists, however, underwent significant metamorphosis. At first he argued that resisting the beast of prophecy was futile, then he had a change of heart and advocated armed resistance to Hitler whether he be the Antichrist or not. Before discussing Hitler, however, there were other possible Antichrists to examine. Benito Mussolini was first.

Norris first began commenting extensively on Mussolini in 1926. This was the period when Norris began to pay much more attention to world affairs and less to local politics. Until the end of his career he made it a point to monitor the European situation in sermons and newspaper articles, always looking for the prophetic angle. In his analysis of Mussolini he often integrated anti-Catholicism with his discussion of world affairs. For example, in a sermon entitled "Mussolini—The Earmarks of the Beast of Prophecy," he told his congregation that the reason the Italian fascist dictator received such favorable press coverage was that the Roman Catholic Church had tremendous influence over the media. As the title of this sermon indicates, Norris began to toy with the idea that Il Duce might be the beast spoken of in the apocalyptic literature of the Book of Daniel.[41]

Norris was not dogmatic on this point, and he always had sense enough to hedge his predictions concerning biblical prophecy. That way, when a more plausible Antichrist emerged, he could shift his focus without completely undermining his credibility as a prophet. In fact, he began to backtrack somewhat on Mussolini as early as 1928. This time he entitled his sermon "Mussolini a Type of the Beast of Prophecy," and said, "I will not say that he is, or that he is not the Beast." He did predict boldly, however, that Mussolini's role would be to restore the old Roman Empire, a necessary precursor to the second coming of Christ in the view of many dispensational premillennialists.[42]

Norris's comments on Mussolini in the late twenties must be viewed in the context of his anti-Catholicism and the anti–Al Smith campaign of 1928. Even after Smith's defeat, Norris feared "papal domination" of the United States. Understandably, then, he spoke out vigorously when Mussolini achieved a concordat with the pope in 1929, and as late as 1931, Norris spoke of the threat of Roman Catholicism and intimated that Mussolini could indeed be the "beast."[43] That year, however, he began to shift his focus to Josef Stalin. As with Mussolini, Norris stopped short of declaring that Stalin was the Antichrist, but in another "Earmarks of the Beast" sermon he listed nineteen ways the Soviet leader fit scriptural prophecy.[44]

In 1933 Norris saw dictatorship everywhere, including in Washington. Norris referred to Franklin Roosevelt as a near dictator and said Congress was merely a "rubber stamp." One month later he accused Roosevelt of using the same tactics as Lenin and Mussolini.[45] Norris believed a day was coming when all the dictators—"like Mussolini, Hitler, Stalin, and Roosevelt"—would get together and run the world, and this was all part of a prophesied world dictatorship.[46] By 1936, Norris's rhetoric concerning the American dictatorship had grown to fantastic proportions as he uttered the following statement:

> Do you know that right now we no longer have any more freedom of communication? You say, "I still say what I please," but did you know that the law that once gave you freedom of air, freedom of telegraph—that has been repealed? Did you know that now there is a law that if the president occupying the White House wanted to, he

could simply touch the button and shut off every radio, control every telegraph, bring every telephone wire down. . . . The Radio Commission is no longer, but now we have what is known as the "Communications Commission." The President has it in his power to remove every one of those men in twenty-four hours time and not give the reason for it. The whole thing is in the hands of the President as it is in the hands of Mussolini, Stalin, Hitler. That is what we have in America right now.[47]

Although Norris would later come out vigorously in favor of resistance to the beast of prophecy, whoever he was, in 1933 he preached that Christians should not oppose what was clearly a fulfillment of Scripture. He urged his congregation to go along with Roosevelt's Blue Eagle program even though the emblem could be the mark of the beast. Citing the apostle Paul's admonition in the Book of Romans that Christians are to submit to their government, Norris claimed that American Christians should accept the Blue Eagle or even the swastika if it came to that. These were signs of prophecy and not to be resisted.[48] Other signs included the League of Nations, disarmament conferences, and all other attempts to bring the world into one community. Norris warned, "My friends, there is no use resisting these things, it is part of God's eternal plan of the ages."[49]

Consistently, throughout the mid-thirties, Norris predicted a worldwide dictator who would fulfill biblical prophecy. He often cited the Book of Daniel and the "little horn," a symbol of rebellion against God, which would arise and take its place among the leaders of the world. Norris was unsure which of the present dictators, if any, would be that "little horn," and he was not dogmatic about when this apocalyptic event would take place. He was sure it would be soon, but he was unspecific as to how soon—days, weeks, months, years, or decades. Perhaps one of the present dictators would step forth as the worldwide dictator, or perhaps there would arise one yet unseen.[50] According to Norris, after the onset of the worldwide dictatorship there was to be a wave of persecution of the Jews unlike anything the world had ever seen.[51] He viewed with alarm, therefore, the anti-Semitism of some of the European dictatorships—citing specifically Spain, Russia, and Germany—and he claimed, but did not attempt to prove, that all the dictators since World War I had exhibited anti-Semitism. In 1936, Norris indicated that the worldwide dictator might be communist, and he warned again that the trend of the present and future was dictatorship. Europe, in his view, was on the brink of disaster with France next in line to fall either to fascism or communism.[52] Norris played one optimistic note that year when he praised Roosevelt for calling attention to religion in one of his speeches. Norris reprinted in his newspaper FDR's call for a "revival of the spirit of religion."[53] Unknown to Norris at the time, this was a harbinger of the vigorous support he would offer the president in the latter's preparedness campaign once World War II began.

Understandably, in the late thirties, Norris focused his attention more and more on Germany. At first, most of what he said was quite positive. In 1937, for example, while traveling in Europe he reported to the *Fundamentalist* that Germany had improved since his visit in 1920. Following World War I and the Peace of Versailles, he reported, there was despair. Now, however, "As you move around among the people, they are happy, they are not in fear. Of course they are under dictatorship but I see no signs of it." Comparing Germany to Russia, where he had been denied entrance, he wrote, "Contrast the communists turning me down with the way I was received in Germany. They gave me every courtesy. I preached in Berlin twice."[54]

Norris even spoke favorably of the national planning that had solved many of Germany's economic problems, but he emphasized that people entered voluntarily into the Nationalist Social Welfare Organization. He claimed there was no unemployment and that even a Jewish shop owner had told him that business was good. "Remember Germany is under a dictatorship, but the people like it," he opined. "Communism and labor troubles are unknown. Business is good. What model will America follow to solve our problems? My faith is stronger than ever in the way our fathers left us."[55] While this final sentence was ambiguous in the context of the rest of the report, it is no surprise that Norris was unrestrained in his praise of the German dictatorship when he had been calling the American government a dictatorship for four years.

During the same month that Norris published his own reports on Germany in the *Fundamentalist*, he also published a pro-German article by a "Professor" Coyus Fabricius. Fabricius was most impressed by Germany's anticommunism, and there is little doubt that this was also an important component of Norris's favorable attitude toward Germany. Fabricius wrote that in fighting against communism, Germany was doing a great act of Christian service. Other nations wishing to pursue Christian policy should follow this lead and ally themselves with Germany because Germany stood for "positive Christianity" against "Neo-paganism."[56] A week later, Norris reprinted an article from the London *Daily Mail* that praised Germany for her efforts toward good relations with

Britain and urged Britain to reciprocate. The *Daily Mail* had been advocating closer relations with Germany for a number of years.[57] Concerning Hitler himself, Norris was impressed but wary. "Keep your eye on that forty-seven year old bachelor," he warned after observing a Nazi demonstration. "He is a teetotaler, a vegetarian, drinks nothing but milk. He is a veritable dynamo. He is Napoleonic in his personality and influence over the masses."[58]

Little more than a year after writing these words, Norris began to reverse himself with regard to Hitler and Germany. In yet another "Earmarks of the Beast" sermon, he warned that Hitler, like Mussolini and Stalin before him, could be the Antichrist. Norris once again cited his belief that a worldwide dictator was imminent and would fulfill biblical prophecy.[59] Unlike some fundamentalists, Norris withdrew from the abyss of Nazi fascism because he abhorred anti-Semitism. Anti-Semitism was the one signpost that indicated to him that all was not right in Germany. Norris believed the Jewish-communist conspiracy theory outlined in the *Protocols* made little sense, since there were both communist Jews and capitalist Jews. Furthermore, he found repugnant Nazi scapegoating tactics used to blame the Jews, who were but a very small percentage of the German population, for all the country's ills, including the loss of World War I.[60] While speaking in Toledo, Ohio, in 1938, Norris condemned Hitler for his persecution of the Jews.[61] From this time forward, with the exception of brief praise for Hitler's antiliquor campaign, Norris forthrightly rebuked the German dictator and nazism.[62]

Norris continued to keep careful watch over international events. During and after World War II, he spent less time interpreting world events and more time advocating that something be done about them. He never wavered, however, in his belief that God was bringing history rapidly to a close. Like other fundamentalists, he lived in tension, in what historian Timothy Weber has called "the shadow of the second coming." Norris believed that although the rapture was imminent, Christians were still commanded to persist in the work of the Lord lest he tarry. Norris therefore continued to fight modernism and a host of other perceived threats to the faith and American culture, while building for a future he claimed would probably not come. Dispensational premillennialism provided for him a construct he would use often in analyzing international events.

Conclusion

The fact that Norris spent so much time and effort analyzing and interpreting international events reveals something about his personality and the nature of his fundamentalist mind-set. He clearly seemed to believe that his readers needed his biblical analyses to supplement, or perhaps even displace, what they heard and read in the secular media. There is no doubt that Norris thought himself much more important than he really was when it came to interpreting world events. This was because he believed, as did nearly all fundamentalist leaders, that dispensational premillennialism gave him insights into Scripture and its relationship to history that others simply did not have. How else can one explain his attempts to convey the insights he gained from his trips abroad to people in high places, even to the president of the United States? Likewise, while overseas, Norris often represented himself as being on a fact-finding mission for the United States. On one trip he tried repeatedly to reach Truman, only to have his calls turned away by White House secretaries. On his return from Europe, he actually wanted to stop by Washington and brief the president. Rebuffed for the final time, Norris, in a fit of sour grapes, slammed down a phone receiver, turned to those traveling with him, and said that he had no time to go to Washington anyway.[63]

Dispensational premillennialism as a method of interpreting world events gave Norris an inflated sense of his own importance. It seems to have fed his ego. He knew things nonfundamentalists could never know, and he could act as the indispensable answer man for his constituency, not to mention as an intelligence source for the president of the United States. He felt justified, therefore, in traveling about the world to play out the role of dispensational prophet. As such, he was more than pastor of First Baptist Church of Fort Worth. He was also a national and international figure who could hold his own with anyone when it came to discussions of world events. Ironically, as is so often the case with populist movements like fundamentalism, Norris, as the populist leader, had become the elite leader. His constituents relied on him for their understanding of the world, its history, and the future, and they could rest assured that even if they could not understand these things, Norris could. It is doubtful whether the average members of First Baptist or Temple Baptist even understood dispensational premillennialism. This did not matter, however, because they could listen to Norris explain these deep matters on Sunday and read about them in Norris's newspaper on Friday. They had normal, everyday problems with which to contend, while Norris took care of the big issues and served as their indispensable dispensational prophet.

5

Motor City Man

By the end of the 1920s, Norris was a well-known fundamentalist figure across the South and in the North as he continued in the roles of populist preacher and dispensational prophet. It was at this time that he also exhibited the worst strands of his nativism in the anti-Smith campaign of 1928. He was already moving toward national prominence within fundamentalism when in the thirties he would broaden his influence even further by adding a northern base to his operations. In the depression-ridden thirties, this move would have financial as well as political and religious implications for Norris's career. In short, it would be a major move.

Norris accomplished this broadened base in late 1934 when he accepted the pastorate of Temple Baptist Church in Detroit. For the next sixteen years he served as head pastor of both Temple and First Baptist Fort Worth. In the autumn of 1934, Norris had preached at Temple in a series of meetings that had also featured the famous evangelist Billy Sunday. The pulpit committee approached Norris with an offer to become pastor. He returned to Fort Worth without giving an answer, then went back to Detroit to preach another revival. Finally, the novelty and excitement of pastoring two large urban churches nearly twelve hundred miles apart proved irresistible, and he accepted the Temple position. When he did so, he announced that his intention was to help the church do battle with the Northern Baptist Convention, which in the view of fundamentalists was moving rapidly toward modernism. True to his word, after becoming pastor, Norris promptly took Temple Baptist out of the convention.[1]

The dual pastorate also enabled Norris to take his populist message north. As he had done a quarter century earlier in Fort Worth, he transformed an urban church into a congregation of common folk. Indeed, according to Norris's Sunday school superintendent at Temple, G.B. Vick, the church's membership consisted mostly of transplanted rural southerners who had come north looking for work in the automobile factories of Detroit.[2] Temple's meteoric growth indicates that these common laborers were hungry for a simple and straightforward gospel message that pitted absolute good against absolute evil.

The advantages of pastoring both churches were obvious: new subscribers to Norris's newspaper, more church revenue for various outreach projects, and wider exposure for Norris himself. Indeed, the Detroit church assumed the funding of the *Fundamentalist,* and Norris began to broadcast on WJR, a Detroit radio station with fifty thousand watts of power. The addition of the Temple church to Norris's duties seems to have been just what he needed. Temple Baptist had eight hundred members when Norris arrived. After two years, Norris reported 4,336 new members for both of his churches, and after five years Temple Baptist alone had added 6,193. By 1946, the combined membership of both churches was twenty-five thousand, and Norris boasted that it was the largest congregation ever under the leadership of one pastor.[3]

Throughout the latter half of the 1930s, Norris used his broadened base to attack the twin forces of modernism in religion and communism in politics. He also worked to organize new fundamentalist churches and eventually another fundamentalist denomination. His method was to go into a town—often where one of his opponents pastored—hold a revival, and organize the converts into a new church. He would then assign one of his protégés as the temporary leader of the new congregation. Finding young men willing to serve as his understudies was no problem for Norris, as Luther Peak's story attests. In 1932, Peak was just a twenty-four-year-old preacher boy and seminary dropout when he wrote a letter requesting that Norris help him start a ministry in a big city where there would be potential for great growth. After accepting the position at Fundamentalist Tabernacle of Denton, which Norris arranged for him, Peak spent the next twenty years in the Norris movement. Like many other aspiring young preachers, Peak was delighted just to get to know Norris, let alone to be taken under the wing of this fundamentalist firebrand.[4]

Norris led many newly formed churches, and many existing ones that were disaffected within their own denominations, into the World Fundamental Baptist Missionary Fellowship, which became an alternative denomination for those who thought of themselves as Fundamental-Baptists. He also founded a Bible institute in 1930 that would evolve into a seminary at which fledgling fundamentalist pastors trained for the ministry.

Norris's move to Temple Baptist symbolized what had in fact been the case for well over a decade by the mid-thirties: he was a popular preacher to the masses and a national fundamentalist leader. If any further evidence were needed, it was supplied in 1937 by Sinclair Lewis, the renowned author of *Elmer Gantry*. Lewis paid First Baptist a visit, saying that he had "satisfied a desire of a great many years standing—I went to hear Dr. J. Frank Norris preach." Obviously impressed with Norris's huge following, Lewis remarked, "I have never seen before so many people at church at once."[5] Norris's move to Temple would also occasion a shift in political thinking, especially with regard to the New Deal.

Norris and the Early Depression

As a result of the election of 1928 Norris became convinced that the Democrats symbolized and supported the pluralization and secularization of America. In the 1930s, Norris had not reconciled himself completely to the fact that the evangelical consensus of nineteenth-century Protestant America had disappeared. He battled, therefore, against any force that he believed mitigated against that consensus. In the thirties, the New Deal symbolized most powerfully what had gone wrong with America.

The 1930s in America was a decade of immense political change with respect to the role of government in society. Before 1933 and the beginning of the New Deal, the national government, except in times of war, was a rather remote institution not directly experienced by most Americans. When Franklin Delano Roosevelt became president and put the state into the service of economic recovery and relief for those suffering the effects of the depression, many were alarmed at the increased role of the federal government. Others, however, welcomed the advent of publicly administered programs designed to help individuals and families. During Roosevelt's twelve years in office, the terms *liberal* and *conservative* took on new meaning as the battle over the government's role in society became the defining issue of American politics.

Religious leaders were divided over the New Deal as were other Americans. Many of the leaders in the so-called mainline denominations welcomed the New Deal. These were individuals who had supported much of modernist theology and were also part of the social gospel legacy. In their concern for the downtrodden, they were relatively unconcerned over the question of which institutions, ecclesiastical or governmental, should aid the needy. Many theological conservatives, however, had been wary of the social gospel all along because it seemed to detract from soul winning and was often wedded to the modernist theology against which they battled. Logically, then, when the government began to advocate what to them looked like the social gospel, and the modernists confirmed this view by actively supporting the New Deal, it appeared to the conservatives as but one more example of the modernist threat to American culture. Norris, after a brief flirtation with the New Deal, came rather naturally to this anti–New Deal position. His political flip-flop coincided with his assumption of the head pastor's position at Temple Baptist Church in Detroit, but before moving to Detroit, he would grope for the proper response to the depression.

After the stock market crash of 1929, Norris, like most Americans, could scarcely believe that the good times were over. Not for two years did he grasp the magnitude of the Great Depression. The first Sunday after the crash he preached on the "Spiritual Lessons from the Twenty-five Billion Dollar Crash." His scriptural text was I Timothy 6:10 and 17-19, which teach in part that the love of money is the root of all evil. Citing financial expert Roger Babson as his source, Norris attributed the stock market plunge to greed and the neglect of the things of God. The crash was God's judgment on America for its mad pursuit of riches.[6] Three months later, after the failure of a large bank in Fort Worth, Norris persisted in his disbelief that the American economic system could actually be in grave danger of prolonged depression. Speaking to his congregation, he asked how many had lost money in the bank closing. According to his stenographer, hands went up all over the auditorium. Norris then told the people that the bank failure was the result of theft from the inside by the bankers. He tried to comfort and calm his parishioners by portraying the bank failure as an anomaly, saying that the city was actually experiencing the greatest growth in its history. Norris believed the economic downturn was a temporary condition. The system itself was sound. The problems resulted only from the unethical and illegal activity of a few greedy capitalists.[7]

Later in 1930, Norris returned to the subject of the depression, calling it God's judgment. Becoming increasingly concerned, he warned his listeners that conditions had probably not gotten as bad yet as they were likely to be in the near future. Norris lumped the causes of the depression into two categories—spiritual and economic. Of the former were such sins as sabbath desecration, crime, disbelief in Scripture, and disregard for the constitution, by which Norris meant violations of prohibition. The economic causes included the aforementioned greed of the capitalists, but now Norris also spoke critically of people who had in the twenties lived beyond their means in the belief that prosperity would continue indefinitely. Norris identified his own silver lining in this cloud of despair when he said that in difficult times the prospects for revival improved because people were more likely to turn to God for answers.[8]

While Norris blamed the depression on generalized spiritual and economic conditions and the judgment of God, others, especially Democrats, faulted the policies of Herbert Hoover. Norris, having campaigned so tirelessly to help elect the president, moved to deflect such criticism. In August 1930, he included in the *Fundamentalist* an article that attributed Hoover's decline in popularity not to the depression itself but to a media blitz by the Democrats. The following March, Norris cited the efforts by Democratic Party chairman John J. Raskob to use the depression to malign Hoover. Norris challenged such negative propaganda, saying that prosperity would return by that summer. He seized every opportunity to praise the president in an effort to turn public opinion in Hoover's favor. In July, he lauded Hoover's debt moratorium, arguing that it would help stabilize Europe and possibly save Germany from Bolshevism. He also reprinted an editorial from the *Washington Post* that praised the president for the arrest and conviction of notorious gangster Al Capone. This editorial compared Hoover to Lincoln for his courage and determination in difficult times. Two weeks later, Norris issued the headline "'A Time of Peace'—Will a Hoover Arise among Texas Baptists?" At the bottom of the same page was a reprint of another editorial, this time from the New York *Times*, praising the president for his debt moratorium.[9]

In the fall of 1931, Norris began to come to grips with the seriousness of the depression. He cited as ominous a protest of farmers at the Texas capitol in Austin, and he warned of greater demonstrations in the near future, perhaps even in Washington, D.C., if the economic problems were not solved. He referred to the French and Russian Revolutions as examples of what can happen if the voices and desires of the people go unheeded. Acutely aware of the potential for class struggle, he mentioned that the depression fell hardest on those at the bottom of the economic system, while many at the top were relatively unscathed. Clearly, Norris was beginning to believe that the ingredients for social upheaval were present in the depression. He urged people to put aside party labels and work together to turn the situation around. Although this reference to political parties was vague, he seems to have been hoping that Democrats would stop criticizing the president and band together with Republicans to buoy the country against the threat of rebellion. Further recognition of the seriousness of the depression came in December 1932, when Norris's newspaper announced that First Baptist Church was converting a large barnlike building into a combination soup kitchen and shelter for the homeless.[10]

Norris's Brief Support for the New Deal

As noted in chapter 3, Norris did not campaign for Hoover in 1932. Neither did he support Franklin Roosevelt. He opposed FDR, but evidently found it nearly impossible to support Hoover with much enthusiasm in the midst of the depression and in the absence of a Roman Catholic opponent on the Democratic side. Once Roosevelt had won, Norris supported his New Deal programs vigorously for the first eighteen months. One month after Roosevelt's inauguration, Norris told his Fort Worth congregation that the nation was passing under a dictatorship but that it was necessary and that he supported it. In a statement that must have startled many in his church, he said, "I am in favor of it [dictatorship]—I don't believe we ought to ever elect another set of Congressmen and Senators. Let them stay at home. They are parasites, and cost us a lot of money." Continuing to what must have been a dumbfounded congregation, he opined, "We are in favor of giving dictatorial powers to our President. Why? It is the last desperate resort. Fifteen million men are looking for bread—that condition cannot continue long."[11]

Norris acknowledged that once the American people relinquished such power to an executive, it would be retrieved only with great difficulty when the depression had abated. He sounded fatalistic about the situation, however, partly because he believed biblical prophecy taught that there would eventually be a worldwide dictator and partly because he could think of no alternative for dealing effectively with the depression. Norris even let Roosevelt off the hook temporarily for supporting the repeal of the Eighteenth Amendment. Citing the Southern Baptist Convention's criticism of the new president, Norris, in what must have confused many who had followed his crusades against liquor traffic, said there were more important issues than prohibition. The Convention's criticism, argued Norris, gave comfort to those on Wall Street who were foreclosing on the homes of those adversely affected by the depression.[12]

By the summer of 1933, Norris was not only in favor of the New Deal but was also issuing a tongue-lashing critique of big businessmen. Exhibiting a strong strain of Texas Populism, he claimed he had more respect for an admitted criminal like Pretty Boy Floyd than for John D. Rockefeller and the other wealthy business magnates who robbed the common people of their fair share of the nation's wealth. A little redistribution of wealth brought about by the New Deal was good and necessary. He compared Roosevelt's policies with those of Old Testament patriarch Joseph. "Joseph took hold of everything in Egypt," Norris said, "and for seven years he took out one-fifth of all the wheat and kept the country alive for seven years of famine." Commenting on the prospect of complete government ownership, Norris went so far as to say, "I am in favor of it because it is prophesied, and I am in favor of it because the present order has broken down and I am in favor of trying something else." The revolution of 1933, as Norris referred to the New Deal, had simply moved control of the government from Wall Street to Washington, D.C., where it belonged.[13]

For taking the side of the commoner against the big businessmen, Norris praised Roosevelt himself, not just his programs. In early 1934, Norris attributed the depression and American involvement in World War I to selfish, wealthy Wall Street speculators. Then, commenting on the debt incurred by the president's programs, Norris said FDR would pile it up, then make the oil interests, railroads, and utility companies pay. This was only justice because those institutions had plundered the country anyway. "'Oh,' but somebody says, 'that is socialism,'" he thundered. "Call it what you please."[14] Norris was unconcerned even with the prospect of socialism coming to America. Two weeks later, he even alleged that Karl Marx was the source of most of Roosevelt's industrial program, but he did not use this supposed fact as criticism of the New Deal.[15]

Aside from possible prophetic implications of the New Deal, Norris supported FDR primarily because he believed drastic action was necessary to thwart a violent revolution by the American people. Until about 1935, the danger of revolution outweighed, in Norris's mind, the threats of dictatorship and socialism. In March 1934, in a sermon entitled "Fifteen Bible Reasons Why I Support Roosevelt's Recovery," Norris said, "America is in the greatest crisis of our history. The issue before us is whether we will have a reign of terror, a bloody revolution, or a bloodless revolution, ordained by the ballot box." In this sermon, Norris sounded like a social gospeler, arguing that since the government could feed the hungry more effectively than the churches could, the churches should support the government in its effort to help the needy. He defended the right of preachers to speak out on economic issues because the Old Testament prophets, Jesus, and the New Testament disciples had done the same. In a statement that was consistent with the theology of the late social gospel prophet Walter Rauschenbusch, Norris said, "There is no use to talk about the destiny of the soul of a man who is shivering in rags, and who hasn't a crust of bread for his hungry children."[16]

Norris also praised recent Supreme Court decisions in this sermon. In a Minnesota case the court had upheld a law that placed a moratorium on foreclosures, and in a New York case the court had upheld a law that fixed the price of milk. Norris admitted that both laws violated the right of contract, but argued that a higher law was at stake—the law of humanity. "That is Roosevelt's program—humanity," he said. He compared these actions to Jesus's admonition to the Pharisees that the Sabbath was made for man and not man for the Sabbath. Likewise, argued Norris, the constitution was made for man and not man for the constitution.

Norris also threw his support behind agricultural legislation that was intended both to aid and regulate farming. If the farmers would not listen to what was best for them, the government would have to tell them what to do. If the farmers overworked and destroyed the land, the government would have to step in to protect the land. The land did not belong solely to the farmer, said Norris. The government, therefore, should act to protect the liberty of all the people.

Returning to the issue of wealth amidst poverty, Norris cited an example from Fort Worth, telling how a wealthy resident had given a $1,500 dinner at a Fort Worth club when nearby lived men, women, and children without shoes for their feet or food for their stomachs. "There needs to be a change in the economic system," he exclaimed. "Why somebody cries, 'socialism;' 'socialism!' To hell with your socialism or what ever you want to call it! People are starving!"[17] Inherent in this statement was Norris's seeming lack of preference for one kind of economic system over another. One paragraph later he said, "'Well,' but you say, 'that is communism.' Suppose it is?" He was clearly more concerned with meeting the needs of those devastated by the depression and with forestalling revolution by the dispossessed than with upholding American-styled capitalism.

Norris also returned to the idea of judgment in the depression, only this time he included the New Deal. His attitude was that while the New Deal may not be what Americans would want under normal conditions, it was part of judgment for the sins that had brought about the depression in the first place. Referring to the Old Testament story of Nehemiah, who had called Israel into account for its indebtedness, Norris explained, "Roosevelt is our Nehemiah today." Then, applying Scripture to the present situation, he said, "'Our lands are mortgaged; our homes are in debt; the bankers have shared usury; we are unable to pay.'" Continuing the judgment theme, he said, "Men have piled up huge fortunes in bonds and stocks—but God took up a collection in 1929, and He is not through yet. So we either have to do it [accept the judgment of God] voluntarily or by force."[18] Norris even toyed with the Old Testament idea of a year of jubilee in which all debts would be canceled and all lands would revert to their original owners. Speaking specifically of government ownership of land in the Old Testament, he said, "It is a part of the Creator's plan that all land belong to all the people, belong to the tribes—every man to dwell under his own vine and fig tree, but no man to have a title to the land. Government ownership of land prevented monopoly; guaranteed man a living."[19]

Norris ended this sermon, "Fifteen Bible Reasons Why [I] Support Roosevelt's Recovery," by contrasting the president with former president William Howard Taft and comparing FDR very favorably to Theodore Roosevelt. "It is said that President Taft never made a mistake," Norris reminisced, "and that Theodore Roosevelt made a multitude of mistakes, but it was Roosevelt who dug the Panama Canal. . . . Courage—action, that's what's needed, and we are getting plenty of it." Having concluded this lengthy apology for the New Deal, Norris would soon become one of Roosevelt's most ardent critics on domestic policy.

Norris's Not-So-Great Reversal

Many scholars have identified as a "Great Reversal" the shift in evangelical politics from nineteenth-century reform-minded progressivism to twentieth-century conservatism.[20] Norris's own reversal was not nearly so "great" considering that his support for the New Deal had been short-lived and somewhat shallow. His about-face can be explained largely by his move to Temple Baptist Church in Detroit.[21] The battle Norris was so eager to join in the Northern Baptist Convention was related to the denomination's avowed support for Roosevelt's policies. The Northern Baptists had experienced a revival of the social gospel during the depression and in 1931 had begun to advocate the type of social action the New Deal was soon to propose.[22] Because of the connection between the social gospel and modernist theology, fundamentalists believed that the battle against the latter necessitated an attack on the former. Furthermore, the government planning inherent in the New Deal looked suspiciously like communism to many conservatives.

Once in Detroit, therefore, Norris threw himself into this battle, which required that he reconsider his position with regard to Roosevelt's programs. Norris's criticism of the New Deal began in the fall of 1934 and revealed the influence, not only of the Northern Baptist fundamentalists, but also of his new friends in Detroit, some of whom came from the ranks of the industrial leaders of that city. In September 1934, he told of a conversation he had had with a leading businessman who had warned him that without a revival of religion the country was headed toward revolution. Applying this to labor unrest, Norris said, "We needn't fool ourselves about these strikes—I don't know who is to blame or who is not to blame, but they show a bad symptom."[23] Norris was just starting to become acutely aware of the dangers of labor radicalism that very shortly he would attribute to communist infiltration of unions, and this was the beginning of his turnabout against the New Deal.

Between September and January, as Norris negotiated and accepted the position at Temple, he began to insist that the New Deal was part of the modernist-communist nexus that was going to destroy America if left unchecked. The complete reversal in his views was explicit by January 1935. "I will not change my policy," he said as he did exactly that. "I will continue to make the same protest. I would rather be banished into oblivion forever with a consciousness of duty well done than to dip my colors in the presence of the greatest menace that ever threatened free people, and that is what the New Deal is, only the American name for Russian Communism." He seemed to have almost forgotten his own earlier support when he asked, "How on earth under heaven any minister can sit idly by in the face of this wet raw deal, as it has well been called. . . . The same atheistic, communistic tyranny that tells the farmer how many rows of potatoes he will plant or the hog raiser how many pigs he can feed—that same tyranny will soon close all the churches in America or turn them into places of atheistic bacchanalian revelry as was done in Moscow, the capital of the U.S.S.R."[24]

The only consistency one finds in these statements with Norris's earlier support for the New Deal is the comparison with communism. Even here, however, he had previously implied that a bit of socialism or communism was necessary during a time of severe hardship and economic depression. Now, his comparison aimed to portray the New Deal as a dangerous threat to religious liberty. Furthermore, where once Norris had gone easy on Roosevelt's support for repeal of the

Eighteenth Amendment, believing there were more important issues, he now used the repeal of Prohibition as one of the leading examples of the godlessness and degradation of the Roosevelt administration. On one occasion he even accused First Lady Eleanor Roosevelt of encouraging girls to drink alcohol and of rushing a carload of beer to the White House immediately after the repeal of prohibition.[25]

Just before Temple's withdrawal from the Northern Baptist Convention, Norris again lashed out at the New Deal, and this time he mentioned FDR specifically as going over to communism. "Whether Mr. Roosevelt intends it or not," Norris charged, "he is today, that is, the brain trust bunch he has around him, they are absolutely carrying out the very program of Karl Marx and Lenin."[26] Where Norris had once referred to Marx's alleged influence on Roosevelt without making judgment or drawing conclusions, he now intended his comments to be interpreted as the worst sort of indictment possible of an American president.

Shortly thereafter, Norris published a booklet entitled *New Dealism (Russian Communism) Exposed*. It contained a speech he had delivered to several hundred businessmen at the Barlum Hotel in Detroit in August 1935. Norris addressed a variety of issues concerning the New Deal in an effort to portray it as the American form of communism. He alleged that the Civilian Conservation Corps received military training so it would be ready to impose martial law should there be an uprising of farmers or some other group. He also charged that the Federal Communications Commission was the government's official censoring agency, aimed at any who might speak out against the New Deal via radio. Norris claimed that on one occasion, before a radio broadcast, he had been instructed to speak only on religion and not on politics lest the station lose its license.[27] As is obvious by the title of the booklet, Norris's primary message was that the New Deal had introduced communist-styled repression in America.

Having made the connection between New Dealism and communism, the next step was to bring modernism into the equation. He did this in an attack on the Northern and Southern Baptist Conventions, which he believed had been infiltrated by modernists who would take the denominations toward communism. For him, modernism, communism, and New Dealism were merely three names for the same threat to American political institutions and Christian orthodoxy. In an attack on the SBC's well-known evolutionist, William Poteat, Norris wrote, "Poteatism is the Southern Baptist name for 'New Dealism,' and 'New Dealism' is the American name for Russian Communism."[28] On another occasion Norris referred to the New Deal and communism as "Siamese twins of the destruction of Christianity."[29] Then, on the title page of his booklet *New Dealism (Russian Communism) Exposed* he pitted modernism and communism against Christianity and patriotism in a brief description of his two churches that read, "Two independent Baptist churches which stand for 100% Fundamentalism and Christian patriotism as opposed to modernism and every brand of communism." Norris was convinced that the battle against modernism necessitated the battle against the New Deal and communism.

Not surprisingly, then, by the summer of 1935, Norris had also adjusted his views on property rights and the redistribution of wealth. Where once he had used the Old Testament to defend redistribution, he now couched his argument in dispensational terms and argued that such would only be possible when Christ returned. On the specific issue of the National Recovery Act and the Blue Eagle Emblem that accompanied it, Norris claimed he still supported them, but primarily on prophetic grounds—that is, because they were part of the end-times prophecy.[30] He had already spoken against the Wagner Act, which had created the National Labor Relations Board. He had told an audience of Detroit businessmen that this law gave a communist the right to force Henry Ford to accept a union that would then tell the automaker how to run his business—a violation of Ford's property rights. He did not, however, advocate resistance to any specific New Deal program at this time because he believed it was futile to oppose what had been prophesied.[31] Later in the decade, Norris would change his view and begin to teach resistance to all evil, even that which had been prophesied in the Scriptures. Presently, he believed such opposition was a waste of time and energy.

That Norris had much to gain personally from his about-face on the New Deal is hardly arguable. The speech he made to the Detroit businessmen was attended by the former governor of Michigan, who closed the meeting by saying, "This address is one of the best, most forceful, and inspiring talks I have heard in a long time, and I was glad to see you give the response to him [Norris] that you did."[32] Norris's stenographer also recorded that the businessmen gave Norris a three-minute standing ovation. This was merely the beginning of Norris's relationship with business leaders in Detroit. He would regularly correspond with presidents and vice presidents of the auto companies.

The new political stance Norris exhibited when he came to Detroit also gained him almost immediate national recognition as an opponent of the New Deal. Nationally known radio personality Stanley High told those in his audience that if they had not heard of

J. Frank Norris, they obviously had not been to the South lately. He presented Norris to the nation as the country's "leading fundamentalist," who had come to Detroit to take on the New Deal. "He's against the New Deal because he's convinced it's communist," remarked High. "In many respects, he's the most potent political force among the Protestant ministers of the nation."[33] Norris's move to Detroit also afforded him greater opportunity to promote himself, both in person and over radio. Each Sunday that he was in Detroit (he had to split time with his Fort Worth church) his earliest morning service originated live from the thirtieth floor of Detroit's Fisher Building and was carried over the city's leading station, WJR. The Sunday evening service was in the auditorium of the Detroit Masonic Temple, which Norris alleged was the largest Masonic lodge headquarters in the nation.

Norris used his new platform to attack Roosevelt personally, portraying the president as a godless man. He had never been warmly supportive of Roosevelt as an individual, but now he took advantage of every opportunity to condemn him for his lack of references to God in speeches. In an extended critique of the administration's lack of religiosity, Norris charged:

> I am going to bring a strong indictment—why from the minute the president kissed the Bible, lifted his right hand with his other on the open Bible, from that day until now—there may have been something, but I am a pretty close observer, I haven't seen one time, in any one address or in one statement by anybody in the Cabinet, or in any department, where they have ever called on God or recognized God; on the contrary, President Roosevelt has surrounded himself with the rankest of atheists—that's the crowd that has charge of the government at Washington.[34]

Two weeks after making this statement, Norris again lamented Roosevelt's lack of religiosity, contrasting the president with statesmen of American history who had called the nation to prayer in times of national distress. In an extended civil religion rendition, Norris related how God had aided national leaders from Benjamin Franklin through Woodrow Wilson and had healed the nation in response to the prayerful appeals of these godly individuals. By comparison, Roosevelt was, in Norris's view, as close to an infidel as the nation had ever had in the Oval Office. Ironically, in the introduction to the sermon in which Norris made the above comparison, he claimed that he had been warning against the New Deal for two years and that his present position was no different than it had always been. Only the first part of the statement was true. Norris had been warning that the New Deal was part of God's judgment and part of biblical prophecy concerning worldwide dictatorship, but he had also supported it as a necessary defense against radicalism and revolution. Now he portrayed the New Deal itself as a form of radical revolution that would destroy the country and the Christian faith.[35]

The following summer, 1936, while attacking Roosevelt's secretary of agriculture, Henry Wallace, Norris returned to the theme of the president's godlessness, saying, "I believe [God] is greatly displeased with an administration, not only which makes no reference to God, which not only violates most of the fundamental laws of the Creator, but denies the existence of God."[36] One week later, Norris reprinted from *Time* magazine an editorial portraying Republican presidential nominee Alfred Landon as much more warmly evangelical than the incumbent president. *Time* corroborated what Norris had been saying about Roosevelt when it charged that the president had never been adept at using God's name in speeches and had recently given up the practice almost entirely.[37]

Norris's change of attitude toward the New Deal coincided with, and was perhaps a result of, his reversal with regard to big business. Where he previously had lashed out at Rockefeller and other magnates, he now found it to his advantage to praise the biggest of all big businesses, General Motors. Speaking over WJR radio in Detroit on November 3, 1935, Norris told how the corporation's executives had graciously provided him with a piece of property for revival services. Having received permission to erect a stone tabernacle on the land, Norris contrasted the attitude of General Motors toward religion with that of the presidential administration, saying, "That's the spirit of Detroit. That's the spirit of the General Motors Corporation. How contrary to the calumny, the demagoguery, that is now being sent throughout the country by this communistic New Deal crowd."[38] Whereas Norris had previously fashioned himself a populist spokesman for the people, he was now an apologist for big business.

By the summer of 1936, Norris, now firmly established in Detroit as well as Fort Worth, was convinced that all ministers had a duty to oppose the New Deal. He announced to his parishioners, "Ladies and gentlemen, I say to you the churches of America, the ministers of America, the mothers of America, the homes of America can't with consistency support such a regime."[39] Norris recognized, however, that most Americans did support the president, and he wasted little time campaigning either against Roosevelt or for Landon during the campaign that year. Immediately following the election, he offered an analysis, which acknowledged that Roosevelt commanded a solid majority from all classes and all ethnic groups. Norris recognized that the president could have been reelected even without winning the South, a rare phenomenon for a Democrat. Norris referred to FDR's reelection as the "Second American Revolution," Roosevelt's own phrase, and he also called it a "Hitler revolution, but with American ballots instead of Hitler bayonets." "Henceforth," Norris lamented, "we will have a planned society. Everybody will be regimented by number. Not only the laborers, but all professional people, doctors, lawyers, and preachers. I am getting ready for my number." Norris believed that the American people had spoken in favor of a planned society by reelecting Roosevelt, and he expressed again his belief that this was part of prophecy and God's judgment for America.[40]

From the election of 1936 until the onset of World War II in Europe in 1939, Norris consistently lambasted Roosevelt and the New Deal. He claimed that there was a dictatorship in Washington and that the president and his administration were doing the work of Moscow. In 1938, Norris attacked what opponents called "the Dictatorship Bill," which was an executive reorganization proposal that would have given the president more power over civil service appointments. Norris used the occasion to list twelve ways the president was a dictator, including his control over banks, money, and tariffs; his "intimidation" of congressmen to get their support for bills favored by the administration; his farm policies, which told farmers what to grow and then fixed the prices of the produce; and his control of the Federal Communications Commission.[41] Norris's critique was clearly an expression of his fear of a strengthened presidency, a fear shared by many conservatives in America, among them the congressmen who had given the reorganization bill its nickname. Lacking political sophistication, he could only charge that this "dictatorship" was identical to that found in the Soviet Union or Nazi Germany. In reference to another executive branch agency, the National Labor Relations Board, which Norris identified as the advance agent of dictatorship, he said, "Does America want the Nazism of Berlin, the Fascism of Rome, or the Communism of Moscow? We have a Dukes mixture of all three."[42]

Norris and Father Coughlin

Significantly, Norris's hostility toward the New Deal generally and the "Dictatorship Bill" specifically helped reverse his opinion of one of the other leading demagogues in America in the thirties, himself another Motor City man, Father Charles Coughlin. Coughlin was one of the best known radio personalities of the 1930s and at one time reportedly received more mail than the president. Back in 1931, Norris had cited the Roman Catholic priest as more dangerous than Al Smith. This was partly because Coughlin at that time criticized the Hoover administration and favored Roosevelt. Norris, however, also charged that Coughlin had a strong tendency to mix comments on workingmen, communism, and World War I soldiers, together with "a little bit of Stalin." Comparing the priest to one of the leaders of the French Revolution, Norris called Coughlin "the Danton of Romanism."[43]

In 1938, however, Norris had completed his odyssey, which saw him oppose FDR, then support the president briefly, before coming around to his vitriolic attacks on the Democrat and his New Deal policies. Coughlin, on the other hand, had flip-flopped only once and now opposed the New Deal as heatedly as Norris. Norris therefore praised the priest, saying, "More than any other voice, the voice of this great American broke the tidal wave of dictatorship at Washington when the Dictatorship Bill was defeated." Instead of the "Danton of Romanism," Coughlin was now the "Savonarola in this 20th century," by which Norris meant one who stood for truth against the political powers of the day. Furthermore, Norris believed that fundamentalists had more in common with Coughlin than with "modernistic machine Baptists." Recognizing that his former enemy was now his ally in the fight against the New Deal, Norris said, "'Consistency is the virtue of fools' and this doesn't bother him [Coughlin] even as it did not bother Jeremiah, John the Baptist, or even Elijah."[44] Norris could have applied that statement to himself as well as Coughlin, for he too had changed his views of Roosevelt and the New Deal. One week later, he reprinted an article in the *Fundamentalist* that called Coughlin the "most fearless, most outstanding and best known Roman Catholic in the world, with the exception of Pope Pius."[45] This issue carried a photograph of the pope. Unfortunately for Coughlin, the pope did not share Norris's enthusiasm. Eventually, in the early forties, the Church silenced Coughlin, bringing to an end his popular radio show. Coughlin lived the remainder of his life much as other priests who never experience national recognition. The once famous radio-priest died in 1979.

Norris would continue his anti–New Dealism rather forcefully for the rest of his life, however, and as the economy took a turn for the worse in the late thirties, Norris moved to highlight the failures

of the New Deal by publishing a modernized, Republican version of
the Twenty-third Psalm:

> Mr. Roosevelt is my shepherd, I am in want,
> He maketh me to lie down on park benches,
> He leadeth me beside still factories,
> He disturbeth my soul.
> He leadeth me in the paths of destruction,
> For the Party's sake.
> Yea, though I walk through the valley of the Shadows of recession,
> I anticipate no recovery, for he is with me. . . .
> He prepareth a reduction in my salary,
> And in the presence of mine enemies,
> He anointeth my small savings with taxes,
> My expense runneth over,
> Surely unemployment and poverty shall follow me
> All the days of my life,
> And I shall dwell in a mortgaged house forever. Amen.[46]

Later in 1938, as off-year congressional elections approached, the
Pittsburgh Sun-Telegraph quoted Norris as saying: "Roosevelt is using
suffering humanity to make himself dictator. His whole scheme—
whether Supreme Court packing, government reorganization, control
of radio, telegraph and telephone or control of WPA—is to put everything under his own control. Only one step remains—to get control of
the next congress. The coming election will determine whether he
will have it."[47] Norris reportedly predicted a revolt of southern conservative Democrats in the new Congress. The following week, the
Buffalo *Evening News* quoted Norris as saying, "There, in truth, is no
Democratic party in America. There is a totalitarian party, however;
call it New Dealism, squealism, ordealism or what have you."[48]

Communism and Organized Labor

In addition to his transformation on the issue of the New Deal,
Norris's move to Detroit seems to have influenced his views of
organized labor. If nothing else, the move northward gave him an
opportunity to address an issue that was hardly noteworthy in the
non-unionized state of Texas. His move to Temple, however, also coincided with the reversal of his view of the relationship of workers
to business leaders. Early in his career, in the late teens and early
twenties, he had consistently taken the side of workers against big
business. For example, in 1919 he had said, "We are glad for the bene-

factions of a Rockefeller, a Carnegie, and a J. Ogden Armour, but I will tell you something that is ten thousand times better and that is a system of justice that will prevent the making of the Rockefellers, the Carnegies and the J. Ogden Armours." In an appeal for better wages, he warned that the churches should not pass by the labor issue the way the Levite and priest had passed by the injured man in the story of the Good Samaritan.[49] In 1920, writing from Egypt, Norris commented that there was no difference between the pharaohs who built their pyramids with slave labor and the modern millionaire business leaders who lived in splendor while their workers enjoyed barely a subsistence lifestyle. On another occasion he called Moses the greatest labor leader ever, having led the Hebrews out of Egypt because their working conditions were too harsh.[50]

In the 1930s, however, as Norris began to develop friendships with the industrial leaders in Detroit, he ceased altogether to support rights of laborers when such rights were articulated by unions. He justified his change of mind by arguing that the labor movement had been infiltrated by communists. Norris hit this issue hard beginning in the mid-thirties. From December 1936 well into January 1937, there occurred in Flint, Michigan, a sit-down strike at a General Motors plant. The workers occupied shop facilities for weeks before management finally gave in and recognized the United Auto Workers union, making General Motors the first major automobile company to unionize.[51] Norris, now firmly planted in Temple Baptist and in the good graces of the top executives of the automobile companies, was incensed by the seizure of General Motors property in Flint. He used the occasion of the strike to begin an intense campaign aimed at organized labor generally and John L. Lewis of the Congress of Industrial Organizations specifically.

Norris charged that the radical activity of 1936 and 1937 had been inspired and masterminded by communists within labor organizations. He claimed with some plausibility that he was in favor of all the things labor wanted, but was convinced that radicalism would ruin the union movement. As shown above, Norris had, in fact, often spoken in favor of working-class people, especially while in Fort Worth, but now the central thrust of his statements changed as he focused not on what laborers needed and were trying to obtain but on the radical means they employed to achieve their goals. Where once Norris had argued that property rights were not absolute, he now said that without property rights there could be no human rights. For this reason, seizure of property through the sit-down strike was wrong. Furthermore, strikes like the one in Flint were "praised by the communists" and led by ex-criminals. Norris alleged specifically that the lawyer who defended the strikers in Flint was a communist.[52]

Although Norris often attacked institutions like Roman Catholicism or communism, whenever possible he attempted to personalize sin. In his worldview, systemic evil emanated from bad individuals. So it was that in the twenties he attacked Al Smith and John Jacob Raskob, and in the thirties he singled out FDR and Lewis. In so doing, Norris exhibited the essentially Manichaean mind-set of fundamentalism that has been identified by historian Richard Hofstadter, and he was also drawing on the American revivalist tradition that has operated from individualistic presuppositions about sin and the need for personal redemption.[53]

Norris went after Lewis in 1936 by saying that the labor leader was an atheist and implying that he was a communist as well. In 1937, in the wake of labor radicalism, Norris stepped up his attack. On January 17, he preached a sermon over WJR radio in Detroit entitled "The Conspiracy of John L. Lewis to Destroy the American Federation of Labor and Become Dictator of the Government." The sermon was covered by the Detroit *Free Press*, the major newspaper in the city, and Norris made thousands of free copies available in booklet form. Norris reasoned in this sermon that Lewis's scheme was to put all workers, from the most skilled to the least, on the same level. "The Industrial Union with its leveling process," he charged, "would put the brains and genius of Henry Ford in the same union with a street cleaner. In short, it means to import the Moscow plan for America." Norris was in essence denouncing the idea of replacing the old craft unions that had been for skilled workers only with CIO unions for skilled and unskilled workers alike. He had come a long way from the days in 1911 and 1912 when in populist fashion he had run off the wealthy elites from First Baptist Fort Worth because he favored the more virtuous common folk. Lewis now played the part of populist, and Norris was the defender of big-business elites. Norris charged, however, that the labor leader had ulterior motives, specifically that he intended to break the American Federation of Labor and replace it with a political organization patterned after the Soviet government. Even more incredibly, Norris blustered, "If the secret messages, if the codes were deciphered, it would be found that Josef Stalin is in daily communication with his first lieutenant in America." Unable to take seriously the problems facing workers, Norris reduced the issue to two evil individuals who were responsible for the communist threat to labor unions.[54]

The argument that labor unions in America had perhaps staved off revolution by securing immediate, short-term goals for workers was lost on Norris. He interpreted strikes as the beginning of a full-scale revolution. Lewis's plan, according to Norris, was as follows: He would use a series of strikes to shut down the industrial capacity of America, then proceed with a continentwide revolution. This, said Norris, was why the communists in America opposed national defense. In the absence of a well-trained and well-equipped army, Lewis could call his workers to arms and immediately there would be a revolution like that which took place in Russia in 1917. "The issue, I say," cried Norris, "is not labor nor hours, nor wages. The issue is, shall we continue to have this free republic where men shall still be free?"[55] Again, Norris failed to appreciate that there were forces that militated against the rights of workers. Instead, he analyzed only the actions of the workers and concluded they were evil. He simply could not acknowledge sin that was depersonalized. If his friends in the automobile companies were good men, then the workers who went on strike against them must be bad—even bad enough to engage in a communist revolution.

Recognizing that a well-organized revolution did not require majority participation, Norris worked the residue of his 1920s nativism into his communist-labor conspiracy theory by arguing that the "unnaturalized and undesirables" who did not have firm roots in America would be the foot soldiers of insurrection. "There is a total of nine million men," he said, "three million un-naturalized and undesirable and six million aliens without citizenship—nine million together! Ladies and gentlemen, that is the crowd that will join the movement to overthrow this government."[56]

In June, Norris took his attack on Lewis to new depths when he reprinted from the Detroit *Free Press* an article written by Henry Ford, charging that the labor leader planned to siphon off union dues for his own use. Ford calculated that if Lewis could pressure the Ford Motor Company into unionizing, and the workers paid their union dues of twelve dollars per worker per year, this would make a "nice sum of $1,200,000 a year for Mr. Lewis to spend as he pleases without being accountable to anybody outside his own group."[57] Earlier that spring, a Buffalo, New York, newspaper had reported that Norris had himself called for a congressional investigation of the CIO. Not surprisingly, the week after the Ford article appeared, Norris claimed that the CIO was threatening to sue him for libel, and later that summer Norris charged that the United Auto Workers union was attacking him and Henry Ford.[58] Once again, without even intending to, he had reduced a complex set of social forces down to a few individuals—himself and Ford against Lewis.

If Norris ever had a shred of hard evidence to support his wild claims, he failed to produce it. What Norris considered evidence was usually simply more charges such as the following, which he cited to prove that labor unions were communist: Moscow supports them; they use violence; some of their leadership is communist; their platform includes the direct action of the old Knights of Labor and the International Workers of the World; they will not obey the law; they violate their own agreements with General Motors; they support intermarriage just like the communists do; and they attack the churches, Temple Baptist in particular.[59] Equally unsubstantiated was his claim that the economic downturn of 1937 and 1938 had been caused by union activities. He reflected that just a year earlier the economy had been improving, "But what a plunge—what a change—what a reversal in twelve months! The sit-down strike, the lawless violent methods of the CIO have been the main contributing factor in paralyzing in so short a time the industrial world."[60] One week later, recognizing that he had gone too far in his denunciation of labor and the National Labor Relations Board, which he had called the "Trojan Horse of dictatorship," he softened his claim by saying that extremes of both labor and capital were responsible for the present economic troubles. He quoted 1 Timothy 6:17–19 concerning the high-mindedness of the rich, and issued a caveat saying, "America is facing revolution, and unless the rich organize and cooperate to relieve suffering a revolution is inevitable."[61]

To stave off such a revolution, the South would have to play a major role. Just as Norris had in the twenties identified the primary modernist threat in the North, so in the thirties he recognized that the union movement was primarily a northern phenomenon.[62] He urged the non-unionized South to aid the fight against the northern labor movement in much the same way that he had previously urged Southern Baptists to join the fight against modernism in the Northern Baptist Convention. He professed optimism that the non-unionists could win just as he had earlier expressed a belief that fundamentalists could defeat modernism. Occasionally, Norris predicted the demise of the CIO, believing that the common people of America who were truly Americans would not long tolerate this communist organization.[63] In one instance he even remarked with mock surprise, albeit prematurely, "Frankly, the CIO collapsed much sooner than I expected."[64]

Norris continued his barrage against Lewis and the CIO through 1938. While he was in Pittsburgh in October, the *Sun-Telegraph* quoted him as saying, "The policies of Lewis and the CIO are dictated from Moscow." This time he cited the Dies committee of the U.S. House of Representatives as his source of information. This committee was charged with the task of uncovering subversive elements in the United States, and Norris praised its work. When the Dies committee was renewed in 1939 for another congressional term, Norris chimed, "There is a new day. America is returning to common sense and plain old-fashioned, everyday Americanism."[65] While in Pittsburgh, he cited Dies committee findings to back his claim that recent sit-down strikes in Detroit had been instigated by a representative from Moscow.

A few weeks after his Pittsburgh address Norris traveled into enemy territory. He had lambasted the Flint strikers for well over a year, so some of the laborites there were ready for him when he arrived. In a crowd estimated at five thousand there were probably as many present who opposed Norris's views on the labor issue as there were supporters. Challenged by a chorus of booing when he began to discuss political matters, Norris responded by unfurling American and Soviet flags and asking the crowd demagogically which one they preferred. He threw the Soviet flag on the floor and stomped on it while one of his attendants waved the Stars and Stripes. The crowd then sang a verse of a patriotic song, but Norris had lost this confrontation and retreated to the safer confines of a straightforward evangelistic sermon, something not even the "labor radicals" in Flint were likely to shout down.[66]

In the late thirties, Norris claimed that he attacked labor unions for the benefit of the laborers, not the capitalists—a point he was sure to argue to his Temple Baptist congregation, which was made up largely of automobile factory workers. Many in Temple Baptist had recently come north for industrial jobs and were probably still wary of union organizations. Norris was able, therefore, to walk a tightrope between labor and capital. In doing so, he pointed out truthfully that he had attacked big business earlier in the decade, and he even sprinkled a few criticisms of capitalists throughout his sermons aimed at labor. He was convinced, however, that the CIO and the other large union organizations existed for political purposes and not for the true benefit of the workers.[67]

In spring 1940, after five years of lambasting the New Deal and organized labor and after nearly two years of preaching against any American involvement in the war in Europe, Norris made it his personal mission to rally support for aid to Britain. He preached a series of revivals in New York, Pennsylvania, Kentucky, and Michigan in which he urged support for Roosevelt's interventionist and preparedness foreign policy, telling his listeners the United States was already in the war. In June, he invited the president's son, Elliot, to Temple Baptist to speak. Norris held the meeting in a convention hall to accommodate the overflow crowd, and the *Fundamentalist* announced the event with a red-lettered headline that read in part, "Calling America to Christian Patriotism and to God—Elliot Roosevelt." The edition that followed the event included a picture of Norris with his arm around Elliot's shoulder as he introduced the younger Roosevelt.[68]

That same month, the World Fundamental Baptist Missionary Fellowship pledged its full support for FDR's preparedness plan. This gave Norris the opportunity to attack the Southern Baptist Convention because its messengers (delegates) had issued what Norris believed was criticism of the president. Acknowledging that no one had been more critical of the New Deal than he had and admitting that he had never voted for Roosevelt, Norris wrote that this was no time to reprove or denounce the commander in chief of the United States armed forces. He described himself—along with Henry Ford and W.S. Knudson, president of General Motors—as one who had been critical of the New Deal but now had recognized the importance of the preparedness effort.[69] Having once placed Roosevelt in the same category as the dictators of Europe, he now cited the president's wisdom in appointing Republicans to important cabinet posts in order to cultivate bipartisan support for foreign policy. Norris contrasted this wisdom with the partisanship Woodrow Wilson had displayed in naming only Democrats to the peace commission that negotiated the Treaty of Versailles following World War I.[70]

In addition to Detroit industrialists such as Ford and Knudson, Norris also cited the stalwart Republican and New Deal critic William Allen White as one who had come over to the president's side. Norris reprinted in the *Fundamentalist* an article written by the nationally recognized editor from Emporia, Kansas, in which White confessed that, although he was a "partisan Republican" who had opposed FDR's domestic policies for eight years, he now supported the president in his campaign to aid the allies. Norris gave this editorial the title, "The Right Attitude of Patriotic Anti-Roosevelt People," and he clearly believed that the time had come to rally behind the president even if his domestic policies were loathsome.[71] Norris nearly endorsed Roosevelt for reelection when he said that the president had "been brought to the kingdom for such a time as this" and asked, "Which of the two men [Roosevelt or Wendell Willkie] would Hitler want defeated?"[72] He did not answer this rhetorical question, and, ironically, after having all but endorsed the president for nearly a year, he confessed after the election that he had not voted for Roosevelt. He did not reveal whether or not he had voted for Willkie, but he reprinted in the *Fundamentalist* a headline from the London *Daily Express* that read in part, "Roosevelt's Election the Blackest Day in Blacked-Out Berlin."[73]

In order to support the president as he had, Norris felt compelled to portray Roosevelt as a politically conservative and fairly religious man. He did this by citing as "right wing" some of FDR's appointments to the National Labor Relations Board and by posing the question in a headline, "Will President Roosevelt Turn Conservative?"[74] Earlier in 1940, Norris had cited Roosevelt's turn toward religion, saying the president had ended one of his speeches with the "flurry of an evangelist" when he had told his audience to "have faith in God."[75] In supporting the president's preparedness campaign, it was important for Norris to believe and to convince others that Roosevelt had moved in his direction and not he in Roosevelt's, for this was the president who had supported the repeal of prohibition and practically created twentieth-century liberalism.[76]

By 1941, Norris was attracting plenty of attention from both religious and secular sources. The state legislatures of both Texas and Georgia invited him to speak in their respective chambers, and he obliged their requests. Ironically, whereas he had been preaching about politics in a religious setting, once in a political setting, he preached primarily religion. In both sermons he stuck to a fairly evangelistic message, urging that in these perilous times the nation needed revival. He even persuaded the Texas legislators to join him in a few verses of the old gospel hymn "Amazing Grace," and his trip to Georgia elicited from the *Atlanta Journal* the headline "Georgia Legislature Is Turned into Revival by 'Flying Parson.'"[77] Later that year, Norris returned to Georgia for a revival campaign and, once back in a religious forum, he resumed his discussion of the war. Various Georgia newspapers covered Norris with headlines such as "Frank Norris Speaks on War," "Dr. Norris Says Lindy Should Be Locked Up," and "Norris to Speak before Defense Rally of Baptists."[78] Significantly, Norris also moved to increase his radio audience in 1941. Formerly, when he was absent from one of his pulpits, there would be no radio broadcast in that city. Beginning in 1941, he worked out a taping system that enabled listeners in both Fort Worth and Detroit never to miss a week of his sermons over the airwaves.[79]

The biggest event in Norris's military preparedness mission was his 1941 trip to England. Norris had by this time attracted the attention not only of state legislatures but of the Roosevelt administration as well. Several cabinet members wrote letters to the British government introducing Norris and urging that he be treated with utmost respect and consideration while there. Secretary of State Cordell Hull wrote to Winston Churchill saying, "He [Norris] is doing marvelous work to arouse the American people from their complacency and to develop thorough understanding of the world war situation and of America's intimate relation to what Hitler and Hitlerism means for civilized countries."[80] Undersecretary of State Sumner Welles wrote to the American ambassador in London, telling him that Norris had the largest congregation in the United States via radio and that he was going to survey the situation in Britain and return to preach about it in America. Welles saw clearly the use to which Norris could be put in propagandizing for the administration's position when he told the ambassador, "I believe [Norris's sermons upon return] will be of the greatest value in bringing home to the American people the dangers of the existing situation and the fundamental problems involved in the present international situation."[81] Similarly, the secretary of the navy, Frank Knox, wrote to his British counterpart that upon return to America Norris would "do much toward promoting the right kind of sentiment over here."[82]

Other notables who wrote in behalf of Norris included former Republican presidential candidate Wendell Willkie and the editor of the *Fort Worth Star-Telegram*, J.M. North. Willkie wrote to Churchill, "The bearer of this letter is the Dr. J. Frank Norris, one of America's most noted Protestant pulpit speakers. He is a man of great force and ability. He can be of incalculable aid in bringing America to a realization of its problem in relation to Nazism."[83] North wrote a general letter to the British press commending Norris for his knowledge of newspaper work and his understanding of "public psychology." He expressed confidence that upon return Norris would do much to cultivate the kind of sentiment that would be invaluable to Britain. The editor also informed the British that Norris had wide influence beyond Texas, a state that was already firmly supportive of more aid to the allies.[84]

While in England, newspapers there reported that Norris had sent a telegram to Roosevelt urging the president to ask Congress for a formal declaration of war, believing that this would bring neutrals in America to the side of the allies. The Reuters news agency also distributed articles in September carrying Norris's prediction that the United States would be in the war in thirty days.[85] Perhaps most important, Norris had an audience with Winston Churchill.

Upon his return, Norris's barnstorming campaign in support of the allies and the Roosevelt administration appears to have been something less than what administration officials had hoped. However, he did what he could to keep the country moving toward entry into the war. He reported on his meeting with Churchill, portraying the English statesman as a devoted Christian. A red-lettered headline in the *Fundamentalist* purporting to be a quote from Churchill read, "I Have the Same Faith I Received from My Mother." Norris emphasized with pride that Churchill's mother was an American and included beneath the quote two pictures of the prime minister autographed for First Baptist Fort Worth and Temple Baptist Detroit respectively. Norris also preached in cities across Texas after his return and received significant newspaper coverage.[86]

When the United States finally entered the war, Norris wasted no time in planning ways he could be of service. Of course, he was far too old to actually fight, but two of his three sons served in various capacities in the armed services—a fact of which Norris was extremely proud.[87]

Norris's own involvement took several forms. He began to preach to the soldiers who were flooding into the ranks of the military. The *Detroit News*, one week after the bombing of Pearl Harbor, reported in an article entitled "Army Evangelical Tour Planned by Norris" that he had asked for a leave of absence from his two pulpits. Norris planned to take a red, white, and blue revival tent to various army training centers. He was also very involved in the World Fundamental Baptist Missionary Fellowship's drive to build a permanent structure at Camp Welters in Texas. Saying it would be a "magnificent temple," Norris believed the building would attract greater numbers of soldiers than the "chicken coups" that were being used for meetings. The Fellowship completed the tabernacle in the summer of 1942, by which time Norris had arranged for ten thousand free copies of the *Fundamentalist* to be sent regularly to the army for distribution and had led both his churches into war bond campaigns.[88] He would continue for the duration of the war supporting the war effort in any way he could.

Conclusion

With some difficulty, one can make sense of Norris's rabid opposition to the New Deal from 1935 forward. Once he made the connection between communism and New Deal policies, opposition flowed naturally. If there was any consistency in his activism, it was that he supported the New Deal in its early years for the same reason he opposed it later. When the Depression began, Norris feared that people would turn to radical ideologies, such as communism, for relief. The New Deal appeared initially to forestall such radicalism by offering assistance from the government that was already in place. Thus, America, in Norris's view, was being saved from radicalism by the New Deal. In its absence, revolution would have been more likely, and America would have been at greater risk.

When Norris became affiliated with Temple Baptist Church in Detroit, he became convinced, or perhaps convinced himself, that the New Deal was itself part of the radicalism against which he had been fighting. The New Deal represented an assault on American political orthodoxy that paralleled modernism's attack on the faith. Furthermore, because he believed that the modernists enthusiastically supported the New Deal, it was natural that he, as a fundamentalist who battled to save Christian orthodoxy from modernism, would also fight to save America from what he believed was politically heterodox radicalism.

This interpretation rests on the assumption that Norris thought through his political positions and sought consistency in his ideology. There is no evidence that this was actually the case. Rather, it seems that his switch from support for the New Deal to radical opposition to it coincided with his move to Temple Baptist, which afforded him the opportunity to associate with the industrialists in Detroit. The allure of these friendships was too much for Norris's ego. He wanted always to be in the public eye, and his primary means of accomplishing this was to be involved constantly in a political fight of some kind. His move to Temple and his reversal on the New Deal allowed him to take the side of the wealthy, influential, and well-known leaders of big business. When he went to Detroit, he left a good bit of his populism in Fort Worth.

This would also explain his support for FDR's preparedness campaign and U.S. entry into World War II. One must bear in mind that the entire nation underwent a drastic change from isolationism to interventionism during the same period that Norris did, so his flip-flop this time was nothing out of the ordinary. Additionally, for Norris, it was the opportunity once again to be found in the good graces of the powerful and influential, even the president of the United States. There can be no doubt that the Roosevelt administration used Norris for its own purposes, but conversely, Norris was willing to be used because he got so much out of the bargain, specifically the opportunity to act in a semi-official capacity in behalf of

America. Just as his role as dispensational prophet gave him an inflated view of his own importance, so in this instance did his trip to Europe, official letters of introduction in hand.

In going to Detroit, Norris's career received a huge boost. In attacking the New Deal and organized labor, he was not only doing what served the interests of his own career and level of recognition but acting consistently with his fundamentalist theology, which sought to save all of America, not just the South this time, from the influences of things liberal. The cultural component in fundamentalism required him to fight against changes that he believed diluted America's nineteenth-century evangelical heritage. He rarely articulated sound reasons for his opposition to Roosevelt's policies and to unions or for switching from isolationism to interventionism, and his real motivation for taking his political positions was usually less than noble. The shameless way in which he switched sides on these issues and the irrational and hysterical ways he often attacked his political opponents led many to question not only his integrity but the soundness of his mind as well. Indeed, the question of character was one that supporters and opponents alike had to consider when confronting Norris. By his way of thinking, however, he was in the same league with the automobile executives of the motor city and the cabinet members in the nation's capital. Fort Worth was fine for a populist, but Norris saw himself as a major player in American affairs, so a major industrial city such as Detroit fit his style better.

6
Sphinx

While Norris's enemies often charged that he had no character, few have doubted that he was one. His need to be in the public eye and his desire to control all facets of his own empire often led him to engage in some of the most outlandish acts imaginable for a fundamentalist pastor. One need think only of some of the events already covered to understand how much this was so. After all, how many pastors in American history have been tried for perjury and arson while leading a movement that thrived during these highly publicized trials? Norris had an almost limitless ability to turn seeming disaster to his own good fortune, but in the quest to advance his own cause he at times engaged in many underhanded acts. Like a mythical sphinx, Norris could be two things at once, a prophet of God and a diabolical schemer. Without a doubt, the most famous event of Norris's entire career was his 1926 trial for murder. Opponents used this against Norris for the rest of his life, and in some ways he never lived it down.

The Murder Trial

As had been the case with the fire of 1912, the events that precipitated Norris's trial for murder resulted from his outspoken attacks on the establishment politicians of the city of Fort Worth. During the summer of 1926, Norris alleged that the mayor, H.C. Meacham, was involved in a scheme to enhance his own business enterprise and a Roman Catholic church and school at the city's expense. According to Norris, Meacham and the city manager, H.B. Carr, were planning to build a street that would reroute traffic past Meacham's downtown store. The mayor, who was Roman Catholic, had also allegedly conspired to aid St. Ignatius School by overvaluing a piece of the school's property that the city intended to buy as part of the street-building endeavor.[1]

The week after Norris made these charges, the red-lettered headline across the top of the *Searchlight* read, "Six Members of First Baptist Church Fired by L.B. Haughey, Roman Catholic Manager of Meacham Dry Goods Co." The article was a stenographic record of the July 11 service at First Baptist when Norris invited the six to come to the platform to tell their stories. At least two told how Haughey had given them the choice of either leaving First Baptist Church or losing their jobs. They chose to remain in Norris's church and were subsequently fired. Norris used this incident to launch into his most severe attacks yet on Meacham and Carr, saying that Carr was an importation from the North and the "missing link" and that Meacham was not "fit to be mayor of a hog pen."[2]

The record of the July 11 service and Norris's vitriolic attacks appeared in print on the sixteenth. The following day was Saturday, and Norris was in his office when a Fort Worth lumberman named D.E. Chipps arrived. Chipps was the mayor's friend and supporter, and he had come to warn Norris to leave Meacham alone. When it appeared to Norris that Chipps was perhaps going to attack him, Norris pulled the night watchman's revolver from his desk and fired four shots, three of which hit the unarmed Chipps, killing him. Norris then called the police, an ambulance, and his wife, and was subsequently arrested and released on bond, pending trial. As he had during the events surrounding the burning of the church in 1912, Norris immediately offered to resign as pastor, but the congregation refused his resignation.[3]

The sermon the following morning was based on the scriptural text "All things work together for good," from Romans 8:28. When this sermon appeared in the *Searchlight* later in the week, captioned above the title were the words "Sermon Preached Is Most Solemn Service in History of First Baptist Church." Indeed, compared to Norris's usual bombast, his words of July 18 were very somber, containing no political references and no mention of the shooting. An insert at the bottom of page one, however, contained a statement by the chairman of the board of trustees saying the shooting was justifiable self-defense.[4] In the weeks that followed, Norris rebounded from his setback and began his attacks anew. Admitting that he was sorry Chipps was dead, he never entertained the notion that the shooting had been anything other than necessary in view of the circumstances. For the most part, his followers agreed with him and stood behind him.

Due to a change of venue and other pretrial maneuvers, Norris's trial did not begin until January 1927, in Austin, nearly two hundred miles south of Fort Worth. The prosecution took only one day to prove that Norris had indeed shot and killed Chipps, but the defense took almost two weeks to prove that Norris had acted in self-defense. Norris's attorney was able to establish that on other occasions Chipps had threatened to kill Norris and that the lumberman had been with Meacham on the day of the shooting. The church bookkeeper gave what was probably the decisive testimony when he corroborated Norris's report that the burly Chipps had threatened bodily harm by challenging the pastor to a fight. Norris himself testified in the trial that he shot Chipps because he thought his adversary intended to kill him.

On January 25, the jury returned a verdict of not guilty. That night Norris returned to Fort Worth and was greeted by a mass of his supporters at his church, and in the year following the shooting itself, First Baptist added two thousand new members.[5] It seems that people were attracted to Norris not in spite of his brushes with the law but in part because of them. Here was a preacher who went to great lengths to pit himself on the side of the common people and in opposition to the power structures of his day. This is not to suggest that Norris concocted ways to land in court. His legal problems stemmed from his extremism in attacking city officials and his compulsive nature, combined in this latter case with the proximity of firearms. Still, however, to the average working-class folks of Fort Worth, he looked a lot like a man who never backed down when confronted by the establishment. In his determination never to be in an inferior position, Norris may have been exorcising psychological demons from a childhood beset by abuse and a sense of inferiority. But to the average Texan in 1926, it looked like he was just fighting against political elites who happened to be Catholic, a fact that could not have been lost on the Protestant residents of Fort Worth. During and after the murder trial, Norris's empire continued to grow in both size and fame, but once again it experienced a disastrous fire in 1929. Coming the same year as the stock market crash and the onset of the Great Depression, the fire did not bode well for the church's prospects. Norris again rose to the challenge and continued to amass a larger and larger empire. In the process, his actions toward his allies were sometimes nearly as underhanded as those directed toward his opponents. Nowhere was this more evident than in his relationship with Luther Peak.

Norris and Peak

In the early thirties, Peak was a young preacher when he introduced himself to Norris by letter, asking the fundamentalist leader for help in establishing a church where there would be potential for growth. Shortly thereafter, Peak attended one of Norris's Bible schools in Fort Worth. Staying for nearly three weeks, Peak was able to get acquainted with Norris. Subsequently, Norris introduced Peak to a new fundamentalist congregation in Denton, Texas, about an hour north of Dallas. The fit was good, and the Fundamentalist Baptist Tabernacle called Peak as its pastor. Peak arrived in Texas to stay in 1934. The Fundamentalist Tabernacle was a satellite in the Norris movement. Many of the churches founded as a result of Norris revival meetings were almost like franchise operations of First Baptist Fort Worth, which served as the epicenter of the independent Baptist movement in Texas. Peak recalled later that he never intended to stay long in Texas. Rather, he wanted to study the Norris movement up close for a few years to learn the techniques that allowed First Baptist to grow into what today would be considered a megachurch. Once in Texas, however, Peak would never leave.[6]

Peak would be associated with Norris in one way or another until the latter's death in 1952. He would serve in various capacities within Norris's empire in Fort Worth, including a stint as president of Norris's Bible Baptist Seminary and even as pastor of First Baptist. During his association with Norris, Peak had to endure the whims of a leader who could be nearly as devious with his associates as he was with his enemies, but Norris was also Peak's ticket to greater influence and visibility within Texas fundamentalism. For Peak, the price of his alliance with Norris was this roller-coaster ride that undoubtedly kept him guessing as to just where he stood with his mentor.

An example of Norris's belief in Peak's potential as a protégé came while Peak was serving his five-year stint in Denton. Norris invited Peak to Fort Worth on Sunday nights to do radio broadcasts. This weekly opportunity to be on the radio allowed Peak to boost his own fledgling ministry at the Fundamentalist Baptist Tabernacle. He would occasionally get to preach his own sermons as well as to pump his church in Denton.[7] By the late forties, Peak had parlayed this radio exposure into his own broadcast hour.

Just as Norris could provide Peak with opportunities the younger pastor was unlikely to get elsewhere, so he could on occasion put Peak in difficult and embarrassing situations. Such was the case in the mid-thirties when Norris invited Peak to come to First Baptist Fort Worth to be an assistant pastor. By this time, Norris was shuttling back and forth from Temple Baptist in Detroit and was therefore in need of frequent pulpit supply in Fort Worth. Peak had filled in occasionally when Norris informed him that he wanted Peak to come as permanent assistant pastor. According to Peak's recollection years later, the congregation in Fort Worth had already voted in favor of calling him. Peak accepted the offer and began to help his Denton congregation find a replacement. Having lined up a new pastor for the Fundamentalist Baptist Tabernacle, however, Peak learned that Norris had hired someone else to fill the assistant's slot in Fort Worth. Norris never gave Peak an explanation, and Peak's wife warned him that this was a clear indication of Norris's willingness to use others for his own purposes. Peak took solace only when he learned from other sources that members of his own congregation had pled with Norris not to take their pastor. In that Norris had personally co-signed the loan on Peak's church building in Denton, the congregation there allegedly even threatened to default if Norris hired Peak. This, of course, would have left Norris with the debt. Accepting this explanation as a rationale, Peak continued his association with Norris. In 1940, when Norris offered him the assistant's position at Temple in Detroit, however, a wary and wiser Peak turned down the offer and accepted a young, struggling church in Dallas. Reflecting later on this decision, Peak remembered that he did not want to be too much under Norris's thumb.[8]

Peak would remain in the Norris sphere of influence, and as such he had not endured the last of Norris's unpredictable ways. In 1947, having already disrupted the annual meeting of the Southern Baptist Convention by verbally attacking SBC president Louie Newton, Norris wanted to do the same at the meeting of the Baptist General Convention of Texas in November. The problem was that Norris could not attend the BGCT meeting because his church had long since been expelled and barred from the state convention. At this time, Peak was serving at the Central Baptist Church in Dallas, which was in good standing in the Dallas Association of Baptist Churches. As such, members of Central were eligible to serve as messengers to the Baptist General Convention of Texas. Norris therefore requested that Peak credential Bill Fraser as a messenger from Central. Fraser was a Norris associate who had agreed to serve as agent provocateur. Peak, recognizing the underhanded nature of such a scheme, not to mention the possible embarrassment for his own church, rejected Norris's overture. Peak erred, however, by leaving town shortly thereafter to attend a conference in Colorado. While he was gone, Norris and Fraser arranged somehow for Peak's secretary to issue a credentials letter, and Fraser attended the Amarillo meeting. When he stood and harangued Newton, as Norris himself had done the previous spring in St. Louis, near riot conditions ensued as others in the auditorium physically removed Fraser from the premises.[9] It appeared once again, to use Peak's wife's words from the thirties, that Norris had "used" Peak.

Somehow, Peak remained tolerant of Norris's ways and stayed close to his mentor. In 1950, when Norris's movement endured a major schism, Peak remained solidly aligned with Norris against the faction that would leave Norris and establish a new fundamentalist denomination with headquarters in Springfield, Missouri. The group that left was headed by G. Beauchamp Vick, who had been serving as the president of Norris's Bible Baptist Seminary while also, for all practical purposes, running the affairs of the Temple Baptist Church in Detroit, where Norris was appearing less and less. When Norris attempted to change the bylaws of the seminary without even notifying the board of directors, Vick and those who aligned with him concluded that they could no longer accept Norris's authoritarian methods. After stormy attempts to reconcile the two camps, Vick and his group left the Norris movement and established the Baptist Bible Fellowship and Baptist Bible College of Springfield.

Throughout the schism, Peak remained a steadfast Norris ally. In a general letter to concerned parties and in ten pages of public testimony taken at the seminary, Peak defended Norris against charges of impropriety and heavy-handedness.[10] Norris may have double-crossed and humiliated Peak in the past, but Norris had also given Peak his start in Texas and had employed him for years as an adjunct professor at the seminary. Over time, Peak had worked his way up within the Norris empire to the point that he was one of a select few to be invited on Norris's 1947 trip to Europe and the Middle East during which, among other things, Norris's party secured an audience with Pope Pius XII. Two years later, Peak had accompanied Norris on a trip around the world.[11] Peak was not about to turn against the Norris movement when its leader was in his hour of greatest need. Peak may well have been convinced that Norris was right in the dispute with the Vick faction, but Peak himself still had much to gain from his alliance with Norris. Such would become evident when Peak succeeded Vick as president of the Bible Baptist Seminary once the schism ended.

After Vick's departure, Norris turned naturally to Peak as a successor. In March 1951, Peak received word that when the trustees held their next meeting, Norris intended to elect Peak as president of the seminary. In this same letter, Norris asked Peak to assume the editorship of the *Fundamentalist* as well, writing, "On the *Fundamentalist*, it is exceedingly important that it be given a permanent leadership and you are the man to take it."[12] Peak was installed as seminary president that summer in what the *Fundamentalist* called a "historical week."[13]

It was while Peak was affiliated with the seminary that he endured yet another embarrassment at the hands of Norris. Peak had brought in fundamentalist preacher B.R. Lakin to conduct a revival at Central Baptist where Peak continued to serve even as he assumed the presidency of Norris's school. Lakin wanted to see the seminary in Fort Worth, so Peak arranged for his guest to speak to the students in a chapel meeting. During the service, Lakin had the students in rapt attention with his wit and charm when Norris entered the auditorium and observed what was taking place. As he walked down the center aisle, Norris stopped behind a student who was well known for his fancy hairstyle. As the attention turned away from Lakin, Norris placed his hand on the student's head and rubbed round and round, ruining the fifties-style coiffure as the other students roared with laughter. Needless to say, Norris had effectively broken up Lakin's meeting. Later, Lakin expressed his shock to Peak that Norris would do such a thing to a fellow preacher, but Peak merely reminded his friend that he had warned him that one could never predict Norris's moods. Years later, Peak chalked up the incident to Norris's jealousy—his inability to accept someone else in the limelight.[14]

Peak's boundless capacity to tolerate Norris's antics would soon pay off even further. The aging Norris, seeming to sense that his empire was crumbling beneath him, recognized that he needed a strong leader to help him shore up his base. He turned to Peak, therefore, as the logical heir of his life's work, inviting his longtime disciple to become pastor of First Baptist Church. Peak accepted, but retained his church in Dallas, just in case Norris "pulled the rug out from under" him.[15] Peak's stint at First Baptist lasted a little more than six months before Norris once again embarrassed him. Peak resigned in June 1952 over a rather cruel practical joke. He was in the sound booth at First Baptist and believed he was preaching to a radio audience. After ten to fifteen minutes he learned that Norris had disconnected the radio feed and was with his longtime Sunday school superintendent, Louis Entzminger, laughing and making jokes about Peak being in his "glass cage" just preaching to himself.[16] The following Sunday, after his morning sermon, Peak read his resignation letter. In it he said nothing of the "glass cage" incident and even emphasized that Norris "has been most congenial and cooperative, and wholehearted in his support of my ministry here, during these months."[17] Recalling these events thirty years later, however, Peak remembered that as he had walked back to his hotel room that night, he had decided that he could endure no more.[18] Norris died two months later, and First Baptist passed into the leadership of Homer Ritchie, a twenty-six-year-old preacher who was about as new to the Norris movement as Peak had been in the mid-thirties when Norris had first extended, then withdrawn, an invitation to be First Baptist's associate pastor.

The clean break with the Norris movement, which Peak was never able to make while Norris lived, came finally in 1956 when Peak led Central Baptist Church out of the independent Baptist movement and back into the Southern Baptist Convention. The *Baptist Standard*, at one time Norris's own newspaper but now the official publication of the Baptist General Convention of Texas, gave Peak several pages in which to explain his return to the Baptist fold following his long sojourn into fundamentalism. Peak made it clear at the outset of his article, entitled "Why We Left Fundamentalism to Work with Southern Baptists," that "in the Fundamentalist movement we were usually in a fight of some kind. If we were not fighting Southern Baptists, Northern Baptists, the National Council of Churches, the Catholics, communism, or modernism, we fought each other." Peak emphasized that while he still believed in the "fundamentals of the faith," he could no longer tolerate the methods and outlook of fundamentalism. In what every Texas Baptist must have recognized as a veiled reference to Norris, Peak described the philosophy of fundamentalism: "It is right to do wrong in order to do right. . . . In the realm of Fundamentalism, preachers may split each other's churches, make war upon one another, print and publish lies and slander against the character of others, and all be accepted as the normal procedure. It is a lawless and anarchistic world under the guise of evangelical Christianity."[19]

In interviews in the early eighties Peak admitted, "If I had it to do over again, I never would have become involved with the nondenominational movement, because I don't think that Baptists were far enough off the track to justify it." With reference to Norris personally, Peak said that while he did not want to be disrespectful of the fundamentalist leader, "I regret that I left my Southern Baptist affiliation and became involved with Dr. Norris."[20]

It appears that despite all he endured at the hands of Norris, Peak was still attracted to fundamentalism largely because he was so drawn to Norris personally. Several times in interviews, after telling of the rather dreadful deeds of Norris, Peak countered with stories of Norris's powerful leadership skills and his personal magnetism. Peak claimed that on one occasion Norris entered a packed sanctuary unannounced, and the people in attendance broke into applause spontaneously. Norris had not uttered a word. In relating this story, Peak ask rhetorically, "Was it communication by the Spirit from one person to another for the whole audience, or just what was it? I couldn't explain it." It seems that part of Norris's appeal for Peak and many others was that they never knew what to expect from him. On some occasions he would preach "like the world was coming to an end," on others deliver a calm Bible lecture, while sometimes he would just toy with his audience and goof around on the platform.[21] Norris played a variety of roles and was everything except boring. Furthermore, for the thousands who joined his churches, turned out to hear him at revivals, read his newspaper, or listened to him on the radio, the vast majority knew nothing of his relationships behind the scenes and probably would not have cared how he treated those with whom he was associated. Even those who knew Norris were often willing to dismiss his lapses as oversights instead of reading them as major character flaws.

Peak insisted that there were many positive things about Norris. In his zeal to win converts to the faith, Norris took a personal interest in those usually ignored by others—African Americans who worked menial service jobs for whites, for example, and common people in the neighborhoods of Fort Worth, Detroit, and the other cities where he preached. Norris reached out to these people with what Peak viewed as genuine compassion. When this was combined with Norris's preaching power, his knowledge of Scripture and history, his energy and enthusiasm, we start to see a person who for all his faults was a whirlwind of excitement that people wanted to see and experience. Nevertheless, Peak's own later regrets about his alliance with Norris suggest that he was dominated and used by Norris and that he could only see the situation clearly after Norris had passed from the scene. In listening to Peak reminisce, one gets the impression that there are times when he wishes he had never met Norris. This is not an altogether unusual feeling among those who left the Norris movement. Peak believed that Norris's jealousy resulted in his running off every good associate he ever had.[22] Recently, Peak reaffirmed his views of Norris and the fundamentalist movement that he led, writing, "We all make mistakes and it would have been far better for me, if I had never aligned myself with Dr. Norris and his movement. For years I gave it my best but I had a hard row to hoe. . . . If I could only live my life over again, I certainly would do it differently."[23]

Norris and Vick

While G. Beauchamp Vick, who succeeded Norris as head pastor of Temple Baptist, could recall both sides of Norris's personality, Vick's recollections of Norris were even more negative than Peak's. Like Peak, Vick became part of the Norris movement when he was a young man. When Vick moved from Kentucky to Fort Worth in 1920 he was at first wary of First Baptist Church and its pastor because Norris attacked Southern Baptist leaders whom Vick had been taught to revere. Norris, however, won over Vick and his wife because he was the only pastor who paid a personal visit to the Vick home, actually welcoming Vick before the furniture had even arrived in town.

Vick was part of Norris's movement off and on during the twenties and early thirties before becoming in 1935 Norris's chief lieutenant in charge of Temple Baptist on the many occasions when Norris could not be in Detroit. After serving in this capacity for a number of years, Norris eventually asked Vick to become president of the Bible Baptist Seminary in Fort Worth. Vick was reticent at first, writing to Norris, "Your word has been law in both the First Baptist Church and the seminary so long, that you would not relish me nor anyone else insisting on carrying out something that you might oppose."[24] Still, Norris persuaded Vick to accept the position. Vick's belief that Norris was unable to accept any challenge to his own authority was confirmed during the schism of 1950. As Vick later recalled the split, Norris had written the new seminary bylaws and instituted them without even consulting the school's board of directors. When the board protested, Norris told the members that they could vote any way they wanted, but the bylaws would remain. He said he would lock the doors of the school and First Baptist Church before he would allow a change. Summing up Norris's approach to institutional governance, Vick remarked that Norris was a dictator who had to control all facets of everything with which he was involved. The extent of this reached even into financial matters where Norris used money raised for a specific project to pay salaries or general operating bills instead. At one point during the schism, Vick learned that enough money had been raised to build a dormitory twice, yet the money was nowhere to be found and the dormitory had not been constructed. Norris simply ignored the generally accepted practices of fiscal righteousness and oversight.[25] After a series of stormy meetings, Vick concluded that he and his supporters would have to leave the Norris movement. They moved to

Springfield, Missouri, and established the Baptist Bible Fellowship and College.

In addition to the institutional matters that divided Vick and Norris, during the schism Vick had to endure frequent public references to his daughter's extramarital affair and subsequent divorce as Norris used this family issue to taint Vick and the others who had departed. Then, when Norris discovered that a member of the Vick faction had been arrested in Phoenix a year before the split for attempting to sodomize a young black male, Norris not only published this revelation but included in the *Fundamentalist* a cartoon showing a white man holding hands with a young black boy while a third person, representing Vick, invited the alleged sex offender to "come on up and preach for us."[26]

Once the schism was complete and Vick and his group had disassociated themselves from the operations in Fort Worth, Norris actually forged a letter to make it appear as if the schism had been a minor breach that had been overcome. This occurred in 1951 when Vick sent several copies of a form letter from Temple Baptist where he remained as pastor until his retirement in the 1970s. The letter was meant to inform supporters of the progress Temple had made in the previous year. Norris somehow got hold of a copy of Vick's letter, placed his own name and address at the top to make it look as if Vick had written it to him, then published it to make it appear as if the two had been reconciled. Vick believed that Norris may have done this to try to rehabilitate his reputation after losing a large contingent of his forces during the schism. Such a letter would have given the appearance that Vick was no longer opposed to Norris. Perhaps most mysterious is that a letter from Vick exposing this forgery and addressed to a man in West Virginia somehow ended up in Norris's files.[27] Vick concluded even earlier than Peak that Norris could not share power and could not be trusted.

Father and Son

The experiences of Peak and Vick were not atypical for Norris. With the exception of Louis Entzminger, the Sunday school superintendent at First Baptist, Norris had a falling out with nearly every individual within his movement who was in any way independently minded. This included his own son, to whom he had relinquished the tight reins of First Baptist in 1944, eight years before he gave them to Peak. After deciding that George should succeed him, Norris merely announced to the church that he was installing George as head pastor. He had consulted neither the congregation nor George himself before taking this action.[28] George had been serving for a time as First Baptist's associate pastor in charge of affairs while the elder Norris was in Detroit tending to Temple. Norris's professional relationship with George and his autocratic style of church administration were revealed regularly in letters he wrote to his son. Norris often included very explicit instructions as to how he wanted First Baptist administered. For example, he wrote this to George: "Find enclosed letter that I want you to take time Sunday morning at 11 o'clock and read to the whole congregation. It doesn't matter what the program is, you hustle everybody in there at 11 o'clock and I don't mean 11:10."[29] The following day Norris threatened to fire the whole church staff unless business was executed in strict accordance with his commands. "I want everything carried out as I direct and I don't want it changed unless I am informed about it," he wrote pointedly.[30] As could have been predicted, Norris was unable to allow George a free hand in leading the church even after he had named George head pastor. Father and son eventually separated in a bitter dispute, and George, along with many members of First Baptist, founded Gideon Baptist Church across town.

After the familial breakup, there ensued a series of letters from Norris to George in which the father berated the son for a host of character flaws, the most frequently mentioned being ingratitude. " I have only regrets for your future," Norris wrote, after accusing George of dishonoring his parents.[31] A few weeks later he was more vitriolic: "You should go back to the day that you were married and pay back to me the blood money we put in your education. You can count the amount. And also include the car. And we could use that library that I selected at great pain and cost." Amidst repeated reminders that he had sent George to the Naval Academy and to the University of Michigan, Norris even sprinkled his letters with references to Lillian's health, implying that George was responsible for illnesses his mother had contracted while she had grieved at her son's departure from First Baptist. Norris also wrote, in a particularly vicious letter, "The day will come in the course of human events when your mother and I will lie cold in death . . . and before the casket lid is pulled down over the faces of those who gave you life, you certainly would remember you stabbed us both in the back." Norris also attacked those who had left First Baptist with George. "You haven't a man around you that has any good level-headed sense and that is unfortunate for you," Norris charged. "You have an ill-tempered, nit-wit crowd, and frankly, I say, I was never so relieved [sic] as to get rid of the whole bunch of them in this church for they have been a blight." The letter was signed, "Yours in deepest and tenderest pity and love."[32]

The next day Norris threatened to expose one of George's associates as a gambler and another as a draft dodger. Even when he tried to be gentle with his wayward son, Norris usually lost control of his pen. Thus, a statement that began, "I shall not cease to pray for you for I feel certain that God laid His hand on you," concluded, "and since He did He will not permit you to play the fool always."[33] A full six months after the original round of correspondence, Norris mentioned, somewhat in passing but nevertheless as part of another angry letter, that he would gladly pay the legal fee for George to change his last name.[34]

All this vitriol directed at George stemmed from Norris's need to dominate his subordinates. A portent of this sort of domination over George had appeared as early as 1940 at about the time George decided to enter the ministry. Norris wrote to George, "I need not advise you. May the Lord direct you." Then, as if to prove that he did in fact need to advise George, Norris outlined an entire week of revival services for George. "But I would preach on judgment, on sin, on hell, on the new birth, on salvation."[35] It was probably no coincidence that Norris listed five themes—just the right number for the five-day meeting George was about to undertake. Little wonder that five years later, when George went his own way, Norris would find such an act so difficult to accept.

Norris and Rawlings

Many of Norris's supporters attested to his inability to deal with individuals he could not control. John Rawlings, who was one of the first students to graduate from the Bible Baptist Seminary, eventually went with the Vick faction during the schism. Later, when he and Vick gave an interview, Rawlings recalled, "I respected him [Norris]. I gave him honor. . . . But, I just never could feel warm and comfortable around him." Vick then interjected, "Don't you think that was partly occasioned, John, by a lack of confidence or trust?" Rawlings replied timidly, "Well, somebody else will have to be the judge of that. I don't know."[36]

Displaying an ambivalence toward Norris much like that of Luther Peak, Rawlings was reluctant to say anything too negative about Norris. With Vick prodding him, however, he eventually told how he had once invited Norris to a meeting in the east Texas town of Tyler. Norris was to appear with Governor Coke Stephenson. Evidently, Norris's address on this occasion was not what Rawlings had hoped. Clearly, this had been by Rawlings's estimation one of the times that Norris played games with the audience instead of preaching forthrightly. Later, when Norris spoke with Rawlings about returning for another appearance in Tyler, Rawlings told Norris that the next time he came he would have to preach the gospel. As Rawlings told this, he began to laugh as he imitated Norris's gravely voice responding, "Well, the hell with you," just before hanging up the telephone. Almost immediately following this humorous story, Rawlings told how he had lost respect for Norris after witnessing his attempts to destroy people. Rawlings then countered with the familiar refrain that he did not want to criticize Norris. In discussing the schism of 1950, Rawlings was willing to let Norris off easy by attributing his viciousness to age and a fear that he had lost Temple Baptist Church because of his own mistakes. With Vick by his side, Rawlings was willing to admit, however, that instead of being proud of young men like Vick whom he had trained, Norris turned on them "like a blind rattlesnake."[37]

In listening to this interview recorded twenty years after Norris's death, one is struck by the psychological power Norris seems to have had over individuals like Rawlings. Rawlings's statements also tell us much about Norris's personality. By nature, Norris seems to have been intolerant of any type of power sharing. His empire may have been populist, but it was not democratic. Much like Huey Long in the neighboring state of Louisiana, Norris ran the show, but he did so in a way that endeared him to the people even as it left some of them, like Peak and Rawlings, wondering if something were not amiss within his personality.

In reminiscing about Norris, some of his followers seem to have been somewhat baffled that a man who had dedicated his energy and considerable abilities to God's work could be capable of such evil. Norris's own daughter testified to her father's ambiguous character even as she bore witness to her ambivalence toward him. She recalled her father as consistently tender with the family, but referred to him as a "dictator" in his public life. She characterized the church business meetings as a "joke." "Every now and then," she recalled, "someone would say: 'We ought to have a business meeting. We haven't had one in three or four years. Then again, maybe we ought to wait until we have some deacons.'"[38] She had also tried to warn her brother George that the arrangement at First Baptist would never work.

Norris and Southern Baptist Leaders

Several Southern Baptist leaders in Norris's lifetime charged that Norris had an autocratic nature. L.R. Scarborough wrote in his undated pamphlet *The Fruits of Norrisism*, "In its [Norrisism's] chief leadership it is the embodiment of autocratic ecclesiasticism. All the privileges and rights of the church leading up to the pastor." Indeed, Norris often acted as if he owned First Baptist Church and had called the congregation to be his parishioners. While he interpreted his actions as consistent with the principle of congregational autonomy, much of what he did could be better described as dictatorship of the rankest sort, and this style seems to have emanated as much from Norris's own personality as from the exigencies of his movement. The organization of Norris's religious empire was a hierarchy of one.

W.A. Criswell, longtime Southern Baptist fundamentalist pastor, grew up hearing two distinctly different views of Norris. "I'd hear my mother and father argue about Frank Norris," Criswell once said. His father was pro-Norris, but his mother despised Norris because he attacked the beloved George Truett. Criswell himself, who ideologically could hardly be closer to Norris, still made a conscious decision to use Truett as his model, and when Truett died in 1944, Criswell succeeded him at First Baptist Dallas. Having adopted Truett's style and Norris's theology, Criswell remembered the two this way:

> Ah, Frank Norris could do anything with a crowd. He could have them weeping, he could have them laughing, he could have them do anything, and when you listened to him you just were moved by him, you know, and you felt that way. He was a gifted man and knew crowd psychology, if there is such a term as that, how to manipulate people, but, oh, underneath Frank Norris there were personal attitudes that were diabolical. They were vicious. But Dr. Truett was the type of a man who built. He was the type of a man to build the institution, to build the school, to build a hospital, to build the church, to build the denomination, and I early sensed that it's that kind of leadership that we ought to follow.[39]

Norris himself saw Texas Baptist leaders like Truett as his natural rivals partly because he had been on the opposite side during the Seventy-five Million Campaign discussed in chapter 2, but more generally because Truett was a leader in a convention that Norris could not control. In addition to occasional public attacks, Norris sent a letter to Truett in 1940 reminding him that all efforts to side-track the Norris juggernaut had been in vain. Norris claimed that he had prospered despite Truett's predictions of imminent demise. What makes this letter doubly revealing of what Criswell called Norris's diabolical side was that it was sent special delivery to reach Truett on Sunday morning, calculated obviously to upset Truett before he entered the pulpit of First Baptist Dallas. Fortunately for Truett, one of his assistants intercepted the letter.[40]

In a similar vein, Norris, at least according to Texas legend, gave J.M. Dawson a free, lifetime subscription to the *Fundamentalist*. Allegedly, Norris had the paper delivered to Dawson's doorstep on Sunday mornings so that when Dawson left his home to lead Sunday services at First Baptist Church Waco, he would have to stumble across Norris on his way. While Norris spent a good deal of time lambasting Dawson as a theological modernist, Dawson never let on that the attacks had the least effect on him, at least while Norris was alive. Some twenty years after Norris's death, however, Dawson told an interviewer how word of Norris's passing in 1952 had caused him to ponder how misdirected Norris's life had been. Off the record, Dawson said that he believed the world would have been better had Norris never lived.[41] Such an assessment is understandable coming from someone who had been savaged regularly by Norris. Although Peak, Vick, and Rawlings would not go that far, it seems highly significant that their stories also reveal a Norris who was capable of acts that at the very least stung the moral sensibilities of fair-minded people; and yet to this day he is revered by followers as the founder of a great movement. These latter-day Norrisites even appropriate their founder's name for the fledgling seminary they operate in Fort Worth, and they call their newspaper the *Searchlight*, in memory of Norris's paper before 1927 when he changed the title to the *Fundamentalist*. Beneath its title are the words "In Memoriam—Dr. J. Frank Norris—20th Century's Foremost Fundamentalist."[54]

While there were plenty of true stories in circulation attesting to Norris's irascibility, certain mythical aspects of his legend are even worse. One story has Norris killing his father-in-law by pushing him off the back of a train, insurance money being the alleged motive. The story is false, but few of Norris's adversaries would have doubted that Norris was capable of such an act.[43] A story that may be true has Norris on the radio lambasting Dawson. When Lillian Norris could endure no more, she allegedly grabbed the microphone and attempted to broadcast an impassioned defense of her husband's archenemy.[44]

Norris and Gerald L.K. Smith

While the alienation between Norris and others within his move-
ment was usually a direct result of Norris's own "diabolical side," as
Criswell called it, on at least one occasion he lost an ally because he
refused to stoop to the level of some other right-wingers of his day.
This refusal led to a temporary split between himself and Gerald
L.K. Smith. Smith was a Disciples of Christ preacher, former ally of
Huey Long, and vitriolic anti-Semite. Norris had recognized the anti-
Semitism in the early forties, but by 1947 he was willing to work
with Smith because both men were calling for a fundamentalist–
Roman Catholic alliance against communism.

In preparation for a Smith rally at First Baptist Fort Worth,
Norris and Smith corresponded heavily in early 1947. Their letters
were laced with affectionate phrases and praise for one another's
work. Norris, however, seems to have been wary of Smith, so he
wrote to his friend M.E. Coyle in Detroit asking for his impression
of Smith. Norris confessed to Coyle, "I once was deeply prejudiced
against him for I thought he was anti-semitic."[45] Norris had already
advertised, however, that Smith would speak at First Baptist. Billed
as a "Mammoth Christian America Rally," Smith's topics were to
include a communist plot to deceive Negroes; why Elliot Roosevelt
is closer to Stalin than any other American; red propaganda on cam-
puses; demagogues in both parties ready to make deals with Stalin;
and who Stalin picked as the next president of the United States.[46]

Following the rally, the Norris-Smith correspondence continued warmly as each kept the other informed in the ongoing anticommunist crusade. Norris, for example, reported to Smith of the cool
reception Henry Wallace had received while speaking in Austin. He
urged Smith to come back to Texas for a second rally, and he hoped
Smith would tear into the "red-hot bunch of communists" at the
University of Texas. Norris wrote gleefully of a possible confrontation in which the National Guard might even be summoned.[47]
Norris received letters from a few of his supporters, however, who
criticized his alliance with Smith because Smith was a racist who
spoke out fervently for white supremacy, something Norris had
ceased to do more than a decade before.[48] This concerned Norris
so much that he wrote to Smith expressing reservations about a
planned second rally. Smith responded with some suggestions, but
the rally was eventually canceled because Smith found that his
schedule would not permit him to attend.[49]

Norris's growing concern over Smith's extremism became so intense that in June he advised Smith to get out of anticommunism al-

together and start a great "soul-winning campaign" instead. Norris admonished Smith: "At your young age, with your experience and with your beliefs in the verities of the Christian faith, if you should come out full fledged for the Pre-millennial coming of Christ and call America to repentance you would silence your bitterest foes and you would challenge America as no man in American history." This was rather strange advice coming from one who had just started an anti-communist campaign against the Southern Baptist Convention and its president, Louie Newton, but Norris may have been making a distinction between anticommunist efforts to save religious institutions and the secular sort of anticommunism in which Smith was heavily involved. Norris implied this when he commended Smith, saying that he had served well as a John the Baptist figure, heralding the coming of the anticommunist movement, but now that both political parties were fully involved, it was time to get back to religious work.[50] Still, Smith may well have retorted that considering the past record, Norris was in no position to steer someone else away from secular politics. Understandably, Norris's advice had little impact. Smith's next few letters failed to acknowledge the admonition and expressed instead his desire to get the Newton issue before the House Un-American Activities Committee.[51]

The break between Norris and Smith came in the fall of 1947 when Smith wrote an article in which he argued that Jesus had not been a Jew. Norris, who had been speaking and writing in support of the formation of the new nation-state of Israel, could not let such an absurdity pass, though he had said things in his own anticommunist campaigns that were nearly as bizarre. He printed a denunciation of Smith in the *Fundamentalist*, citing Smith's fine reputation as an anticommunist crusader, but condemning such an irresponsible and theologically heretical idea. Norris wrote, "Gerald discredits his whole movement by such a preposterous and untrue statement. . . . Incidentally, that was the chief stock in trade of Hitler and Goebbels and Company."[52] Smith responded with a scorching letter to Norris complaining, "For one who knows better, I think you rather over did it in trying to make me look like Hitler and Goebbels." Then, as if to confirm Norris's concern, Smith continued, "I suggest that in your anxiety to please some of these hooked nose kikes that curse the name of Jesus Christ that you go a little easier on some of your brethren in Christ." Smith also issued a veiled threat when he reminded Norris that a court had ruled recently that it was libelous to even imply that someone was a nazi.[53]

In January 1948, Smith went after Norris in his own magazine, *The Cross and the Flag*. In an article entitled, "Frank Norris the Paradox," he portrayed Norris as confused and inconsistent on seventeen different issues. Smith wrote, "He curses the Pope, he praises the Pope. He curses the Jews, he praises the Jews. He praises Gerald Smith, he curses Gerald Smith. He is against the Roosevelts, he is for the Roosevelts."[54] The root of the problem, charged Smith, was that Norris would do anything to keep himself in the public eye. Smith was wrong about Norris cursing the Jews. But on Norris's willingness to switch positions on other issues to enhance his own notoriety, Smith had him pegged.

Several months later, after Jewish statehood had been achieved, Smith criticized all Zionists and Norris by name. Since Smith believed that the Jews were behind many of the communist conspiracies, he viewed Norris's support for Israel as softness toward communism. The final chapter in the rift between the two appears to be Norris's comments concerning Smith's publication of Martin Luther's tract against the Jews, *The Jews and Their Lies*. Norris doubted the authenticity of the work, saying, "I am wondering if it is another forgery like the famous Protocols." Smith responded, telling Norris, "The fact is that in his early life he [Luther] petted the Jews about as you do now, but experience taught him the error of his ways."[55]

Norris would have done almost anything to battle left-wing politics and theology, but he would not criticize the Jews, because this would have been a violation of his premillennial dispensationalism, one of the roots of his fundamentalist theology, which included the belief that the nation-state of Israel had to be reconstituted before the second coming of Christ. Smith was correct, however, in accusing Norris of manipulating events to keep himself in the public eye. Such was the case, it seems, in the Helen Douglas affair of 1947.

Norris and Helen Gahagan Douglas

Douglas was a congresswoman whom Norris and others had accused of being communist. When she was scheduled to speak in Fort Worth at the Paschal High School auditorium, Norris wrote to the school board protesting that Douglas had "a communistic record that is undisputed." When the board caved in to Norris's intimidation and denied Douglas use of the school facility, Norris fired off a letter to the congresswoman informing her that she was welcome to use the First Baptist auditorium for her speech. Norris told her, "Regardless of opinion, pro and con, I believe in free speech, and the sky is the limit on anybody who speaks in the First Baptist Church auditorium."[56]

Norris may have been maneuvering to deflect criticism for the upcoming Smith rally at First Baptist by having Douglas speak there first. That way, when he was criticized for having a racist anti-Semite at First Baptist, he could argue plausibly that he did not endorse all who spoke in his church auditorium. Or he may have done it to prove that he really did believe in free speech, since he had made statements on several occasions that implied that subversives did not enjoy that right. Whatever Norris's motive, at least one follower from Kansas laid bare the inconsistency when he asked Norris why he believed in free speech for Douglas and not for SBC president Louie Newton, whom Norris had attempted to silence during the SBC meeting of 1947.[57] Whatever Norris's motives were, he succeeded as usual in remaining visible to the general public, and he was not reluctant to use underhanded means to achieve this end.

Whether in his dealings with his opponents or supporters, Norris was often capable of acts that were outside the parameters of moral propriety and human civility. His public preaching and leadership endeared him to thousands, but his actions behind the scenes revealed him as a mysterious and unpredictable enigma all too often capable of taking the moral low road.

7

Anticommunist ‖

As Norris progressed through his career he latched on to a variety of political and religious issues. Although he always seemed to be battling on several fronts, there was usually one dominant issue during a given period. He would often tackle such an issue for several weeks, then drop it and go on to another. At other times, he would take on a major theme for a much longer period and attempt to connect it to other disputes. This was the case with anticommunism. As has already been seen, this was an underlying motif as he sparred with the New Deal, organized labor, the Northern Baptist Convention, and even the Southern Baptist Convention when he attacked Louie Newton. He began to discuss communism in the early twenties, became consistently and outspokenly anticommunist by the mid-thirties, and adopted anticommunism as his lead issue for the final six or seven years of his life.

Fundamentalism and Anticommunism

Practically from the outset of the Bolshevik revolution in Russia in 1917, Americans have been fearful of communist infiltration of the United States. One need only recall the Red Scare of 1919 and A. Mitchell Palmer's raids on Russian immigrant workers to see that this has been so. Later, especially after World War II, the fear of communism became twofold—infiltration from within and takeover by the expansionistic Soviets from without. The anticommunist movement then advanced on both fronts with renewed vigor as the world entered into the cold war (1945–1989).

Anticommunism has long been one of the leading political tenets of the fundamentalist movement in America. Just as fundamentalists in the second decade of the century made a connection between the German militarism of World War I and German phi-

losophy that had produced higher criticism of Scripture and, therefore, modernism itself, so they later identified modernism with
communism. For Norris, domestic communism was an outgrowth
of modernism, just as modernism had been a product of German
philosophy. The same philosophy undergirded all movements and
ideologies that deviated in any way from orthodox theology or the
American way of life as perceived by Norris. Once he became convinced that communism was a serious threat to America, it was a
short step to attribute this threat to the theological heresy called
modernism, which had provided the underpinning for most other
social and political dangers.

It took several years for Norris to make the connection between modernism and communism. This also seems to be true of
the fundamentalist movement as a whole. During the twenties the
struggling Soviet Union was scorned but not yet feared. Most serious
anticommunist activities of the fundamentalists began in the early
thirties. Fundamentalist opposition to communism grew steadily,
and by the end of World War II, anticommunism was practically an
article of faith.[1]

Norris's Early Consideration of Communism

Norris's first comments on the Soviet Union were favorable in many
respects. In 1920, when he traveled to Europe, he reported his observations on Russia to the *Searchlight*. Although he viewed the collec-
tivism of the state negatively, he said that it was a misconception
that a bunch of bad men ruled the Soviet Union. "No shrewder or
more far-sighted set of men govern any country today," he wrote.
"They have put everybody to work. The head-cutting off stage is
past." Bolshevism, in his view, was the "natural reaction against
long-standing oppression through the centuries."[2]

Norris maintained a fairly objective and reasoned view of
the Soviet Union throughout 1920, recognizing and condemning
state persecution of the Russian Orthodox Church, but also praising
many positive reforms made by the new regime. He noted that
Russia was a broken and crippled country under the last czar and
that the Bolsheviks had brought many qualified leaders into government service. They were responsible for new farms and schools and
a return to some semblance of order in society. Norris believed that
the western attitude toward Russia needed adjustment, and he condemned American interference in the revolution. "We have no right
to dictate to Russia or any other country what sort of government
they should have," he argued, and he pointed out that the United

States did not attempt this with other countries. In perhaps a veiled reference to the activities of Attorney General Palmer, whose raids had taken place largely in the spring of 1920, Norris said that the Soviets were not anarchists and that the American people had been misled into believing they were.[3] Even the term *bolshevik* for Norris signified radical opposition to oppression. He relished being referred to as the "arch-bolshevik" of the Southern Baptist Convention, and he listed Abraham, Moses, Elijah, John the Baptist, Jan Huss, Savonarola, and even George Washington as other bolsheviks of history.[4]

Another Reversal

Norris did not discuss Bolshevism much from 1922 to 1930. The issue had faded from his interest as he gave attention and energy to other more pressing issues like evolution, prohibition, the anti-Catholic crusade, and his own murder trial. In the thirties, however, he revisited the topic of Soviet communism, and he displayed a completely different attitude. In an article on prohibition he digressed into a short discussion of Bolshevism: "There is no small Bolshevik element in this country and it can no longer be laughed out of court. Unemployment is rampant and the great army of idlers will gather around the standard of any man who waves the red flag of discontent and Bolshevism." Clearly, he had become concerned that in the midst of the economic downturn, Americans would be enticed to radical solutions. Much of the world, in his view, was succumbing to communism, including the labor government of Great Britain, which, according to Norris, was practically controlled by the ideology of Bolshevism. He believed communism was making a strong bid for complete control of Europe.[5]

Norris never again took a mediating position on the issue of communism. In 1931, he preached a sermon entitled "The World-Wide Sweep of Russian Bolshevism and Its Relation to the Second Coming of Christ." As the title indicated, he was attempting to put communism into a prophetic context. The *Fundamentalist* republished this sermon periodically throughout the next two decades, but one wonders why. It was far from being representative of Norris's more mature thought regarding communism, and it was actually one of his poorer sermons on the topic. At this stage in his anticommunist development he had not yet honed his rhetoric into the crisp and belligerent attack that developed later. He cited as alarming the Russian attempt to operate a "moneyless" economy with equality of the races and an absence of a caste system. He failed to make it clear, however, just why these were of such concern. Even on the subject of collectivization, he did not argue that the threat to freedom and individual initiative was the key problem. He stated again, as he had the year previous, that Russian Bolshevism was on the move into Asian nations like China and the British colony of India. Then he argued curiously that the final aim of the Soviets was a move against Britain, the United States, and the Jews. Perhaps most significant for the future was that he equated atheism in America with communist atheism in the Soviet Union. Soon he would broaden the connection between religious philosophy and communism.[6]

A year later, in a sermon entitled "The Red Menace of Communism," Norris quoted from reports alleging that public schools and other American institutions were being infiltrated by the communists. He cited a particular Fort Worth teacher who was supposedly teaching the ideology, and he said that many teachers' salaries were subsidized by communists. He concurred with the view that publicly supported universities should not harbor communists or even professors who required students to read communist literature. By this time, Norris viewed the threat as even more severe than the threat of Roman Catholicism, and he even advocated that Protestants and Catholics put their differences aside to join in the fight. The first time he delivered the "Red Menace" sermon, Norris asked for volunteers to destroy a Russian flag. When several volunteered, he invited them forward, saying, "All right, come up here and do it. Demolish it. Get up here on the platform. Do you have a knife? Cut it to pieces! Tear it to pieces! Step on it, boys! Trample it underfoot!" Two of the "boys" proceeded to cut the flag into pieces, after which someone handed them an American flag to unfurl as the choir broke into the song "Columbia, the Gem of the Ocean."[7]

Also, in 1932, Norris attacked Baylor University for inviting religious activist Kirby Page to be a commencement speaker. Page was an active socialist and editor of *The World Tomorrow*, a pacifist journal. He did not support Marxism, however, and he was critical of class warfare and militarism. In much the same way that Norris believed that all forms of evolutionary thought were equally evil, so he was unable to distinguish between a democratic socialist and a thoroughgoing communist of the Soviet variety. Norris wrote to the acting president of Baylor, accusing Page of communism and demanding that he not be allowed to speak at Baylor.[8]

Most of Norris's ideas with regard to communism were in place by 1932, but he was not yet ready to make the issue a regular part of his endeavors. There was still the hope of saving prohibition on the national level, then on the state and local levels. By 1935 or so, when prohibition was dead on all but the local level, Norris began to discuss communism regularly. Most important, however, was that he became pastor of Temple Baptist in Detroit in 1935. This appears to have been a major factor in his taking up the anti-communist crusade with such vigor, just as it was a major factor in his turnabout against the New Deal. The issue of communism was much more intense in the North than in the South, and Norris found a ready audience for a campaign against the Northern Baptist Convention based on the charge that the denomination had been infiltrated by communists.

As Norris led Temple Baptist Church out of the Northern Baptist Convention, he cited as his principal motivation that the NBC had endorsed communism. In July 1935, Norris published "Why Temple Baptist Church Withdraws from the Northern Baptist Convention," in which he outlined his beliefs concerning the communist infiltration of American institutions. The two leading centers of communism in America were the universities and the denominational headquarters. Claiming to have read most of Lenin's works, Norris told his new congregation that the leader of the Russian Revolution had had a plan to infiltrate the schools and pulpits of America. "Hear me friends," he implored his parishioners, "you Baptists especially, the scheme is what? To Sovietize the churches of America, to honeycomb the public schools, then the red propaganda can go unmolested."[9] Norris was particularly fond of these types of conspiracy theories as he conjured up images of communist subversives serving on local school boards, on university faculties, and in the headquarters of Protestant denominations.

Norris also equated with communism any social action that was close to the New Deal in its thrust and purpose. The resolution Temple Baptist presented to the NBC implied that the convention had aligned itself with a particular political and economic program and that such an action was a violation of the Baptist principle of separation of church and state. The resolution accused the convention of pressuring its member churches into accepting "the Communistic plan of Karl Marx," and it equated communism with the New Deal, saying, "The 'Social Action Commission' sums up, sets forth, and advocates essentially the revolutionary, communistic plan of Soviet Russia, which is better known by its American Brand of 'New Dealism.'" Norris told the congregation that he could turn to fifty places in the writings of Marx and find expressions identical to those uttered by members of the Social Action Commission, and he charged that the commission and Russian communism, especially in its two principal American forms, were essentially identical. He also claimed there were more than forty organizations in America that were similarly tainted by communism, including the American Liberty League, the League for Industrial Democracy, and the American Civil Liberties Union.[10]

Although Norris himself had dabbled in social Christianity from time to time, he now attacked the social gospel, charging that Satan regularly twisted such preaching into support for communism and that concern for social justice turned attention away from evangelism. He therefore vigorously opposed any attempt by the NBC to bring Christian action to bear on social and economic conditions. Norris unleashed some of his most vicious rhetoric in attacking convention leaders, saying that he had more respect for professed infidels like Thomas Paine or Robert Ingersoll than for "these little modernistic, lick-the-skillet, two-by-four aping asinine preachers who want to be in the priest's office so they can have a piece of bread, and play kite tail to the Communists."[11]

Conveniently forgetting how he had attempted to change the course of politics himself, and failing to recognize that he would continue his political involvement throughout his career, Norris uttered the following a month later: "So, therefore, our business this afternoon, as believers, is not to regulate or legislate or change any form of government on earth—for they are beyond our control, but it is ours to see when these things come to pass, that the end of the world, the final hour is at hand." Ironically, in the same address in which he made this statement, he urged the NBC to take a political stance on prohibition in opposition to the Roosevelt administration.[12] Norris was vexed by the issue of when it was acceptable for religious leaders and institutions to become involved in politics. His guiding principle at this time, if indeed there was one, was that Christians should eschew any action that resembled the social gospel, the policies of the Roosevelt administration, or the activities usually associated with communism.

Norris's rhetoric can be attributed largely to his love for a new fight and his desire to thrust himself into the public eye. As with his anti–New Deal stance, he seems to have convinced himself that anticommunism was also part of his new crusade to save America now that Prohibition was no longer viable. He envisioned the departure of Temple Baptist Church from the Northern Baptist Convention as the start of a mass movement, and he claimed that three hundred other churches had followed Temple's lead.[13]

An American Holy War against Communism

Norris's crusade necessitated that he combine nationalism and religion together in a veritable holy war against communism. In other words, he became an avid participant in American civil religion. In announcing an anticommunist campaign that he had launched over WJR radio in Detroit, he said, "Surely there are enough patriotic people that will rally to support the greatest cause under the shining stars, namely, the defense of our flag, our constitution, our Bible, our homes, our churches, our souls."[14] The extent to which he would blend biblical and national themes was illustrated further in this statement: "We will not bow down to the red flag, regardless of what name it comes to us under. We still hold our allegiance to the greatest flag that was ever unfurled to the breezes. We will still hold the Bible of our fathers and mothers. We still believe Jesus was buried in Joseph's new made tomb."[15]

On other occasions he referred to the founders of America who, when signing the Declaration of Independence, "got down on their knees and prayed for God to guide them," and presidents who had called the nation to prayer during times of national crisis.[16] Perhaps most revealing of Norris's civil religion in the service of anticommunism was his statement in the spring of 1936: "The seven thousand, the Holy remnant, with the spirit of Valley Forge, of Culpepper Court, of Gettysburg, or the Alamo, will win and save America for God, home, and native land."[17]

By that spring, communism had subsumed all other political issues. He traveled to Rochester, New York, for a revival meeting with his stated purpose to battle communism. The red-lettered headline in the *Fundamentalist* read, "Christianity and Communism Will Clash Next Month in Rochester."[18] While there, he spoke of the communist attempt to infiltrate churches, using some of his most extreme rhetoric yet. He charged, "The first scheme is to sovietize the churches of America. This hydra-headed monster hates the name of the churches, blasphemes Christ, the head of the churches, denies the existence of God. Its purpose is to honeycomb the churches, to use the churches as a means of propaganda." Norris then announced that one hundred thousand copies of the Rochester address were being printed for distribution. He encountered vocal opposition that led to a very ugly scene, all of which his stenographer recorded for publication. While he was speaking, there was a disturbance and someone shouted, "Call the police." Norris countered that he did not need police protection but would handle the situation in his own way. He then said to the hecklers, "You fellows, let me show you something—something you never saw in your life—a thing I have used in the West." The stenographer recorded that he pulled up his sleeve, but did not say what he revealed beneath it. Norris then asked, "I want to know if there are twenty young men in this audience over 21 and under 30, free, single and white, who are not afraid, and you are willing to stand for God, home and native land—stand up." According to the stenographic report more than fifty men leaped to their feet to assist in silencing the opposition. Norris then instructed them, "Now I want about a dozen of you who are standing to go up into the gallery to see that these Communists behave themselves. . . . I am not going to permit this bunch of Communistic Divinity students to come down here and disturb the meeting."[19] Norris seems to have assumed that the hecklers were students from the liberal Rochester Divinity School nearby.

On other occasions that spring Norris charged that the communists had placed a book about their Five-Year Plan in a Fort Worth school for the purpose of introducing communism to the students. When he complained to the superintendent, the book was removed. Norris also did all in his power to keep Japanese Baptist Toyohiko Kagawa from speaking in American churches, alleging that he was a communist who advocated revolution. He traveled to the Southern Baptist Convention meeting in St. Louis armed with a resolution urging the cancellation of Kagawa's address to a joint meeting of Southern and Northern Baptists. While in St. Louis, he held his own meeting in competition with the convention and delivered the same address he had given while in Rochester.[20]

Shortly after the St. Louis convention, Norris spoke at the Masonic Temple in Washington, D.C., and renewed his charge that the New Deal was communist and had made America "an annex of Moscow."[21] He continued his attack on Roosevelt's administration into the summer when he singled out Henry Wallace, secretary of agriculture. The headline in the July 31 issue of the *Fundamentalist* summed up his argument by saying, "Secretary of Agriculture Member of the President's Cabinet Advocates 'Totalitarian' or Communistic State." In the affixed article, Norris quoted from Wallace's book, *Whose Constitution?* But the quotes simply did not say outright what Norris alleged that they did—namely, that Wallace favored totalitarian communism. He also referred to Kagawa, saying that Wallace and the Japanese Baptist leader were in the same league.

In August 1936, Norris entered the fray of a local political battle in Detroit. Evidently, one of the candidates running for a judicial position was an alleged communist, or at least Norris believed he was. Equating communism with atheism, Norris told the Temple Baptist congregation that communists could not take oaths because they did not believe in God. Oddly, in that same sermon Norris said an atheist had the same rights as anyone else, then made the claim that communists, because they were atheists, could not hold office or testify in court cases. By mid-August when Norris delivered this sermon, he had for the most part exhausted the issue and was ready to move on to other topics. His parting shot was his declaration that there were essentially three religious groups fighting communism. The Protestants in Europe had given up the fight, he said, leaving the Roman Catholics, Lutherans in America, and the fundamentalists.[22] Norris would return to the issue in the spring of 1937.

Communism as a Form of Modernism

In the twenties Norris had seen evolution as a form of modernism, but in the thirties and forties communism took the place of evolution. Although Norris engaged in a full-blown political crusade against communism, he also sought often to portray communism as a theological system that was a variant of modernism. He often argued that any solution to the communist threat in America would have to include a revival of religion. He, of course, meant a revival of fundamentalist Christianity, for in his view, many nonfundamentalist religious leaders and groups were part of the problem. Tainted by modernism, they had become variants of the communist threat. Norris, therefore, trained his sights on one of fundamentalism's favorite targets, the Federal Council of Churches. During a trip to Buffalo in 1937, the newspapers there covered his assault on the Council. The *Express* quoted him as saying, "In our very midst we have ministers who are openly condoning Soviet principles, who are working for the downfall of the United States government in conjunction with John L. Lewis and his Committee for Industrial Organizations."[23] Norris had earlier written letters to the Reverend Samuel McCrea Cavert, president of the Federal Council, warning him that he was going to expose the communistic activities of the Council.[24] Shortly after a major sit-down strike at a General Motors plant in Flint, Michigan, Norris read over the radio a letter he had written to the congressional committee that was investigating the strike, telling its chairman that "it would be a proper source of inquiry for your honorable committee to examine the financial records of the Federal Council of Churches and ascertain the source of their income, especially since they have declined to open their financial records."[25]

Later, in a pamphlet entitled *The Federal Council of Churches Unmasked*, Norris charged that Council leader and Methodist minister Charles Webber had worked behind the scenes to help organize the sit-down strike. Norris also cited evidence, allegedly provided by the Bureau of Naval Intelligence, that the Federal Council was a radical, subversive organization. In Norris's view the Council had said much in opposition to nazism and fascism but nothing against communism—always a telltale sign of leftism.[26] Furthermore, Norris charged that the Federal Council was closely associated with the American Civil Liberties Union, making the two organizations "interlocking directories" in the service of the Soviet Union. Norris believed that nearly all liberal organizations and journals, political or religious, were communist backed. He listed specifically *The World Tomorrow, Christian Century, Survey*, and the *New Republic*.[27]

Norris did not stop with the Federal Council of Churches and other truly modernistic organizations. Once World War II was over and the cold war had begun, he stepped up his attack on leaders in the conservative Southern Baptist Convention. This was especially true in 1947 when Louie D. Newton was the convention president. Norris launched another extended anticommunist offensive that year because he concluded that Newton was tainted by communism. Newton had, in fact, traveled to the Soviet Union and returned with some favorable impressions. He apparently reported that there was much freedom of worship in the Soviet Union and that Baptists should soften their attitude toward Russians. Norris had made similar comments himself in the twenties, but times had changed and so had Norris. Newton qualified his statements by admitting that his observations were based on limited and perhaps inadequate exposure, but this was immaterial to Norris. Immediately after Newton's statements, Norris launched a campaign against the SBC president that would continue for more than a year.[28]

Norris charged that Newton was either incredibly naive or a "cold-blooded propagandist for the Russians and their American communist fifth columnists." It became apparent rather quickly that Norris preferred the latter interpretation. He lambasted Newton not only for his statements concerning the Soviet Union but for allowing the American Russian Institute to publish the journal Newton had written about his trip. Moreover, the introduction to the journal was the work of Methodist bishop Bromley Oxnam, who Norris said was "one of the most aggressive pro-Communistic, modernistic, Russian appeasers to be found anywhere in the United States." Norris created a twenty-point indictment of Oxnam that accompanied his criticism of Newton.[29]

By April 1947, Norris had devised a plan to oust Newton from the presidency during the convention meeting scheduled for the first week of May in St. Louis. He wrote privately that he was going to expose Newton and that he viewed this as the "major fight of my life."[30] At the preconvention pastors' conference on May 6, Norris rose during Newton's sermon, and from the floor he informed those present that he had some questions he wanted to ask the president about his communist affiliations. Amid cries of "Throw him out," Norris was physically restrained from the platform until the police arrived, by which time Norris had resumed his seat.[31] As covered in the previous chapter, Norris employed the same tactics at the Baptist General Convention of Texas meeting that fall, but this time he sent a surrogate credentialed by Luther Peak's secretary to try to interrogate Newton. Norris admitted proudly to the Fort Worth *Press* that he had recruited and instructed the individual who precipitated the events.[32]

Following the Southern Baptist Convention meeting, Norris expressed great satisfaction with his actions, and he continued to dog Newton's every step. Writing the week after the convention, he told his friend M.E. Coyle in Detroit about the whole affair, saying, "I arose and challenged Louie Newton and his Soviet appeasers and threw the whole thing into pandemonium. I more than succeeded in getting the issue before the people, namely, that it was Newton and his henchmen attempting an appeasement with Moscow."[33] On May 29, he wrote to Speaker of the House Sam Rayburn, volunteering to appear before the Un-American Activities Committee, and in another letter that day he told a fellow pastor that he hoped to expose the "Southern Baptist conspiracy" before that committee.[34] In yet a third letter that day, he wrote to Coyle, informing the General Motors executive that he was to appear before the House Un-American Activities Committee. He predicted, "While the fight is terrific I am absolutely certain we are going to win and save America."[35] Norris had claimed earlier that month in the *Fundamentalist* that Newton was going to be investigated by the congressional committee, and in June he wrote to committee chairman John Rankin to tell him that the congressional hearings had not gotten to the "tap root" of the problem, which was "the communistic boring within ecclesiastical organizations." He told the chairman that the communists had infiltrated the Methodists and the Southern Baptists.[36] Later that summer, believing that

Newton had done enough damage by visiting the Soviet Union, Norris wrote to Secretary of State George C. Marshall in an attempt to keep the SBC president from gaining entry into Yugoslavia.[37] Norris's attacks on Newton continued well into 1948. For the rest of his life, Norris viewed Newton as a communist sympathizer.

The reason Norris jumped into this issue so viciously is that Newton's statements had solidified Norris's belief that modernists and communists were of one mind. He viewed Newton and many other Southern Baptist leaders as modernists, and he now seemed convinced that communism was perhaps an even more serious threat than he had previously believed. It was bad enough that communists had permeated labor organizations. It was much worse that they had infiltrated the Southern Baptist Convention. Furthermore, the issue of communism gave Norris one more populist weapon to use in his running battle with the Southern Baptist leadership. This issue served to keep Norris in the public eye and allowed him to vent more of his hatred for the SBC leaders.

In the late forties, and especially around the time of the Newton affair, Norris made quite explicit his charge that modernism and communism were of the same root. He charged that all modernists, not just Newton, had defended Russia. In an article in 1948 in which he outlined the differences between fundamentalist Baptists and Southern Baptists, three of his ten differences were related to opposition to communism. He said the SBC was soft on communism and that the leaders of the convention were aligned with the leaders of the Federal Council of Churches, the leading modernist institution in America, which was aligned with Josef Stalin. When Southwestern Baptist Theological Seminary in Fort Worth invited the president of the Northern Baptist Convention to be its commencement speaker in 1948, Norris charged that the Northern Convention was known for its modernism and its appeasement of Russia. In the same article he criticized Baylor University for having an evolutionist speak at the inauguration of the new president there.[38] This completed in Norris's mind the evil triad of evolution, modernism, and communism. The next year, an Abilene, Texas, newspaper quoted Norris as saying, "There has been a trend in the schools of the nation toward modernism and evolution theories for the past 30 years." Then, while speaking to the Texas State Legislature, he cited evolutionists and communists as "two sides of the same question."[39]

Also in 1948, Norris had placed in the Fort Worth *Star Telegram* an advertisement that filled two full pages of the newspaper. The bold-faced caption read, "Christianity or Communism," and a cartoon showed a figure representing communism in the act of pulling down a cross. Beneath the illustration was a resolution that had been adopted at the convention of fundamental Baptists in Fort Worth in October. It read in part: "Because of the increasing threat of World War III, and because the Americans were sold out to Joe Stalin at Teheran, Yalta and Potsdam, and because of additional pussyfooting and [the] compromising attitude of the government toward Moscow and Joe Stalin and his gangsters, Therefore, Be It Resolved . . . , that we desire to go on record in declaring that the time has come and long past for judgment to begin at the house of God—in good old America."[40] The words and the visual image of the cartoon vividly illustrated the fundamentalist belief that communism was attempting to do what modernism had endeavored to do for decades—defeat orthodox Christianity and America. Compared to the typical stance following World War I, the fundamentalist focus had now shifted ideologically from modernism to communism and geographically from Germany to the Soviet Union.

Aligning With Catholics to Fight Communists

Norris felt the threat of communism so acutely that in the forties he would align himself with Roman Catholics in the anticommunist effort. Although he obviously disagreed with much of Roman Catholic theology, at least the pope in Rome was resolutely against communism, which was more than Norris would say for liberal Protestants. In this respect, the heresy of Protestant modernism was worse than the heresy of Roman Catholicism because the former was a threat not only to theology, but to America as well.

In 1945, Norris began to outline explicitly his desire to align with anticommunist Roman Catholics. He said there were two great powers in the world standing against communism—Great Britain and the Roman Catholic Church. Historic enemies since the days of Henry VIII, they had now come together in a great battle. Later that year, when Winston Churchill was ousted and the Labor government came to power, Norris would change his mind about Great Britain, but he had made his point—in the face of the communist threat, historic enemies may have to rethink their attitudes toward each other. He said that in America the choice was to align either with communists or with the Roman Catholic Americans who opposed communism.[41]

Norris's alignment with Roman Catholics solidified in 1947 as he was battling Louie Newton within the Southern Baptist Convention. Early that year, writing to Coyle at General Motors, himself a Roman Catholic, Norris expressed his desire for an alliance between fundamentalists and Catholics against communism. As the convention meeting in St. Louis approached, Norris told Coyle that he planned to speak on why all patriotic Americans, Catholic and Protestant, needed to band together. Following the convention, after Norris had been criticized for working with Roman Catholics, he told Coyle that Protestant ministers who were in sympathy with communism wanted to precipitate a fight over Roman Catholicism to divert people's attention from the real issue. He cited specifically Joseph Dawson, who like Newton was one of the best known Baptist pastors in the South, as Stalin's fifth columnist. He told Coyle, "I am uncovering the whole conspiracy of these ministers masquerading under the term 'Protestant Christianity' who are dragging the red herring of Roman Catholicism across the trail in order to confuse the minds of American business."[42]

That summer Norris made these private accusations public. In a July edition of the *Fundamentalist* he wrote that though Baptists certainly had doctrinal differences with Roman Catholics, at least there were no bishops or archbishops who supported communism. Then, while on one of his several world tours, he succeeded in gaining an audience with Pope Pius XII. Several newspapers reported this rare meeting of the pontiff with a fundamentalist pastor. Norris was quoted after the meeting as saying the pope was "the last Gibraltar in Europe against communism."[43]

The issue of communism turned Norris completely around with regard to Catholicism, and some of his right-wing allies criticized him on this point. T.T. Shields, Canada's leading fundamentalist and longtime Norris friend, called Norris's trip to Rome "folly." Shields admonished Norris that Hitler and Mussolini had both been Roman Catholics and that the Catholic Church had failed to stand against them. Norris, however, was no more persuaded by Shields than he had been by his enemies in the Southern Baptist Convention. In fact, Norris twisted Shields's criticism into support for Stalin, issuing a headline that read, "What Dr. T.T. Shields Stands For When He Praises Stalin."[44] Norris argued that he himself was following the same strategy as Winston Churchill when the latter aligned Great Britain with the Soviet Union to defeat Hitler. Likewise, in Norris's view, his own praise of the Roman Catholic Church constituted an alignment of necessity against the greatest threat in the world.[45] Recognizing that this new stance toward Catholicism was controversial, Norris defended it again publicly at an outdoor rally in Fort Worth. He was quoted as saying in this address, "I will join anyone to oppose communism, even though I do not agree with them on some things. The world is on fire, and I'll take my stand with the Catholics before I will with Joe Stalin and his cutthroats and criminals."[46]

Just as Norris twisted Shields's statements, so he misinterpreted warnings by some Southern Baptist leaders who opposed on church-state grounds the Truman administration's plan to send an ambassador to the Vatican. Norris reasoned that opposition to an ambassador was tantamount to anti-Catholicism. And, since the Roman Catholic Church was against communism, opposition to the Church was softness toward the Soviet threat. He said, "The Baptist preachers attacking President Truman in his efforts to stop Communism are certainly doing the bidding of Stalin. . . . The issue for America in the world is not the union of State and church, but whether we will have a church or no church, a State or no State, God or no God."[47]

That Norris failed to see the Baptist basis for opposing an ambassador to the Vatican illustrates the degree to which his fundamentalist activities had steered him away from his Baptist heritage. This is especially true in light of his own position three years later when he wrote to Truman, urging that the president not appoint a successor to Myron S. Taylor, who had been serving as the U.S. representative to the Vatican.[48] When Truman persisted with his plan to appoint an ambassador, Norris reprinted in the *Fundamentalist* a series of articles by fundamentalist leader Carl McIntire opposing the confirmation on First Amendment grounds. By this time, Norris was firmly allied with McIntire and his International Council of Christian Churches, which McIntire had formed in opposition to the Federal Council of Churches.[49] As was the case so many times in Norris's career, he played either side of an issue depending on what point he was trying to make at the time. When he was forming his alliance with Roman Catholics against communism, he portrayed Baptist criticism of the Truman administration as evidence of anti–Roman Catholic sentiment and the actions of the Truman administration as evidence of anticommunism. Four years later, however, after the Alger Hiss trial and during the McCarthyite accusations that the Truman administration was riddled with communists—accusations that Norris believed—he came out against the administration on the appointment of an ambassador to the Vatican. Norris supported separation of church and state only when doing so did not interfere with his anticommunist crusade or other fundamentalist endeavors.

The Final Crusade

A commendation by the Texas legislature capped off Norris's intense three-year crusade against communism in the late forties. The resolution citing Norris praised him for his knowledge of world affairs and his efforts to gather "factual and statistical data on subversives." When a Tarrant County representative offered the resolution, there were moans and groans from some Norris critics in the legislature, but the measure passed by a forty-five to thirty-five vote.[50] Norris was invited to speak to the legislature as a result of the resolution honoring him, and of course he accepted. He traveled to Austin and gave an address summing up his anticommunist endeavors of the preceding three years. He told the legislators he was more afraid of the internal threat of communism than of the external threat of the Soviet Union. This was consistent with his often-stated view that the United States should have and could have defeated the Soviets militarily at the conclusion of World War II. Norris had an unbridled confidence in America's military might, but the military was virtually powerless against internal subversives. Only legislatures and courts that heeded his words and the words of other anticommunist public figures could defeat the threat from within.[51]

In his speech to the Texas legislature, Norris identified three types of communist subversives that were the most threatening to America—radical communist labor leaders, professors, and clergymen. He had had much to say in the forties about the labor leaders and clergymen, and he took this opportunity to hit hard at university professors. Concerning academic freedom, he said, "It is the greatest misnomer and the most dishonest thing that was ever perpetrated on an honest people." Arguing that radical professors were immune from being fired because of the power of education associations, he urged the legislators to pass a law cutting off funds to universities that harbored communists. Norris then rambled from one topic to another, telling stories in a kind of evangelistic testimony. Although the speech's lack of organization clearly revealed the effects of age, Norris was still capable of holding his audience, and he was very entertaining. The stenographer recorded applause and laughter throughout the address. Norris's fusion of fundamentalist theology with rabid anticommunism in service to America was nowhere more evident than in his closing words to the legislature. Having said nothing about communism for most of the second half of the speech, he still closed with what amounted to a cold war, civil religion creed: "I believe in God and in the Son of God, and in the Word of God that lives and abides forever. To hell with Joe Stalin! Good Night."[52]

By the 1950s, one could hardly introduce Norris without identifying him as one of America's leading anticommunists. When the mayor of Fort Worth presented Norris to a large crowd at LaGrave Baseball Field, he said, "He has been one of the strong advocates of one hundred percent Americanism. He has opposed every form of un-American activity and has been most outspoken in his opposition to foreign isms. His stand on the subject of Communism is known from one side of the country to the other."[53] Norris, however, was past his prime and unable to sustain his crusade into the next decade with the same sort of tireless energy that had animated him during the forties. As Joseph McCarthy came to the fore, Norris was forced to leave the battle to others. He even relinquished control of the *Fundamentalist* to one of his associates, who attempted to keep the crusade alive with articles on the Hiss trial and other such affairs.[54] Illustrative of Norris's support for McCarthy was a letter he wrote to Tom Connally in 1950. Norris told the Texas senator, "On this investigation that McCarthy, Tydings, et al. have stirred up, it is more and more apparent to the people that there is 'something rotten in Denmark.'"[55] Interestingly, Connally expressed ambivalence when he replied, "With relation to the McCarthy charges and the hearing before the Tydings Committee, [I] have to say that the Committee is doing a good job investigating. Mr. McCarthy has not as yet produced a single witness or a single record to substantiate his charges."[56] Norris, however, persisted in his support for the Wisconsin senator, writing to McCarthy in 1952, "You make your case most conclusive [sic] and like the prophet in his day, you are ahead of your time. More strength and power to you."[57]

Norris's anticommunism dominated his political thinking to the very end of his life—so much so that when he made a few feeble attempts to address other issues, such as civil rights, he ended up talking about communism. For Norris, all other political issues in the late forties and early fifties were related to the issue of communism. The modernist-communist nexus was so pronounced, believed Norris, that it was impossible to be a modernist without being a communist as well. The religiously orthodox were also politically orthodox. Fundamentalists, in Norris's scheme of things, desired to save America by either maintaining the status quo or by turning back history to the nineteenth-century evangelical consensus—prior to modernism. The modernists were politically heterodox communists who wanted to change America religiously, socially, and politically.

The Search for an Anticommunist, Anti–New Deal President

Throughout the forties, Norris's anticommunist activities meshed with his anti–New Deal political stance. Having nearly despaired of ousting New Dealers from the American government in 1940, Norris would gear up once again for the search for a presidential candidate who would end the New Deal, which in Norris's mind was just a step or two from all-out communism. As of 1940, Norris and others who opposed the Roosevelt administration had made little progress in scaling back the New Deal. He was saddened that year when a conservative magazine, the *American Mercury*, carried an article by conservative Michigan senator Arthur H. Vandenburg, entitled "The New Deal Must Be Salvaged." All this seemed to indicate the futility of governmental reform. "There was a time when the ministry of America gave its greatest efforts to prohibition," Norris lamented nostalgically. "But today we need to preach the gospel of the New Birth to save drunkards from hell." Then, in what sounded like a disillusioned repudiation of twenty years of political involvement, he said, "And we would have been better off if we had continued the preaching of this same gospel of the individual, rather than the foolish course of reforming the nation."[58]

Although Norris sounded as if he were getting out of politics, he was not. During the war years, however, he would find himself an ally of the president he had maligned for the previous five years, and he turned his attention to the immediate external threat posed by Nazi Germany.[59] He still would have preferred a Republican in the White House, and to this end he offered his support to presidential nominee Thomas Dewey in 1944.[60] Prior to the election that year, however, Norris actually did very little in the way of overt campaigning, and when FDR died in April 1945, he even praised the president for his leadership during the war. Then, when Harry Truman became president, Norris seemed ambivalent. He recognized that most of the new president's policies did little to turn back the changes wrought by the New Deal, but Norris had trouble making up his mind as to whether he should support Truman's tough, anticommunist foreign policy or condemn him for being too much like Roosevelt on domestic issues. Norris liked Truman's cold war rhetoric and solid stand against the Soviet Union, but he also recognized that most of those in Truman's administration were of the "New Deal crowd."

For the next several years, therefore, Norris alternated between support for and opposition to Truman. In 1947, he favored the president against liberal clergy who opposed the president's plan to aid the governments of Greece and Turkey, which were threatened by internal communist revolutions. At this time, Norris was convinced that the clergymen were themselves communists, but he did not believe Truman was. He told Sam Rayburn, Speaker of the House and fellow Texan, that it would be a masterful political stroke to expose the communist leanings of the liberal periodical, *Protestant*, before the House Un-American Activities Committee. Norris even offered to appear before the committee at his own expense. In the same letter, Norris indicated to Rayburn his belief that the South was solidly behind the president, and Norris seemed to imply that he was also.[61] A few weeks later, a new newspaper in Fort Worth issued the headline "Frank Norris Resolves to Back President Truman, v., Henry Wallace and Louie Newton." This was while Norris and others were accusing Newton of modernist and communist leanings. This headline was further evidence that in 1947 Norris still saw Truman as a bulwark against communism with liberal and even moderate church leaders on the opposite side.[62]

One year later, writing to Coyle at General Motors headquarters, Norris revealed a change of opinion, saying that the South was in revolt and would not vote for Truman. Norris seemed pleased with this turn of events because it would mean the end of Roosevelt's New Deal dynasty. He also indicated that he was planning to barnstorm the South to preach the gospel, "the one and only cure for all un-American and unchristian nostrums."[63] During the election campaign of that year, Norris played on both sides. Writing to candidate Dewey, he again expressed his desire to see an end to sixteen years of New Deal policies, and he told the Republican, "Without question, you have victory in the bag, but it is a long time till November 2nd."[64] Then, in October, revealing a change of heart toward Truman's foreign policy, he told Dewey that the international situation was the key and that there was still time to "unmask the unholy alliance that is existing between Washington and Moscow." Continuing, he said, "It is commonly believed that Truman doublecrossed Marshall and the latter came home to resign unless Truman quit playing hide-and-seek with Joe Stalin—'good old Joe.'"[65] Ten days later, he told Dewey that he hoped the election, now just a week away, would be the start of a two-party system in Texas.[66]

During the same period that he corresponded with Dewey, Norris was also in communication with Truman. Norris wrote positively to Truman at the beginning of 1947, saying, "It is both amazing and gratifying to see your stock rising."[67] When the 1948 campaign season began, Norris continued to encourage the incumbent. In June, he accused the Republicans of hypocrisy and urged Truman to attack them.[68] The following month, after Truman's address to the Democratic National Convention, Norris wrote, "You are more than President of the United States, you are just 'Harry Truman' to the common people." Continuing the endorsement, he wrote, "You machine-gunned the whole Republican crowd."[69] In September, he told Truman, "Texas is in the bag and one teriffic [sic] blast against communism and Joe Stalin like you gave once to a joint session of congress will cinch the victory."[70] Little more than a month later, however, Norris predicted to Coyle that Truman would lose.[71]

The events of the late forties, especially in foreign policy, caused wild swings in American public opinion toward the president. Norris's mood changes toward Truman, however, reveal little logic or consistency. He seems to have seen himself as a shrewd, behind-the-scenes politician who, by secretly telling each camp what it wanted to hear, would retain his influence with the victor, whomever that might be. Another possible explanation is that he was now seventy years old, and given the fact that he suffered memory lapses in the final years of his life, he may have been unaware that he had pledged his support and predicted victory to both candidates. It must also be kept in mind, however, that little in Norris's long career would suggest that he was above the sort of duplicity he displayed during the campaign of 1948.[72]

When Truman won reelection, Norris was not dismayed, and wrote to Senator Connally that even his industrialist friends in Detroit were ready to support the president now that he had been elected in his own right. Norris quoted the head of Chrysler as saying, "The time of needling the president should be over; he is our president and we should support him."[73] Norris recognized that Truman's election meant that the "New Deal crowd" would still be in power, but he hoped that the Texas leadership in the House and Senate would offset the liberal leanings of the administration. Alluding to the apostle Paul's admonition that Christians should be in the world but not of it, Norris told Coyle that Rayburn and Connally were "in the New Deal crowd yet they are not wholly for it."[74]

As late as the spring of 1950, Norris still supported Truman, at least in part, and even called himself "one of the original Truman Men."[75] By 1951, however, in the wake of the Alger Hiss trial and other anticommunist rumblings of the early McCarthy era, Norris had soured on Truman almost completely. By then, Norris had finished his long stint at Temple Baptist, but it mattered little. His transformation to the right wing of the Republican Party, which had begun during the Al Smith campaign, had been completed during his early days in Detroit. Having written privately in November 1951 that "Truman has lost Texas,"[76] in December, Norris informed a friend, "I am letting you know of the plans I have to throw myself into this presidential election. There are moral and religious issues involved as well as political. Truman has ruined this country, and there is no doubt he is running it in sympathy with the communists."[77] In addition to the charge that Truman was tainted with communism, Norris also listed the appointment of an ambassador to the Vatican as a reason Texas would not support Truman, another example of Norris's willingness to stand on either side of a church-state issue in order to serve his larger purposes.[78]

In January 1952, Norris even suggested to Senator Connally that Truman be impeached. "It would be a proper suggestion for you to have him impeached," Norris wrote. "It would be a matter of honor to the United States and you have the courage to do it."[79] Norris did not suggest on what grounds such a preposterous proposal should proceed.

Periodically, throughout 1952, Norris encouraged no less than three Democrats to run against Truman for the presidential nomination. In January, he told Rayburn to run. Nine days later he told Senator Estes Kefauver that he should seek the nomination and that, if Kefauver did open a presidential campaign, the First Baptist auditorium in Fort Worth would be available to him free of charge. That summer, Norris offered the auditorium to Averill Harriman should he agree to seek the nomination.[80] It appears that Norris wanted someone, perhaps anyone, to defeat Truman for the nomination. Strangely, in May, Norris wrote to Truman, telling the president that if the Republicans nominated conservative Robert Taft, "he will be easy pickings for you."[81] Then, ironically, Norris even urged Truman to run for reelection. He told the president, "You are the only man that can unite the Democratic party and hold office for the great masses of the common man." Norris received a reply from the president's personal secretary informing him that Truman would not seek reelection and thanking Norris, perhaps sarcastically, for "the friendly interest which prompted you to write."[82]

Now in the final months of his life, Norris seems to have been exhibiting the loss of memory mentioned above. His rather confusing relationship with Democrats in 1952 notwithstanding, however,

he was clearheaded about his choice of a Republican. Dwight Eisenhower was the first Republican candidate since Hoover for whom
Norris showed genuine enthusiasm. Although he had clearly preferred the Republican Party since 1928, Norris had often resigned
himself to the fact that the Democrats had a lock on the White
House. Clearly, Eisenhower was the man Norris believed could end
the long reign of the New Deal machine. Norris began to predict
that Ike would carry Texas long before the general even secured the
Republican nomination, and when Eisenhower succeeded at the Republican National Convention, Norris fired off letters to several
congressmen around the country, informing them that Eisenhower
was the choice of Texans.[83] He wrote letters to Eisenhower himself
on the tenth, eleventh, thirteenth, and sixteenth of July, informing
the new Republican standard-bearer that he was ready to campaign
vigorously for the party that fall. To vice presidential nominee Richard Nixon, Norris predicted victory in Texas. Praising the avid anticommunist prosecutor, Norris told Nixon that the Hiss case was an
example of the corruption within the Democratic Party.[84] On July 18,
he told his radio audience that he planned to throw himself into the
campaign with the same vigor and enthusiasm that had animated
him during the presidential contest of 1928. Although he was actually far too old for that type of intense crusade, he spent the final
few weeks of his life campaigning for Eisenhower and Nixon over
radio. He praised Nixon for his dogged pursuit of Hiss and predicted
that the Californian would expose many more communists once he
became vice president.[85]

Norris's words regarding Ike's religion were reminiscent of his
laudatory remarks about Hoover nearly a quarter century before.
"He is a Christian," Norris said emphatically. "He believes in the
fundamentals like I do . . . like you do."[86] With words like these
gracing the airwaves, it was little wonder that the Eisenhower campaign leaders invited Norris to their headquarters for a personal
meeting with the candidate. Following the meeting, Norris reported
that Eisenhower's platform was "God, Home, and Mother." As he
had done throughout his life, Norris defended his role in politics,
saying, "Well, I'm in it [the Eisenhower campaign] because of the
issues involved. I was in it in 1928. I am in it every time. I have been
in campaigns here in Texas. . . . I have my opinion. I have my convictions and I believe you can have yours."[87]

Norris's death just days later robbed him of the opportunity
to continue campaigning for Eisenhower. There is little doubt that
he would have gloried in that work, for as many scholars have

acknowledged, Eisenhower's rallies were more like religious crusades than political campaign stops. Norris would have relished
the outpouring of civil religion that accompanied the first victorious
Republican presidential effort since Hoover had defeated Smith.
No doubt, Norris would have interpreted Eisenhower's victory as
America's salvation from the communistic New Deal and a return
to God and right religion.

8

The Race Card ‖

In the summer of 1995, messengers to the Southern Baptist Convention annual meeting in Atlanta approved a resolution recognizing the responsibility the denomination bore for its past complicity in racism. In addition to acknowledging "the role that slavery played in the formation of the Southern Baptist Convention," the resolution cited the failure on the part of many Southern Baptists to support civil rights initiatives as well as their outright opposition to such measures. While the authors attempted to steer clear of the touchy issue of whether one generation can repent for the sins of its forefathers, in perhaps the most telling clause the resolution read: "We apologize to all African-Americans for condoning and/or perpetuating individual and systemic racism in our lifetime."[1]

In striking contrast to the 1995 resolution, Southern Baptist pronouncements on the race issue during Norris's lifetime typically failed to even question the basic institution of segregation. Individual leaders concerned about race sometimes decried poverty among black people and inequalities in the funding of white and black schools, but rarely did any official body of Southern Baptists question segregation. That was left to a few courageous individuals, whose advocacy most often fell on deaf ears, and a few state special interracial committees, which sometimes excoriated Southern Baptists and their convention for a lack of action on the race issue. More typically, problems of race were seen as individual problems that should be addressed only through evangelism aimed at individual sinners. The idea of attacking the systemic and institutional aspects of race seems to have been for the most part out of bounds even for the state Baptist social-service committees that were instituted explicitly to deal with social problems.[2]

This is not to single out the Southern Baptist Convention as uniquely grievous in its failures on the race issue. With regard to the civil rights movement itself, historian Andrew Manis has argued that there were two civil religions in the region—a black one for which civil rights gains became a fulfilled hope, and a white civil religion that interpreted civil rights successes as a disappointment. Manis quotes southern historian George Tindall as saying that "the idea of a peculiarly pure Americanism in the South, with overtones of Anglo-Saxon racism and anti-radicalism, became an established article of the regional faith." Manis then maintains that after World War I, Southern Baptists carried forward this regional faith.[3] While one of the strong arguments of this biography is that Norris was not a typical Southern Baptist, on the issue of race he was, in fact, very representative of mainstream Southern Baptist views.

Norris rarely addressed the race issue head-on. It is for this reason that this chapter is the shortest in the book. Had he lived into the 1960s, he would have been forced, no doubt, to deal directly and more comprehensively with race because he would have been confronted by the civil rights movement. For him, as for most southerners before the fifties, however, race was the nonissue that was more important than all other issues. The racial situation, while extremely important, was not up for debate. Segregation and white supremacy were taken for granted, part of the natural order of things. Norris usually made statements on race as part of a broader point that had to do with something else, such as modernism, Catholicism, or communism. In the vernacular often used in politics, Norris usually played the race card as a trump to beat his opponent's best hand.

Modernism and Race

Typical of this approach were lines he penned while visiting Harry Emerson Fosdick and John D. Rockefeller's Park Avenue Baptist Church in New York City. While lashing out at the theological modernism those two individuals epitomized, he incorporated the racism so prevalent in the South in the twenties. He charged specifically that part and parcel with the modernist attempt to scuttle traditional Protestantism were Park Avenue's efforts to destroy racial barriers. Just before Norris's visit there, the church had hosted a marriage ceremony that joined a black Filipino and a white woman. "The main purpose of the Rockefellers," Norris therefore charged, "is to break down all distinctions in doctrine, in denominations, in race—in short, STANDARDIZE all things. Is not this the 'mark of the Beast'?"[4] Two points seem worth highlighting here. First, the question of whether the easing of racial barriers was good or bad was not open for consideration any more than the issue of Christ's deity or resurrection. Second, modernism was a threat to all things traditional, hence, all things southern.

If there was a distinguishing mark to Norris's racism it was that on this issue, as with all others, he was given to violent rhetoric. Even a few months after his trip to Park Avenue, he was still inflamed by the interracial marriage that had occurred there. When he returned to a discussion of the race issue, Norris skirted the edge of advocating murder when he said, "I can name you a people south of the Mason-Dixon line that if a negro should take a white girl's hand in marriage that girl would be without a negro husband before the sun arose the next morning." That was descriptive and perhaps true, but he went further, placing his imprimatur on lynching when he said that in such a case, he would gladly perform the funeral.[5]

Race as Part of Norris's Nativism

Similar to his discussion of race in the context of modernism, Norris also addressed the issue as part of his broader effort to help defeat the Democratic nominee for president during the anti–Al Smith campaign covered in chapter 3. In this instance, race was a political, as compared to theological, card. Norris was at the height of his nativistic phase during that campaign, so the race issue fit well with his wider political activities aimed at Catholics and immigrants. During the summer of 1928 he remarked, "What a conglomeration, Tammany Hall, Roman Catholicism, bootleggers, carpet bag politicians and negroes. What will the white people of Texas do?"[6] He also criticized Smith and other Tammany Hall politicians for appointing blacks to positions in government in New York. Speaking in Dallas, he said succinctly, "Ladies and gentlemen, Tammany is black and wet."[7] Then, in October, to an Alabama audience, Norris hit the race issue hardest, detailing Smith's transgressions as follows:

> He believes in social equality. He approves of miscegenation, the intermarriage of negroes with whites. He associates with negroes. He stoops to social equality to get negro votes. He ran for the New York Assembly on the same ticket with negroes. He has negro members of his legislature. He has taken the negro away from the Republican Party. He has made the negro believe that he will be welcome in the White House when he is elected. If he is elected it will be because the negro and the foreign-born vote enables him to carry the East while the South remains solid.[8]

As was often the case, Norris here attributed to his sinister opponent almost omnipotent power, even to name his own legislature, but on the matter of race, several significant points jump off the page. First, equality for African Americans necessitates approval of racial intermarriage, which was anathema to the southern mind and considered by Norris to be the height of violation of God's created order. Two, Smith cannot be sincere; he was only stooping to social equality to get black votes. In doing this, Smith was part of the Democratic effort to steal black votes from the Republican Party. Three, blacks themselves are portrayed as Smith's dupes, made to believe they will be welcome in the White House if Smith wins. Finally, African Americans are classed with the foreign born, the implication being that they are somehow less American than whites.

Norris portrayed Smith as antisouthern because the candidate had not spoken in favor of Jim Crow laws, and he also attributed the integration of New York schools to Smith. Norris lamented the poor white children who would not only have to go to school with African Americans but perhaps even be taught by black teachers. He also spoke with alarm at the election of a Democratic congressman from Missouri who was black. Norris said the congressman had been handpicked by Tammany Hall. "Once this country puts a negro 'democrat' in Congress and a negro-loving 'democrat' in the President's chair," he warned, "the south is doomed. We will have to battle against our own party as well as the opposition to maintain our white supremacy."[9]

In the October issues of the *Fundamentalist*, Norris debated the race issue with Senator Pat Harrison, one of Smith's staunch supporters and campaign leaders. Norris had sent several questions to Harrison, and he printed the senator's answers. This exchange showed how sensitive even northern Democratic politicians were to charges of coddling the "black" vote. Harrison essentially denied that Smith had acted favorably toward African Americans, saying the candidate was not responsible for their appointment to positions in the New York government, had not supported integrated schools, and did not support mixed marriages. After printing Harrison's refutation of the charges, Norris issued a whole new set of allegations. Clearly, there was no way to satisfy Norris on this issue when he would always have the last word through his newspaper. In fact, Norris entitled Harrison's reply, "National Democratic Headquarters Dodging on Tammany Hall and Negro Question," a very misleading headline considering that Harrison had answered each of Norris's allegations on race directly and thoroughly.[10]

As he would later in his career when lashing out against communism, Norris employed the political technique of attributing to his opponents all that he and his constituents found offensive. For example, since he was opposed to social equality for blacks, Roman Catholics were believed to be in favor of equality. In 1929, Norris would say that a Roman Catholic church in Fort Worth had given prominent seating to African Americans in its services. "Now, that is some of the Roman Catholic social equality in Fort Worth, Texas—take that and smoke it," he said. "Yes, the Roman Catholic church stands for absolute racial equality with the negro. . . . I am opposed to sending negroes to Congress or negroes holding any official position with the white people of this country."[11] Again, it should be pointed out that Norris was not here or elsewhere addressing the race issue on its merits. Rather, he was using his region's unchallenged assumptions about race to attack his political enemies, just as he had used these assumptions to attack his theological enemies when he was visiting Fosdick's church in New York.

Norris and the Klan

If the Roman Catholic Church supported racial equality, something that is perhaps more arguable than Norris let on, then what organization was standing for southern segregation and white supremacy? The obvious answer was the Ku Klux Klan. While Norris was not, as far as I can tell, a member of the Klan, he often spoke favorably of that group. He made several references to the Klan during the 1920s, and many of these, like his broader statements on race during the anti-Smith campaign, were in the context of his anti-Catholicism, but understandably the race question lurked over in the corner of most of his references to the Klan. In May 1928, during the campaign, he had published in the *Fundamentalist* an anti-Smith article by Klan leader Hiram Wesley Evans, an act that was indicative of several years of his being, if not enthusiastically supportive, at least soft on Klanism. As early as 1922, he had pitted local judge James Wilson on the side of bootleggers and the Knights of Columbus over against the Klan and Prohibitionists. On that occasion Norris had said, "I hold no brief for the Ku Klux Klan," but he also cited a recent lawsuit filed against the organization by "a bunch of low-browed, disreputable leeches on society, against some of the most honorable citizens of Fort Worth."[12] Norris was, of course, correct in saying that the Klan included some of the most "honorable" citizens of Fort Worth, for this was long before it became disgraceful to be a member of that society. In the 1920s the Klan was broadening its appeal and becoming as strong in some areas of the North and West as it was in the South, largely because of the perceived threat of immigration of Roman Catholics to those regions.[13]

In 1924, Norris alternately criticized and praised the Klan in a series of articles, arguing ultimately that one had as much right to be a member of the "KKK as the K. of C. [Knights of Columbus]."[14] He sometimes pitted the Ku Klux Klan against Catholic interests such as the Knights, believing firmly that the real threat to the South was the latter. This is understandable. African Americans were, by Norris's way of thinking, under control in the segregated system of white supremacy. Roman Catholics were actually increasing in numbers as well as economic, social, and political clout. Recall from chapter 6 that in the mid-twenties Mayor Meacham of Fort Worth was Catholic. This was deeply troubling to Norris, so much so that his reaction led directly to the shooting of D.E. Chipps and his own trial for murder. By contrast, he certainly had no worries that an African American would run for mayor anytime soon. Blacks were suppressed by segregation. Since Catholics could not be similarly kept down, they had to be shut out, hence Norris's support for tight immigration restrictions and his vigorous campaign to freeze out Smith and other Catholic politicians.

In 1924, Norris even opposed a resolution to the SBC denouncing the Klan, his stated reason being that Catholics would have appreciated any slap at the KKK. Again, his view was that the Klan should not be an issue among Baptists because Catholics were the real issue. He even argued that those who denounced the Klan had been duped by the Catholic Church.[15] On another occasion Norris mildly chided the Klan but then praised the organization for running W.E.B. Du Bois out of the state to keep the civil rights leader from making a speech on interracial marriage. Norris claimed this time that the Klan treated law-abiding black people just fine, the implication being that anyone who challenged segregation was not "law-abiding," which was technically true. Once again he threw the Catholic issue into the mix by saying, to a cheering crowd, that a person had as much right to join the KKK as the Knights of Columbus.[16]

Communists and Race

In the early thirties, in addition to Catholics, Norris began attributing integrationist views to communists as well. While trying to head off a visit to Baylor by socialist activist Kirby Page, editor of

The World Tomorrow, Norris wrote this: "He carries his communism into practical application by repeatedly advocating social equality with the negroes."[17] Norris believed it scandalous that Page had a black secretary. This would be one of the many times that Norris would refer to racial equality as part of a communist plot, just as he had in the twenties accused Catholics of being in favor of racial equality. Once again, Norris came around to the haunting specter of interracial marriage, charging that communists, like the Catholics and modernists, advocated intermarriage between whites and blacks. This was, in Norris's view, bad for blacks and intolerable for whites. "And I tell this crowd," he exclaimed to an audience made up largely of transplanted southerners at Temple Baptist in 1936, "the North, South, East or West will never submit to a white girl married to a negro man."[18] Significantly, speaking here from his Detroit pulpit, Norris included the North, East, and West along with the South, essentially believing that some southern principles were national and universal.

The racial views Norris expressed in the twenties and thirties remained constant through the rest of his life. In an address to the Texas legislature in 1949 he reiterated the idea that communists supported the intermarriage of blacks and whites because they wanted to form a "mongrel race."[19] Why communists wanted to do this was unclear. At the end of his career Norris continued to tie all desegregation efforts to communism, and he had a lot of help in doing so, some of it coming from Congress. In 1950, the *Fundamentalist* issued the headline "Committee on Un-American Activities Made Full Investigation of National Association for the Advancement of Colored People, the Urban League, and Southern Regional Council."[20] The intent of such a headline was clearly to taint all civil rights groups as communist. Norris's anticommunism in these instances served to justify views that were typical of the southern, white middle class at that time. Purporting to believe that any attempt to change the racial status quo was really a communist plot to destroy America, he resisted any move toward a more moderate position. As has been seen, however, he could just as easily employ anti-Catholicism or the fundamentalist battle against modernism to justify racism. It was a given that Norris would never question the racial caste system of his day. He was too southern for that.

Implicit in Norris's racial views, as exhibited in the anti-Smith campaign, was his belief that African Americans could be duped by forces that wanted to bring about social change in America. While he rarely if ever tackled the issue of black voting rights (Why would he?

It was moot during his lifetime.), he typified the southern belief that blacks could be easily swayed by Al Smith and Democrats or by communists. Another hint of this came through when he advertised a rally to be held at First Baptist by Gerald L.K. Smith. Billed as a "Mammoth Christian America Rally," Smith's topics, as advertised by Norris, were to include a "Communist plot to deceive negroes."[21] Such a phrase rings with the southern paternalism of that period in southern history—the view that African Americans were akin to children who had to be protected from the evil and crafty communists.

The Implications of Norris's Racial Views

As can be seen, Norris's implicit views on race included the great southern fear of interracial sex. This has been illustrated above by his numerous references to interracial marriage. As with segregation itself, the evil here was never discussed but, rather, taken for granted. The ugliest example of this came while Norris's empire was experiencing its schism in the early fifties, specifically when Norris tried to taint the entire dissident faction led by G.B. Vick, which had left Fort Worth to go to Springfield. The cartoon of a Vick associate soliciting sex from a young black boy, cited in chapter 6, brought together the themes of race, homosexuality, and predatory sex abuse of children.

On other occasions Norris's very typical and implicit racism surfaced even when he was at his most progressive. In 1920, while advocating that the Texas legislature do more for education, he said, "I want to see an administration that thinks more of the education of children of the state than it does of cattle, ticks, boll weevils, and hog cholera." Then, in criticizing low pay for educators, he dropped a line about how deplorable it was when the "negro" laborers working on the new church auditorium at First Baptist were paid more than teachers.[22] Again, as with the cartoon illustrating sex abuse, an already deplorable situation was portrayed as worse because of the race of those involved.

Norris did not live to see the flowering of the civil rights movement, but if he had cared to look, he could have seen its sprouts. Just two years before his death a major desegregation case came out of Texas. In *Sweat v Painter* (1950) the U.S. Supreme Court ruled that a hastily formed law school for black students did not meet the *Plessy v Ferguson* (1896) standard of separate but equal. The new law school was separate, but it could hardly be deemed equal to the well-respected University of Texas. The University of Texas Law School was forced, therefore, to admit black students. This case was one that paved the way for *Brown v Board of Education* (1954), which would strike the death knell for *dejure* segregation. Neither the Sweat decision nor any of the other events of the early fifties seem to have had any effect on Norris's racial views. At that time, he was locked so securely into the issue of communism that he was unable to even consider the race issue on its own merits. Attempts to desegregate were just communist-inspired agitation that had another hidden agenda for moving America away from God's ordained order. Fittingly, then, in a radio broadcast less than two weeks before he died, Norris summed up his own views on the race question with the following statement: "Well, God didn't make them [blacks] that way [equal]. It's hard to go against God's laws." He said that he liked blacks, employed them, and was their best friend, "But I am not in favor of them coming into my home and sitting down with my family, and marrying my daughter."[23]

As with many southerners, there was another side to Norris's racism. He is remembered by at least one of his associates as being compassionate toward those usually ignored or oppressed by society. Luther Peak, in reflecting on Norris, specifically cites African Americans who worked menial jobs for whites among those toward whom Norris showed compassion.[24] Even this, however, is typical of a large segment of southern genteel society in his day. The eminent interpreter of southern religion in the 1960s, Samuel Hill, put the situation like this: "The Southern white [who] says he has genuine affection for the Negro, means what he says. . . . He is often kindly, protective, even generous in his dealings with his black neighbor. He has yet to see, however, that Christian love is not present when kindliness, protectiveness, and generosity are extended toward another on condition that he is not regarded as a full person."[25] As Norris himself said, he liked African Americans and was their best friend; he bore little animosity toward people merely on account of the color of their skin. There was, however, a racial caste system that was created not by humans but by God. It was sinful for modernists, Catholics, communists, or the NAACP to tamper with the social order. While Norris in some instances had certain theological ideas that molded his agenda, here his theology was shaped by his southernness. The race issue highlights again the ways in which Norris quite naturally adapted northern fundamentalism for a southern audience.

This is certainly not to say that northern fundamentalism was free of racism, but the racism of northern fundamentalists was more apt to be anti-Semitic than anti–African American. William Vance Trollinger Jr. has shown how William Bell Riley, perhaps the North's leading fundamentalist, turned to anti-Semitism during the 1930s. Trollinger argues that Riley's views and his efforts to peddle the *Protocols of the Wise Elders of Zion* were born of his frustration after years of failing to get the fundamentalist agenda adopted in the Northern Baptist Convention.[26] When one considers the two fundamentalist Geralds—Winrod and L.K. Smith—Riley appears to be by no means the sole or most vitriolic of the anti-Semites who were associated with northern fundamentalism. Even considering these individuals, it seems a contested issue as to whether or not there was anything inherent in fundamentalism that necessitated anti-Semitism. Some have argued that dispensational premillennialism could foster it in certain instances. For Riley and some others, dispensational premillennialism meant that although Jews had played the major role in God's historic drama during the Old Testament dispensation of law, and they would play a similarly important role again at the end of history during the millennium, in the meantime Jews were enemies of Christ and under severe judgment. Not all fundamentalists, not even a majority, interpreted dispensational premillennialism in this way and, as has been discussed in this work, dispensational premillennialism even steered some like Norris away from anti-Semitism. Historian Timothy Weber, who has done some of the best work on premillennialism, is probably closest to the mark when he argues that most premillennialists were at worst ambivalent toward Jews while many remained sympathetic.[27]

Anyone who might use Norris in the South and Riley in the North to argue that fundamentalism was or is necessarily given to racism of various kinds would do well to remember that Billy Graham, a product of southern fundamentalism, desegregated his revival services long before secular universities in the South, probably the region's most liberal institutions, were integrated.[28] Rather than an inherent racism, the problem fundamentalists have faced is how to discern when one is defending the Bible as opposed to defending one's culture. Given that fundamentalism after World War I made an explicit connection between the defense of orthodox Protestant theology and the maintenance of the culture that was presumably built on scriptural principles, it is understandable just how easily the faith became captive to the culture on such matters as race. This was the essence of Norris's racism.

Conclusion ‖

If anything emerges from a study of J. Frank Norris, it is that he was an extremely complex individual. A bundle of contradictory forces, he was fundamentalist yet Baptist, populist yet elitist, southern yet northern, and Democrat yet Republican. When he was on the attack on any issue, he was usually crude and vicious. When he was explicating Scripture or teaching, he could be calm and rational. At times he was positively eloquent and profound while at other times sinister or silly. As it was with his public preaching and teaching, so it was with his life as a whole. Stories abound of the shameless Norris who would do anything no matter how evil. Others remember him as a concerned man of God. He was a persuasive preacher who cared deeply about people's physical and spiritual needs, and yet he was also a villainous *real politik* who acted as if the parameters of civility, let alone Christian morality, did not apply to him.

Because he thought the stakes were so high, Norris fought ruthlessly and never wavered in the belief that he was right and that God supported what he did no matter how extreme. Norris believed that people who had opposed him and First Baptist down through the years were actually opposing God and accordingly fell under judgment. The sheriff who served the indictment on Norris for the 1912 fire had been hit by a train. The prosecutor in the subsequent trial had died an untimely death. A chairman of the board of deacons who opposed Norris early in his tenure at First Baptist had suffered a long, lingering death from disease. August Busch of the Anheuser Busch Brewing Company, who opposed prohibition, had committed suicide by shooting himself in the head. H.C. Meacham, mayor at the time of the Chipps killing, had ended in ruin. Norris believed these tragedies were related to the fact that the individuals involved had opposed him. The Scriptures teach, "No weapon that is formed against thee shall prosper; and every tongue that shall rise against thee in judgment thou shalt condemn." In a classic case of hubris, Norris applied that verse to himself and to First Baptist Church.[1] His life and work had prospered, while his enemies, at least by his account, had suffered judgment. What greater evidence was there that his ends and means were acceptable to God? What greater evidence was there that his ends justified his means? Norris was indeed a complex figure—much of the time irascible and even sinister. W.A. Criswell pegged him accurately as having a diabolical underside.

Norris was often most vehement when attacking a position he had previously held himself. On several major issues he headed off in one direction only to reverse field. It appears that the world was becoming more complicated than he preferred and that he was unable to take mediating positions amidst the complexity. Instead, he grabbed on to a position and ran until he found himself in an intellectual cul-de-sac or on what he perceived to be the wrong side of the fight. He would then turn and come roaring out in the opposite direction, attacking most severely those who still held the view he had just discarded. This happened during his New Deal reversal, with regard to aid for Britain and France in the early stages of World War II, and again in his attitude toward Germany once the cold war had begun. In each of these instances he seemed threatened most by his former views and tried desperately to kill the old Norris as if it were a ghost that haunted his conscience.

There is another way of interpreting these reversals. Norris often started off with populist instincts on issues like labor relations, communism, and the New Deal, but then after a quick and instinctual burst of rhetoric, he would put his finger to the wind and learn that the position he had adopted was not conducive to the fundamentalist movement he wanted to lead. Like many would-be leaders, therefore, he then tried to discern which direction the fundamentalist parade was headed so he could run to get to the front of it, giving the appearance that he was one of its leaders.[2] That a figure like Norris could succeed in this effort reveals something important about American culture. In times of stress, uncertainty, and transition, such leaders as Norris, Huey Long, Father Coughlin, and Gerald L.K. Smith attract followers because they present simple answers for difficult social and political problems. Norris could reverse himself on a variety of issues without losing his following partly because the masses often like leaders who believe fervently in something almost regardless of what that something is. His followers appreciated the sincerity, tenacity, and simplicity of his attacks as if those attributes were more important than the actual message

Norris preached. In all of his reversals, however, it was not difficult to detect a consistency that endeared him to the common people. Whatever position Norris took on a given issue, the underlying theme of his crusading efforts was that the virtue of plain and simple folk was being subjected to a sinister cabal carried out by educated elites. He was successful in portraying himself as a defender of the people even when in fact he rubbed shoulders consistently with the automobile company magnates of Detroit and unwittingly did their bidding against the leaders of the labor movement.

Norris hoped to recapture nineteenth-century America as he perceived it. He yearned for a homogeneous society where people held common values that were consistent with evangelical Protestant orthodoxy—a place where American institutions reflected and supported those values and where those institutions were responsive to the common person. In his analysis of what America was supposed to be, he, like the fundamentalist movement itself, embodied the influence of both premillennialism and the Puritan tradition. This was never more apparent than when he would condemn America in one sermon, saying the nation was doomed to the destruction that was scheduled for the end of the present dispensation, and then in his next sermon praise the nation as a shining example of what Christian civilization could be. As George Marsden has indicated concerning early fundamentalists generally, they could not decide whether America was Babylon or the new Israel. For Norris, America was both. Intended to be a new Israel, or "city on a hill" as the Puritans were fond of calling their society, the nation was more and more resembling Babylon or even Sodom and Gomorrah. He asked, therefore, what had happened, and concluded that modernism was causing the precipitous degeneration of culture. He never understood that the changes of the first half of the twentieth century were brought about by a multitude of forces and that the transformation was for the most part irreversible. Rather, since he had settled on one cause, he envisioned only one solution: attack and destroy modernism in theology and all its secular manifestations in politics and culture.

In this respect he was much like others of his lifetime who protested against the prevailing trends of twentieth-century America. Alan Brinkley, in his study of Huey Long and Father Charles Coughlin, specifically mentions their underlying desire to recapture an America "in which the individual retained control of his own life and livelihood; in which power resided in visible accessible institutions; in which wealth was equitably (if not necessarily equally) shared." Brinkley cites also their "urge to defend the autonomy of the

individual and the independence of the community against en-
croachments from the modern industrial state."[3] Something very
similar to this also motivated Norris except that he framed the question in primarily theological terms. He identified theological modernism as the all-encompassing force that had rendered impotent the
once dominant evangelical Protestant consensus and brought about
the deterioration of culture.

It was not just what Norris said and did, however, that made
him successful in garnering followers for his movement. He was also
suitably fitted to the times in which he lived. Just as the American
nation itself was under tremendous stress in the thirties and forties,
so was fundamentalism. The dislocated state of American economic
and social institutions was mirrored by the disarray of the fundamentalist movement. Fundamentalism has always been a complex and
contradictory movement. Marsden has written recently, "Fundamentalism was a peculiar blend of sectarianism and aspirations to
dominate the culture. . . . Its most conspicuous unifying feature has
been militancy."[4] While some became militant because they were
fundamentalists, Norris became a fundamentalist, in part at least,
because he was militant by nature. He was especially well suited
to the period after the Scopes trial of 1925 when fundamentalism became increasingly reactionary and anti-intellectual. Norris helped
create this climate and also flourished within it. The more astute and
sophisticated fundamentalists reevaluated the failed tactics that the
movement had employed in the twenties and then emerged as the
neo-evangelicals in the forties, having rejected the militancy of
fundamentalism. In the meantime, Norris and those of his ilk moved
into the resulting vacuum. Norris was a bridge between sophisticated leaders in early fundamentalism—James Gray, Curtis Lee
Laws, and the Princeton theologians—and social reactionaries in the
thirties and forties—Carl McIntire, Gerald Winrod, and Gerald L.K.
Smith. At the same time, J. Gresham Machen was the primary exception to the nadir of fundamentalism and thereby served as the bridge
from Gray, Laws, and the old Princeton theologians to neo-evangelicals Edward G. Carnell and Carl Henry. It was Norris, however, and
not Machen, who epitomized fundamentalism during its darkest
days from 1926 to the 1940s, and he also symbolized what had gone
wrong with the movement—its Manichaean and cultic tendencies.[5]

All this is not to say that Norris can always be taken at face value.
He was often driven by less-than-pure motives. As he fought his many
battles, he always had one eye on his own fame. To ensure that he was
never ignored, he often engaged in activities that bordered on sheer

lunacy. Politically, Norris moved consistently toward the right, which coincided with the enhancement of his own social status, especially when he seized the reins of Temple Baptist and began to come into frequent contact with the leading industrialists in Detroit. Earlier in his career, before the fundamentalist-modernist controversy had reached titanic proportions, and before he had developed much of a reputation, he had often alienated the rich people in his Fort Worth congregation by tailoring the church's ministry to the needs of the working class. In populist fashion, he had also lashed out at big businessmen for their brutal treatment of laborers. Later, however, he became such a reactionary conservative that he would not even consider an issue like racial equality on its own merits or in light of biblical teaching. Instead, he interpreted it merely as part of the modernist-inspired degeneration of culture he had been battling for most of his career. However complex and mixed his motivations were, in the end his ideology conveniently fit his increasing prestige and elite status.

As he moved to the right, however, Norris became for many fundamentalists a voice of protest who identified destructive trends in America. Something in his rather crude worldview touched a responsive chord within them, and the politicians and industrialists who treated Norris with respect recognized that many of his constituents were theirs also. There is no evidence that he had any influence over those politicians and industrialists, but he served them well as a barometer that indicated the trends and desires of fundamentalists and others who felt completely alienated from the very institutions that supposedly represented them. Sadly, his insatiable desire to be in the good graces of the powerful made it possible for these elites to use him for their own purposes. When he told the automobile workers in his Temple congregation that the primary goal of labor unions was to destroy all that was good about America, this was precisely what the industrialists would have liked those workers to believe. Still, even as he unwittingly did the bidding of the rich and powerful, Norris often articulated the dissatisfaction and protests of his listeners in a way that made sense to them. Many who were bewildered by the changes they saw in American society, who believed they had lost all influence, saw in Norris's tirades an explanation for what had gone wrong. In other words, he verbalized the discontent and vexations of a voiceless mass of dislocated fundamentalists. Norris failed them, however, because he offered no viable solution beyond the naive hope that somehow one big victory against their modernistic foes would usher America back to its golden age. Over time, many fundamentalist intellectuals grew weary of being viewed as part of a movement that included the likes of Norris.[6] Fundamentalism, in their view, had not only proven itself bankrupt as a cultural and political force but it only remotely resembled the evangelical consensus that had prevailed in the nineteenth century. That consensus had been progressive, while fundamentalism of the thirties looked only to the past.

Perhaps Norris's most successful contribution to fundamentalism was his effort to help shift the center of gravity of the movement from the North to the South.[7] He tried to preserve and defend the South from the modernist threat, which was largely northern. He sensed correctly that the South was less pluralistic and more conservative than the North, but he also realized that it would not remain so for very long. Clinging to the belief that the South was more righteous and orthodox than the North, he hoped to fashion a southern fundamentalism before it was too late. Few of his regional brothers and sisters within the leadership ranks of the Southern Baptist Convention followed him, because the threat was not yet imminent.

In the late twentieth century, as the South has indeed become industrialized, pluralistic, and more secular than ever before, fundamentalists in the Southern Baptist Convention have taken up Norris's battle. It is a fitting commentary on the regionalism of America that what Northern Baptists and northern Presbyterians went through in the twenties, Southern Baptists have experienced in the eighties. In religion, no less than in industrialization and urbanization, the South has lagged behind the North by about a half century.

In an odd sort of way, from a fundamentalist perspective, Norris could be considered a visionary who was ahead of his time in identifying changes that threatened the cultural homogeneity of the South. How can one account for the fact that Norris became a reactionary before there was much against which to react? On this point we come again to Norris's complex nature. He was both a southern and national fundamentalist: national in the sense that he recognized that the forces threatening the North would soon come southward as well, and southern enough to believe his region could battle those forces more successfully than the North and maybe even save the North in the process.

If visionary in one respect, however, he was also a rascal in another. His opponents and often even his supporters saw this. He would not have minded being called a rascal, for he had certainly been called worse, and he sometimes referred to himself as a Southern Baptist Bolshevik. He might have added only that if he were a rascal, he was God's rascal.

Notes ‖

Introduction

1. Homer G. Ritchie, Norris's immediate successor at First Baptist Fort Worth, has told me that privately some of the new leaders of the Southern Baptist Convention have expressed their admiration for Norris even though publicly they do not recognize any connection to him. Homer G. Ritchie, interview by author, tape recording, Fort Worth, 26 May 1992.

2. C. Allyn Russell, *Voices of American Fundamentalism: Seven Biographical Studies* (Philadelphia: Westminster Press, 1976).

3. The most biographical of these dissertations is Clovis Gwin Morris, "He Changed Things: The Life and Thought of J. Frank Norris" (Ph.D. diss., Texas Tech University, 1973). See also Charles Lynn Walker, "The Ethical Vision of Fundamentalism: An Inquiry into the Ethic of John Franklyn Norris" (Ph.D. diss., Southwestern Baptist Theological Seminary, 1985), Danny E. Howe, "An Analysis of Dispensationalism and Its Implications for the Theologies of James Robinson Graves, John Franklyn Norris, and Wallie Amos Criswell" (Ph.D. diss., Southwestern Baptist Theological Seminary, 1988), and Royce Measures, "Men and Movements Influenced by J. Frank Norris" (Th.D. diss., Southwestern Baptist Theological Seminary, 1976). There are several biographies of Norris written by former associates, e.g., Louis Entzminger's *The J.Frank Norris I Have Known for Thirty-four Years* (Fort Worth: privately printed, 1948), E. Ray Tatum's *Conquest or Failure?* (Dallas: Baptist Historical Foundation, 1966), Roy E. Falls, *A Fascinating Biography of J. Frank Norris: The Most Outstanding Fundamentalist of the 20th Century* (Euless, Tex.: Faith Baptist Church, 1975), and most recently, Homer G. Ritchie, *The Life and Legend of J.Frank Norris, "The Fighting Parson"* (Fort Worth: privately printed, 1991).

4. C. Allyn Russell, letter to author, 5 October 1992.

5. Barry Hankins, "The Strange Career of J. Frank Norris; or, Can a Baptist Democrat Be a Fundamentalist Republican?" *Church History* 61 (Sept. 1992): 373-92.

6. Probably the two best discussions of this in recent years are Nancy Ammerman, *Baptist Battles* (New Brunswick, N. J.: Rutgers Univ. Press, 1990), and Bill Leonard, *God's Last and Only Hope: The Fragmentation of the Southern Baptist Convention* (Grand Rapids: Eerdmans, 1990). See especially Leonard's

chapter 2, "Denominationalism: The Shape of the SBC." Leonard calls the effort to keep diverse theologies together under the umbrella of the convention the "Grand Compromise."

7. For the best analysis of the fundamentalist eclipse following Scopes and how fundamentalism was remade as neo-evangelicalism, see George Marsden, *Reforming Fundamentalism: Fuller Seminary and the New Evangelicalism* (Grand Rapids: Eerdmans, 1987).

8. George Marsden, "From Fundamentalism to Evangelicalism: A Historical Analysis," in *The Evangelicals: What They Believe, Who They Are, Where They Are Changing,* ed. David F. Wells and John D. Woodbridge (Grand Rapids: Baker Book House, 1977), 147

1. The Making of a Populist Preacher

1. Nathan O. Hatch, *The Democratization of American Christianity* (New Haven: Yale Univ. Press, 1989), 211 and 214.

2. Norris himself estimated more than 1.5 million subscribers in 1945, but this was obviously an exaggeration. It was hard to determine the exact distribution because he gave away so many free copies and had others sold on street corners. One man told me that as a boy in Waco he sold the *Fundamentalist* for a nickel and was allowed to keep all the money he collected. Norris was obviously more interested in circulation than profit. Roger Edens, interview by author, 20 September 1989. The paper was called the *Searchlight* from 1917 to 1927.

3. While there are many examples of this, see Connally to Norris, 13 June 1949, 28 January 1950, 24 January 1951, and 10 July 1952, Norris Papers. Norris's papers are stored at the Southern Baptist Historical Library and Archives in Nashville. Microfilm sets may be found at several Baptist institutions including Baylor University's Texas Collection and Southwestern Baptist Theological Seminary's Roberts Library. Citations in this work refer to the microfilmed set of Norris papers at the Texas Collection, Baylor.

4. Falwell has been quoted as saying, "In my own personal life, I have been greatly influenced by his [Norris's] ministry, as men trained by him were instrumental in leading me to Christ and training me for the ministry." See Homer G. Ritchie, *Life and Legend,* 270.

5. Hill County, Texas, Deed Records, 1889, book 28, p. 146. Norris recalled the move late in life in his own newspaper. See "A Visit to My Boyhood Home and My Mother's Grave," *Fundamentalist,* 16 September 1949, 1.

6. Louis Entzminger, *Norris I Have Known,* 35. Norris is the only source for this story and many others like it. The only other published book-length biographies of Norris have been written by his former associates: Tatum, *Conquest or Failure?;* Falls, *Fascinating Biography;* and Homer G. Ritchie, *Life and Legend.* See Morris, "He Changed Things." A brief published account of Norris's life is the aptly titled chapter "Violent Fundamentalist" in C. Allyn Russell's *Voices of American Fundamentalism.*

7. Tatum, *Conquest or Failure?* 28–29; Falls, *Fascinating Biography,* 25; and Entzminger, *Norris I Have Known,* 33. In all these accounts Norris is presumably the only source. For the court records see *State of Texas v John Shaw,*

cases 3113 and 3114, box 29, Hill County, Texas, district clerk; and *Criminal Minutes,* vol. H, 349 and 357, Hill County, Texas, district clerk.

8. Morris, "He Changed Things," 37–38; see also D.G. Bouldin, "The J.M. Dawson–J.F. Norris Controversy: A Reflection of the Fundamentalist Controversy among Texas Baptists" (M.A. thesis, Baylor University, 1960). Dawson was pastor of First Baptist Waco for much of the time Norris was in Fort Worth. Norris attacked Dawson unmercifully for years, but Dawson refused to be drawn into the fray by Norris's accusations.

9. Russell, *Voices of American Fundamentalism,* 23; and Bouldin, "Dawson-Norris Controversy," 16-17.

10. E.P. Kirkland to F.S. Groner, 27 October 1922, Norris File, Roberts Library, Southwestern Baptist Theological Seminary, Fort Worth. This letter is published in H. Leon McBeth, ed., *A Sourcebook for Baptist Heritage* (Nashville: Broadman Press, 1990), 488. As of 7 January 1991, this letter could no longer be located in the Norris file. I have a photocopy of the letter, which I received from McBeth.

11. Entzminger, *Norris I Have Known,* 65; Tatum, *Conquest or Failure?* 73; and Morris, "He Changed Things," 44.

12. "Inside Story of First Baptist Church," *Searchlight,* 16 June 1922, 3.

13. Tatum, *Conquest or Failure?* 81 and 85; Morris, "He Changed Things," 44-45. One of the ironies of fundamentalist history is that the McKinney Avenue Baptist Church building, which Norris had built in 1907, is now the Hard Rock Cafe of Dallas.

14. Morris, "He Changed Things," 53-61. Dawson later revealed that he believed Norris's hatred for him began when Dawson received special recognition from the Baylor president at their graduation in 1903. Dawson also recorded that Norris had been a vicious and cruel young man while at Baylor, often making fun of a student who stuttered. See Bouldin, "Dawson-Norris Controversy," 16.

15. J. Frank Norris, *Inside History of First Baptist Church, Fort Worth, Texas and Temple Baptist Church, Detroit* (privately published, n.d.), 27-29.

16. "Inside Story of the First Baptist Church, No. 3," *Searchlight,* 21 July 1922, 1-2.

17. Falls, *Fascinating Biography,* 32-33.

18. "Inside Story of First Baptist Church, No. 3."

19. "Inside Story of First Baptist Church, No. 5," *Searchlight,* 4 August 1922, 1.

20. Ibid., 2. Perhaps the most humorous example of Norris's sensational sermon titles was "Should a Prominent Fort Worth Banker Buy the High-Priced Silk Hose for Another Man's Wife?" Norris joked facetiously that when he announced this title, three bankers called him to confess, but none of the three was the man he had in mind. See Morris, "He Changed Things," 115.

21. Tatum, *Conquest or Failure?,* 116-17; Danny E. Howe, "An Analysis of Dispensationalism and Its Implications for the Theologies of James Robinson Graves, John Franklyn Norris, and Wallie Amos Criswell" (Ph.D. diss., Southwestern Baptist Theological Seminary, 1988), 150-51.

22. "Inside Story of the First Baptist Church, No. 6, " *Searchlight,* 11 August 1922, 1.

23. Morris, "He Changed Things," 90-92.

24. Entzminger, *Norris I Have Known*, 84. For a discussion of this populist impulse in American Christianity see Hatch, *Democratization of American Christianity*, 210-19. This same populist approach was employed by William Bell Riley at First Baptist Minneapolis. See William Vance Trollinger Jr., *God's Empire: William Bell Riley and Midwestern Fundamentalism* (Madison: Univ. of Wisconsin Press, 1990), 16-18.

25. "Inside Story of First Baptist Church, No. 7," *Searchlight*, 15 September 1922, 3; and "Inside Story of First Baptist Church, No. 8," *Searchlight*, 22 September 1922, 1.

26. Morris, "He Changed Things," 92–94. The most recent book on this aspect of Fort Worth's history is Richard F. Selcer, *Hell's Half Acre: The Life and Legend of a Red-Light District* (Fort Worth: Texas Christian Univ. Press, 1991).

27. "First Baptist Church Damaged, Firemen Have Very Hard Battle," Fort Worth *Record*, 12 January 1912, 7; "Diabolism in Fort Worth," Fort Worth *Record*, 5 February 1912, 14; "Anonymous Letters Warned Pastor That Church Would Be Destroyed, Mr. Norris's Life Also Threatened," Fort Worth *Record*, 6 February 1912, 1; "Rev. J. F. Norris Is Indicted, Pastor of First Baptist Church Must Answer Charges of Perjury," Fort Worth *Record*, 2 March 1912, 3.

28. The first quote is in "Dr. J. Frank Norris's Home Destroyed by Fire," Fort Worth *Record*, 3 March 1912, 3; the second quote is in "Burning of Norris's Home Is Shrouded in mystery, Officers Without a Clue," Fort Worth *Record*, 3 March 1912, 1.

29. "Rev. Mr. Norris Indicted for Arson, Hurrying Here to Answer Charge," Fort Worth *Record*, 29 March 1912, 1.

30. "Rev. J.F. Norris Tenders Church His Resignation," Fort Worth *Record*, 28 March 1912, 1; "Norris's Resignation Refused by Baptists, Decision Unanimous," Fort Worth *Record*, 1 April 1912, 1; and "Norris Acquitted of Perjury, Song Service in Courtroom," Fort Worth *Record*, 25 April 1912, 1.

31. "Norris Arson Case to Jury Saturday; Arguments Are On," Fort Worth *Star Telegram*, 23 January 1914, 1.

32. "Jury Acquits Norris on the First Ballot; Trial Ends Abruptly," Fort Worth *Star Telegram*, 24 January 1914, 1. See also Judge George E. Hosey, "Resume of the Norris Cases," 29 November 1927, L.R. Scarborough Correspondence, Roberts Library, Southwestern Baptist Theological Seminary, Fort Worth. Hosey was convinced that Norris had indeed burned First Baptist. Years later, possibly at the request of Norris's enemy, Scarborough, he wrote this brief account of the trials of 1912 and 1914. Hosey wrote that the judge in the 1914 trial was a Norris supporter.

33. Tatum, *Conquest or Failure?*, 116.

2. From Populism to Southern Fundamentalism

1. Hatch, *Democratization of American Christianity*, 214-19.

2. George M. Marsden, *Fundamentalism and American Culture: The Shaping of Twentieth-Century Evangelicalism, 1870-1925* (New York: Oxford Univ. Press, 1980), 4.

3. See William R. Hutchison, *The Modernist Impulse in American Protestantism* (Cambridge: Harvard Univ. Press, 1976).

4. Marsden has written recently that the fact that modernism sought to save Protestantism is perhaps the single most important point to consider in understanding modernism. See Marsden, *Understanding Fundamentalism and Evangelicalism* (Grand Rapids: Eerdmans, 1991), 32.

5. Martin Marty, *Pilgrims in Their Own Land: 500 Years of Religion in America* (Boston: Little, Brown, 1984), 297-307. For a discussion of evangelicals who did not reject Darwin see David N. Livingstone, *Darwin's Forgotten Defenders: The Encounter between Evangelical Theology and Evolutionary Thought* (Grand Rapids: Eerdmans, 1987).

6. Marty, *Pilgrims in Their Own Land*, 303. For a discussion of the Princeton Theology in the early twentieth century see Mark A. Noll, *Between Faith and Criticism: Evangelicals, Scholarship, and the Bible in America* (Grand Rapids: Baker Book House, 1986), 47-48, 51-56. On Princeton theologian Benjamin Warfield and his views of science see Marsden, *Understanding Fundamentalism and Evangelicalism* , 122-52. Arguably the last of the Princeton evangelicals was J. Gresham Machen, who became the most articulate intellectual defender of the conservative position during the fundamentalist-modernist controversy. See D. G. Hart, *Defending the Faith: J. Gresham Machen and the Crisis of Conservative Protestantism in Modern America* (Baltimore: Johns Hopkins Univ. Press, 1994). In Common Sense philosophy, as well as in Bacon's inductive method, a premium is placed on plain observation and categorization of facts. This approach to science eschews theorizing and was therefore at odds with the science of Darwin.

7. Quoted in Marty, *Pilgrims in Their Own Land*, 305.

8. Marsden, *Fundamentalism and American Culture*, 119.

9. Ibid., 122. For a brief but helpful summary of Mullins's theology, see Fisher Humphreys, "E.Y. Mullins," in *Baptist Theologians* ed. Timothy George and David S. Dockery, (Nashville: Broadman Press, 1990), 330-50.

10. Marsden, *Fundamentalism and American Culture*, 141.

11. Ibid., 149.

12. Ibid. For a discussion of the populist impulse in American Christianity see Hatch, *Democratization of American Christianity*, 210-19.

13. Marsden, *Fundamentalism and American Culture*, 164.

14. Curtis Lee Laws, "Convention Side Lights," *Watchman-Examiner* 8 (20 May 1920): 652.

15. See Ray Ginger, *Six Days or Forever: Tennessee versus John Thomas Scopes* (New York: Oxford Univ. Press, 1958).

16. For a discussion of the battle in the Northern Baptist Convention see Roland Tenus Nelson, "Fundamentalism and the Northern Baptist Convention" (Ph.D. diss., University of Chicago, 1964). See also Trollinger, *God's Empire*, 52-61.

17. Marsden has written recently that "almost all" fundamentalists by the sixties were Baptists. See *Understanding Fundamentalism and Evangelicalism*, 4.

18. See Marsden, *Reforming Fundamentalism*.

19. See Trollinger, *God's Empire*.

20. James J. Thompson Jr., *Tried as by Fire: Southern Baptists and the Religious Controversies of the 1920s* (Macon, Ga.: Mercer Univ. Press, 1982), 77 and 79.

21. Homer Ritchie of Fort Worth, Texas, interview by author, tape recording, 26 May 1992, Fort Worth.

22. "Roman Catholicism and Modernism," *Searchlight*, 8 June 1923, 1; "The Rockefeller-Fosdick Conspiracy to Liberalize the Baptist Denomination," *Searchlight*, 5 June 1925, 1.

23. "War against Modernism Making Glorious Progress," *Searchlight*, 25 May 1926, 1.

24. William Estep, "Baptists and Authority: The Bible, Confessions, and Conscience in the Development of Baptist Identity," *Review and Expositor* 84 (fall 1987): 599.

25. Ritchie, interview.

26. "Texas Baptists Repudiate Dr. Norris," *Christian Century* 41 (25 December 1924): 1672.

27. For an excellent recent discussion of the establishment status of the SBC, see Leonard, *God's Last and Only Hope*, 92-96. See also John Lee Eighmy, *Churches in Cultural Captivity: A History of the Social Attitudes of Southern Baptists* (Knoxville: Univ. of Tennessee Press, 1972), 41-56.

28. It should be noted here that fundamentalism in the early twenties included many who would not be comfortable with the militancy of the movement after 1925 or so. Gray was one of those.

29. "I Want the Evolutionists out of Baylor and the Books of the Denomination Opened," *Searchlight*, 29 September 1922, 1-2. Norris here alleged that he was ordered to join the campaign or be considered uncooperative. For a good discussion of the Seventy-five Million Campaign see Thompson, *Tried as by Fire*, 15-20, 195-200.

30. "A Statement and a Pledge," L.R. Scarborough Papers, Roberts Library, Southwestern Baptist Theological Seminary, Fort Worth. Scarborough also authored a pamphlet entitled *The Fruits of Norrisism* (n.p., n.d.), in which he characterized Norris's movement this way: "In its chief leadership it is the embodiment of autocratic ecclesiasticism. All the privileges and rights of the church leading up to the pastor."

31. BGCT *Annual*, 1922, 15-17 and 19. That same year a committee report at the Southern Baptist Convention took similar action on the issue of the teaching of evolution in Baptist colleges, even saying that one could not believe both the Bible and modern textbooks on the issue of the origins of humankind. See Southern Baptist Convention *Annual*, 1922, 35.

32. Grove Samuel Dow, *Introduction to the Principles of Sociology* (Waco, Tex.: Baylor Univ. Press, 1920), 42. For Brooks's statement on the Dow case see BGCT *Annual*, 1922, 154-55. Dow had asked Brooks to read the manuscript before the book was published, but Brooks did not have time. When the book appeared in print, Brooks read the work, met with Dow, and showed the professor the offending portions. It seems that Dow's primary offense was his refusal to interpret the Genesis account of creation as a definitive scientific explanation of the origins of humankind.

33. *Annual, BGCT* 1923, 18-21. For a discussion of the BBU and Riley's role in its formation see Trollinger, *God's Empire*, 57-60. By the early 1930s, the BBU was defunct. Rising from its ashes, however, was the General Association of Regular Baptists, which remains as a viable conservative evangelical denomination.

34. The Brooks statements can be found in BGCT *Annual*, 1924, 59-60. The amendment is on page 16. For a history of Norris's attacks on Baylor see BGCT *Annual*, 1927, 22-28.

35. As with the BBU, Riley was the moving force behind the formation of the WCFA. See Trollinger, *God's Empire*, 37-44. For a discussion of dispensational premillennialism and Norris's role in it, see chapter 4.

36. "The 'Baptist Beacon' of Minneapolis Combines with the 'Searchlight' of Fort Worth, Texas," *Searchlight*, 28 May 1926, 6. A year later Riley was miffed when Norris changed the title of his newspaper to the *Fundamentalist*. Riley interpreted this as an attempt to make it appear that the Fort Worth paper was the official organ of the World's Christian Fundamentals Association. This began an alienation of the two leaders. G.B. Vick, interview, Baylor University Institute for Oral History, 26 July 1973, tape 1. See also Trollinger, *God's Empire*, 42-43. Holding tent meetings adjacent to the Southern Baptist Convention's annual meeting for the purpose of disrupting the denomination was one of Norris's favorite maneuvers.

37. William Jennings Bryan, "Bryan's Last Letter," *Searchlight*, 31 July 1925, 1. I use the word *allegedly* concerning this letter because no one could possibly have known with assurance that this was Bryan's last letter. The letter appears to be authentic, however. I am referring to Bryan as a fundamentalist only because he sided with the movement during the final years of his life in the evolution controversy. While it is problematic to view him as such, it does seem that in the twenties he was viewed by everyone as America's most famous fundamentalist.

38. *Searchlight*, 14 August 1925, 2. C. Allyn Russell says Bryan was practically boycotted by the leading fundamentalists, none of whom came to the trial. Some were at fundamentalist conferences while others were vacationing. See Russell, *Voices of American Fundamentalism*, 184-85.

39. That Norris changed the name of his school to include the term *Baptist* seems peculiar in light of the fact that just a year later he changed the title of his newspaper from *Searchlight* to *Baptist Fundamentalist*, then promptly dropped *Baptist* from the new title.

40. "World Convention on Fundamentals of the Faith," *Searchlight*, 7 July 1922, 1; "Evangelist to War on Moderns," *Searchlight*, 30 January 1925, 1. The second article was a reprint from the Chicago *Tribune*, 22 January 1925. For a discussion of the importance of World War I for the development of fundamentalism, see Marsden, *Fundamentalism and American Culture*, 42-64, and for a discussion of the northern fundamentalist reaction to Germany see ibid., 149.

41. "The Rockefeller-Fosdick Conspiracy to Liberalize the Baptist Denomination," *Searchlight*, 5 June 1925, 1. Norris had begun as early as 1922 to identify Rockefeller money as the driving force in the modernist advance within the Northern Baptist Convention. See "World's Convention on Fundamentals of the Faith," *Searchlight*, 7 July 1922, 1.

42. "What Attitude Will Southern Baptists Now Have toward the Northern Baptist Convention?" *Searchlight*, 11 June 1926, 10.

43. Stories abound of the personal nature of this rivalry, including the lifetime subscription to the *Searchlight* and *Fundamentalist* that Norris afforded Dawson free of charge. Supposedly, Norris attempted to have the newspaper delivered to the Dawson home on Sunday mornings before Dawson would leave

for First Baptist Waco where he was pastor. Norris's charges were often front-page news on these editions.

44. "The Verbal Inspiration of the Scripture," *Fundamentalist*, 13 December 1929, 1 and 3. Norris later published an article comparing Baylor and the University of Chicago. See Reilly Copeland, "Baylor University Compared with University of Chicago, Dr. Brooks with Dr. Harper," *Fundamentalist*, 14 October 1927, 1. This article was based on an academic comparison that a Baylor public relations official had made—a comparison meant to flatter Baylor by putting the Waco university in the same class as the University of Chicago. Copeland, however, used the comparison as evidence that Baylor was becoming like the modernistic Chicago school.

45. Joseph Dawson, "John Erskine's Life of Jesus Is Sincere but Controversial," Dallas *Morning News*, 11 November 1945, sec. 4, p. 8. For Norris's attack on this review see *Fundamentalist*, 7 December 1945, 1, 3, and 5.

46. Thompson, *Tried as by Fire*, 90.

47. "Dr. J.R. Sampey's Hand Called," *Searchlight*, 25 December 1925, 1 and 3. For Norris's earlier praise of Sampey, see "Inside Story of First Baptist Church," *Searchlight*, 16 June 1922, 3.

48. See Thompson, *Tried as by Fire*, 78-79, for examples of their orthodox beliefs.

49. "Shots on the Wing," *Searchlight*, 28 August 1925, 1.

50. See for example "Roman Catholicism and Modernism," *Searchlight*, 8 June 1923, 1-2.

51. "Four Ways to Begin Life," *Fundamentalist*, 5 January 1945, 3 and 6.

52. For a discussion of fundamentalism and the Bible see Timothy P. Weber, "The Two-Edged Sword: The Fundamentalist Use of the Bible," in *The Bible in America: Essays in Cultural History*, ed. Nathan O. Hatch and Mark A. Noll (New York: Oxford Univ. Press, 1982), 101-20.

53. "Address to the World Fundamental Convention Held at Los Angeles," *Searchlight*, 28 July 1922, 1.

54. "World's Convention of Fundamentals of the Faith," *Searchlight*, 7 July 1922, 1.

55. "Rome Invades Protestant America," *Searchlight*, 2 July 1926, 1.

56. Weber, "The Two-Edged Sword," 116

57. "Address to World Fundamental Convention," 1-2.

58. For this argument applied to fundamentalists in general see Marsden, *Fundamentalism and American Culture*, 220-21; Weber, "The Two-Edged Sword," 115-16.

59. "Address to World Fundamental Convention," 2.

60. Weber, "The Two-Edged Sword," 113.

61. "Genesis 12," *Fundamentalist*, 22 December 1944, 2 and 6.

62. "Is the Great Tribulation Prophesied by Jesus at Hand?" *Fundamentalist*, 5 January 1945, 5.

63. "Bible Baptist Seminary Now Legally Gives All and More Degrees than Any Other Seminary," *Fundamentalist*, 12 October 1945, 1. A check of the American Bible Society, Tichendorf, Westcott-Hort, Textus Receptus, Alexander Souter, and Nestlé texts reveals that none of them includes a demonstrative pronoun before *great tribulation*. Norris may have believed that the context re-

quired the word *the*, but he was in error in saying that the word appeared in the Greek. Had Norris been using the parallel passage in Mark 13:24 he would have been closer to the mark in his translation.

64. "Genesis 12," 2.

65. "Method of Study in the Bible Baptist Seminary," *Fundamentalist*, 3 August 1945, 1 and 4. With all Norris's traveling, it's questionable how much attention he paid to the details of the seminary. In 1945, he wrote an article for the *Fundamentalist* outlining the degree requirements. The next week, his assistant, Louis Entzminger, who was running the seminary at the time, wrote another article correcting Norris's errors. See Norris, "Bible Baptist Seminary Now Legally Gives All and More Degrees than Any Other Seminary," 1 and 8; and Louis Entzminger, "Bible Baptist Seminary Adopts Enlarged Curricula to Include Three More Degrees, *Fundamentalist*, 19 October 1945, 1 and 6.

66. "The Two Courses Taught Next Year by Dr. J. Frank Norris," *Fundamentalist*, 22 June 1945, 1.

67. *Fundamentalist*, 19 January 1945, 5; and 9 February 1945, 7. The list required two issues of the newspaper to complete.

68. The Verbal Inspiration of the Scripture," *Fundamentalist*, 13 December 1929, 1, 3, and 6.

69. Joseph Dawson, *The Light That Grows: Sermons to College Students* (New York: Doran, 1923), 43-44.

70. Other SBC leaders pointed this out. See Thompson, *Tried as by Fire*, 94.

71. "The Verbal Inspiration of the Scripture," 3. This confession, in booklet form called the *Baptist Faith and Message*, was modeled on the New Hampshire Confession of 1833. See William L. Lumpkin, *Baptist Confessions of Faith*, rev. ed. (Valley Forge: Judson Press, 1969), 390-400.

72. "'I Want the Evolutionists out of Baylor and the Books of the Denomination Opened,'" *Searchlight*, 29 September 1922, 2; and "Address on Evolution before the Texas Legislature," *Searchlight*, 23 February 1923, 2. The quotation is from the first reference.

73. "The Verbal Inspiration of the Scripture," 3. "Some Fruits of Evolution among Texas Baptists," *Fundamentalist*, 4 November 1927, 2. The quotation is from the first reference.

74. "Address on Evolution before the Texas Legislature," 1-4.

75. Ibid., 2.

76. Ibid., 4.

77. *SBC Annual*, 1922, 35.

78. James Thompson argues persuasively that there was a small party of theistic evolutionists in the convention and that there were others like E.Y. Mullins who were prepared to accept various facets of the theory. The latter group maintained, however, that while God may have used evolution in His creative process, humankind did not evolve from lower species of life. See *Tried as by Fire*, 114-15.

79. *Searchlight*, 21 August 1925, 1.

80. "Dr. Mullins Evades Again," *Searchlight*, 25 June 1926, 3; and Lumpkin, *Baptist Confessions of Faith*, 391. Although the Texas bill never came to a vote in the Texas Senate, Governor Ma Ferguson in 1925 simply banned textbooks that contained any discussion of evolution.

81. Hatch, *Democratization of American Christianity*, 213-14.

82. "'I Want the Evolutionists out of Baylor and the Books of the Denomination Opened,'" 2.

83. "When a Church Is Not a Church," *Fundamentalist*, 15 June 1945, 1. Although Norris did not say so specifically, in this article he seems to have been reacting to churches that were threatening to leave his World Fundamental Baptist Missionary Fellowship. Several times in the article he spoke of "troublemaking" churches.

84. See Norris to Eloise Vick, 23 July 1949, Norris Papers, Texas Collection, Baylor University.

85. Luther Peak, interview by Bill Pitts, April 1982, Oral History Memoir, Texas Collection, Baylor University, Waco; and Homer Ritchie, interview by author, tape recording 26 May 1992, Fort Worth.

86. B.H. Hilliard, "Unscriptural Practice of Ordaining Deacons," *Fundamentalist*, 16 November 1945, 2.

87. C.E. Matthews to Whom It May Concern, 1 May 1922, L.R. Scarborough File, Roberts Library, Southwestern Baptist Theological Seminary, Fort Worth; and E.P. Kirkland to F.S. Groner, 27 October 1922, in Leon McBeth, ed., *Sourcebook for Baptist Heritage*, 488. The first letter appears to have been solicited by Scarborough during the height of the controversy over the Seventy-five Million Campaign. Matthews had been formerly Norris's Sunday school superintendent at First Baptist. He claimed that the church office regularly gave departing members their letters of membership without knowledge or vote of the congregation. Kirkland, who had known Norris from boyhood, claimed that Norris once told him that Baptists believed and fought for many things not contained in the Scriptures. He concluded, "I write in evidence that the Rev. J.Frank Norris has never been in full accord with the organized work of convention Baptists of Texas."

88. F.S. Groner to E.P. Kirkland, in McBeth, *Sourcebook for Baptist Heritage*, 488.

89. J.B. Rounds, "Northern Baptists No Longer Baptists," in "What Attitude Will Southern Baptists Now Have toward the Northern Baptist Convention?" *Searchlight*, 11 June 1926, 10. For the allegation that Norris allowed someone to join First Baptist without baptism, see C.E. Matthews to Scarborough, 23 November 1921, and Lyn Claybrook to P.A. Thornton, 5 July 1923; both in Scarborough Correspondence, Southwestern Baptist Theological Seminary.

90. See chapter 6 for examples of Norris naming his own successors.

91. John R. Rice, "Why I Am a Big F. Fundamentalist," *Fundamentalist*, 2 March 1928, 3.

92. Norris once referred to Bible Baptist Seminary in the headline, "Seminary the West Point and Annapolis of the Lord," *Fundamentalist*, 19 October 1945, 1.

3. American Nativist

1. Marty, *Pilgrims in Their Own Land*, 376-77. For a history of Prohibition, see James H. Timberlake, *Prohibition and the Progressive Movement, 1900–1920* (Cambridge: Harvard Univ. Press, 1963).

2. Sydney E. Ahlstrom, *A Religious History of the American People* (New Haven: Yale Univ. Press, 1972; Garden City, N. Y.: Image Books, 1975), 2:348-51.

3. Quoted in Marty, *Pilgrims in Their Own Land*, 376.

4. Lewis Gould, *Progressives and Prohibitionists: Texas Democrats in the Wilson Era* (Austin: Univ. of Texas Press, 1973), 289-90. The degree to which Southern Baptists were active in Prohibition in the late nineteenth century to the exclusion of other social issues is covered in Eighmy, *Churches in Cultural Captivity*, 41-56.

5. Norris did not start his own newspaper until 1917, and the secular press, with the exception of his arson and perjury trials, did not cover his activity heavily before the twenties. Also, there are no Norris personal papers extant from before 1928. The fire of 1929 destroyed most of what he had collected before 1928. This makes it difficult to track his involvement in politics, but it appears from early issues of the *Searchlight* that he was not nearly as heavily involved in Prohibition in the teens as he would become in the twenties.

6. *Fence Rail*, 26 January 1917, 2. For a few months Norris called his newspaper the *Fence Rail* before changing the name to the *Searchlight* and then, in the late twenties, to the *Fundamentalist*.

7. *Searchlight*, 31 August 1917, 1; and *Searchlight*, 26 October 1917, 1.

8. *Searchlight*, 7 August 1919, 2.

9. Gould, *Progressives and Prohibitionists*, 95-97; Timberlake, *Prohibition and the Progressive Movement*, 170. The quote is from George B. Tindall, *America: A Narrative History* (New York: Norton, 1984), 994.

10. *Searchlight*, 9 June 1922, 1. This issue contained reprinted correspondence between Norris and Hall, as well as between Norris and Wilson.

11. "Judge Wilson, K.C.'s, Ku Klux Klan and Bootleggers," *Searchlight*, 12 May 1922, 1.

12. "J. Frank Norris Sermon on Judge James C. Wilson," *Searchlight*, 9 June 1922, 2; "Some Undisputed Facts of Judge Wilson's Record," *Searchlight*, 9 June 1922, 1; and "Turning On the Light," *Searchlight*, 23 June 1922, 1.

13. "J. Frank Norris Sermon on Judge James C. Wilson," 2.

14. *Searchlight*, 16 June 1922, 1.

15. *Searchlight*, 23 June 1922, 1-4. At one point in this sermon Norris remarked with surprise that he had been speaking for more than two hours.

16. "Norris in Contempt of Court? Sued for Libel?" Fort Worth *Press*, 29 June 1922, 1; reprinted in *Searchlight*, 7 July 1922, 1; "Norris Declares He Welcomes Any Probe of Charge," *Searchlight*, 29 June 1922, 1. For the articles praising Wilson see *Searchlight*, 21 July 1922, 1; "Bootleg Doctors and the Rosser Incident," *Searchlight*, 8 August 1924, 1; and "The Wages of Sin," *Searchlight*, 12 March 1926, 2.

17. "Turning On the Light," 1-3.

18. "Shall the Catholics and Boot-Leggers Elect the Next United States Senator?" *Searchlight*, 28 July 1922, 1.

19. "Hon. Felix D. Robertson: A Plea for Fair Play," *Searchlight*, 18 July 1924, 1.

20. *Searchlight*, 25 July 1924, 5; and "Sermon Delivered Sunday Night to Audience of Ten Thousand," *Searchlight*, 1 August 1924, 1. Political

advertisements appeared frequently in the *Searchlight*. Most appear to have been paid for by the candidates.

21. See *Searchlight*, 1 August 1924, 1; *Searchlight*, 8 August 1924, 1; and *Searchlight*, 22 August 1924, 1.

22. "Election of Ferguson as Governor of Texas," *Searchlight*, 29 August 1924, 1. For ads for Butte see *Searchlight*, 3 October 1924, 2, and *Searchlight*, 24 October 1924, 5.

23. "Wages of Sin," *Searchlight*, 12 March 1926, 2.

24. "J. Frank Norris Sermon on Judge James C. Wilson," 2; "Roman Catholicism versus Protestantism," *Searchlight*, 14 July 1922, 1.

25. "Roman Catholicism versus Protestantism," 1.

26. "Shall Roman Catholicism Rule Tarrant County?" *Searchlight*, 21 July 1922, 1-2. For another vivid description of the massacre see "Shouldest Thou Help the Ungodly?" *Fundamentalist*, 24 June 1927, 5.

27. "Shall the K of C Control Our Public Schools?" *Searchlight*, 5 May 1922, 1.

28. "Roman Catholicism versus Protestantism," 1-2.

29. "Rear Them Protestants," *Searchlight*, 4 August 1922, 1.

30. "Sermon Delivered Sunday Night to Audience of Ten Thousand," *Searchlight*, 1 August 1924, 1-4.

31. "Roman Catholic Control of N.Y.," *Searchlight*, 11 January 1924, 2.

32. "The Boy v. the Bootlegger," *Searchlight*, 25 March 1927, 1.

33. "Why the U.S. Should Continue to Refuse Demand of K.C.'s to Interfere in Mexico," *Searchlight*, 10 September 1926, 1-5.

34. "J. Frank Norris Sermon on Judge Wilson," 2.

35. "Robertson vs. Jim Ferguson: Rum, Romanism, Russianism, the Issue," *Searchlight*, 1 August 1924, 1. The phrase to which Norris alluded originated in the presidential campaign of 1884 when a minister who supported James G. Blaine against Grover Cleveland accused the Democrats of being the party of "Rum, Romanism, and Rebellion."

36. "Sermon Delivered Sunday Night to Audience of Ten Thousand," 3.

37. "The Reign of Law vs. the Reign of Anarchy," *Fundamentalist*, 12 August 1927, 4.

38. "Rome Invades Protestant America—The Eucharistic Conference in Chicago," *Searchlight*, 25 June 1926, 4.

39. "The Conspiracy of Rum and Romanism to Rule This Government," *Searchlight*, 5 February 1926, 1 and 6.

40. "Roman Catholic Control of N.Y.," 1-2.

41. "The Conspiracy of Rum and Romanism to Rule This Government," 6.

42. For a full discussion of Norris's involvement in presidential campaigns see Barry Hankins, "The Fundamentalist Style in American Politics: J. Frank Norris and Presidential Elections, 1928-1952," *American Baptist Quarterly* 11 (March 1992): 76-95.

43. See *Searchlight*, 26 March 1926, 1; and *Searchlight*, 16 April 1926, 1 and 9.

44. Charles C. Marshall, "An Open Letter to the Honorable Alfred E. Smith," *Fundamentalist*, 22 April 1927, 4-6.

45. "Why Al Smith Should Not Be President of the United States," *Fundamentalist*, 20 May 1927, 1-2, and 4. Norris cited the case correctly as *Watson v Jones* (1872).

46. James Hennesey, "Roman Catholics and American Politics, 1900-1960," in *Religion and American Politics from the Colonial Period to the 1980s*, ed., Mark Noll (New York: Oxford Univ. Press, 1990), 313.

47. "Why Al Smith Should Not Be President," 6-7. For Norris's eulogy of Bryan see "W.J. Bryan, the Fundamentalist," *Searchlight*, 7 August 1925, 1-2.

48. Norris to R.B. Craeger [*sic*], 20 May 1927, Norris Papers. The man's name was Creager. Norris misspelled it the first few times he wrote to him.

49. "Talk about Religious Freedom and Intolerance," *Fundamentalist*, 17 February 1928, 3; "Address on the Candidacy of Al Smith," *Fundamentalist*, 2 March 1928, 2 and 6; and "Al Smith Habitual Drinker," *Fundamentalist*, 17 August 1928, 1.

50. Norris to Fairfax Cosby, Los Angeles, 5 May 1928, Norris Papers.

51. Norris to Fairfax Cosby, Los Angeles, 12 May 1928, Norris Papers.

52. "Address on the Candidacy of Al Smith," 7; and "Salvation through Christ versus Salvation through Romanism," *Fundamentalist*, 16 March 1928, 1.

53. Norris to Connally, 25 January 1928, Norris Papers.

54. Connally to Norris, 25 February 1928, Norris Papers.

55. L.R. Scarborough, "The Ground of My Opposition to Putting Governor Smith in the White House," *Fundamentalist*, 31 August 1928, 1, 3-4, and 7.

56. "President of Southern Baptist Convention Misused by Al Smith," *Fundamentalist*, 5 October 1928, 1-2 and 7; "Dr. Truett More Misunderstood than Ever," *Fundamentalist*, 12 October 1928, 1; "Dr. Truett Makes Another Statement," *Fundamentalist*, 19 October 1928, 1 and 8; and "Will Dr. George W. Truett and Other Texas Leaders Remain Silent on Al Smith?" *Fundamentalist*, 20 July 1928, 1.

57. *Fundamentalist*, 27 July 1928, 1

58. "Will the Baptist Standard Continue Its Silence in the Present Crisis?" *Fundamentalist*, 13 April 1928, 6.

59. "The Baylor University Al Smith Club," *Fundamentalist*, 26 October 1928, 1-2.

60. "President Mullins on the Sad Plight of Democrats," *Fundamentalist*, 20 July 1928, 1-2. For a concise discussion of Mullins's efforts in behalf of prohibition see William E. Ellis, *A Man of Books and a Man of the People* (Macon, Ga.: Mercer Univ. Press, 1985), 209-15. Ellis writes that prohibition drew Mullins into politics for one of the few times in his life.

61. James S. Vance to Norris, 14 September 1928, Norris Papers. Emphasis in the original.

62. Norris to James S. Vance, 8 October 1928, Norris Papers.

63. Norris to R.B. Creager, Brownsville, Texas, 26 November 1927; and Norris to Creager, 19 March 1928, Norris Papers.

64. Norris to Hon. James W. Flood, Chicago, 17 September 1928, Norris Papers.

65. "Appeal by Pastor to First Baptist Church Sunday Morning April 15th," *Fundamentalist*, 21 April 1928, 1; "Greatest Victory in Texas since San Jacinto Day, April 21, 1836," *Fundamentalist*, 11 May 1928, 1.

66. "Local Politics," *Fundamentalist*, 29 June 1928, 1.

67. "Assassin Admits He Was Influenced by Roman Catholic Nun," *Fundamentalist*, 3 August 1928, 1.

68. "Six Thousand Dallasites Enthusiastically Cheer Name of Hoover Monday Night," *Fundamentalist*, 24 August 1928, 4.

69. Norris to Mordecai Ham, 17 September 1928, Norris Papers.

70. *Fundamentalist*, 15 June 1928, 8.

71. "Herbert Hoover and Prohibition v. Al Smith and the Brass Rail," *Fundamentalist*, 22 June 1928, 8.

72. Norris to R. B. Creager, 29 August 1928; and Creager to Norris, 6 September 1928, Norris Papers.

73. *Fundamentalist*, 7 September 1928, 1; and Norris to Mordecai Ham, 17 September 1928, Norris Papers.

74. Norris to Lon F. Anderson, Brooklyn, New York, 27 August 1928, Norris Papers.

75. *Fundamentalist*, 14 September 1928, 1; *Fundamentalist*, 21 September 1928, 1; William Ward Ayer, Gary, Indiana, to Norris, 12 September 1928; and Norris to Ayer, 17 September 1928, Norris Papers.

76. "Six Thousand Dallasites Enthusiastically Cheer," 1 and 4.

77. "Al Smith and the Negro," *Fundamentalist*, 19 October 1928, 4.

78. "Hoover Win to Be Celebrated Here," Fort Worth *Star Telegram*, 7 November 1928, 1; "Supporters for Hoover Here Celebrated," Fort Worth *Star Telegram*, 8 November 1928, 3; John R. Rice, "A Worthy Tribute to Dr. Norris," *Fundamentalist*, 9 November 1928, 1. It should be noted that only in the Rice article was the head of the Hoover Democrats quoted as saying that Norris had done more than anyone to put Texas into the Republican column.

79. "And the Mule under Him Went Away, "*Fundamentalist*, 9 November 1928, 1.

80. "For the Time Is Come That Judgment Must Begin at the House of God," *Fundamentalist*, 16 November 1928, 1 and 8.

81. Judge J.M. Combs, "Report on Laymen's Work," BGCT *Annual*, 1928, 113-14; and "Convention Politicians Slap Ministry in the Face," *Fundamentalist*, 23 November 1928, 1.

82. "And the Mule under Him Went Away," 1 and 4. Norris read the telegram during this sermon.

83. *Fundamentalist*, 30 November 1928, 4.

84. The charges of embezzlement appeared in a boxed item in the *Fundamentalist*, 7 December 1928, 1. There was no title. For the two headlines see John Bond, "Anger and Despair . . . ," *Fundamentalist*, 14 December 1928, 7; and "Rome Defies Protestant America," *Fundamentalist*, 1 February 1929, 1. John Bond was identified as the "Rome Correspondent" to the *Fundamentalist*.

85. "Hoover an Inspiration to Every American Boy," *Fundamentalist*, 16 November 1928, 6; and "A New Era for America," *Fundamentalist*, 15 March 1928, 7 (quote).

86. Norris to Mordecai Ham, 11 March 1929, Norris Papers.

87. R.B. Creager to Norris, 14 March 1929, Norris Papers. For Norris's recommendations on appointments see letters from Norris to Creager, 26 January, 5 March, 2 April, 6 May, and 18 June 1929, Norris Papers.

88. "A New Era for America," *Fundamentalist*, 15 March 1929, 7; and "Fort Worth to Be Dry as Sahara," *Fundamentalist*, 29 March 1929, 1.

89. "Rome Attacks President Hoover and the Constitution," *Fundamentalist*, 26 April 1929, 1 and 6.

90. "When the Wicked Beareth Rule the People Mourn," *Fundamentalist* 4 July 1930, 1-2 and 7.

91. *Fundamentalist*, 2 May 1930, 8

92. "The Governor's Race," *Fundamentalist*, 18 July 1930, 3; "Roman Catholics Spend One Million Dollars Fighting Earle B. Mayfield: Dying Testimony of Man Who Raised the Funds," *Fundamentalist*, 25 July 1930, 1; "Moral Issues in the Governor's Race," *Fundamentalist*, 25 July 1930, 3 and 6; and "Three to One Victory for Bone-Dry Prohibition," *Fundamentalist*, 1 August 1930, 1 and 8.

93. *Fundamentalist*, 29 August 1930, 1.

94. "Why the Bootleggers Are Fighting Bob Stuart," *Fundamentalist*, 11 July 1930, 1 and 8.

95. "They Drink and Forget the Law," *Fundamentalist*, 6 June 1930, 2; "The Governor's Race," *Fundamentalist*, 18 July 1930, 3; and "Moral Issues in the Governor's Race," *Fundamentalist*, 25 July 1930, 3.

96. "Dark Underground Conspiracy of Raskobism, Romanism, and Liquor Exposed—Raskob Gives $250,000 a Year to Malign Hoover," *Fundamentalist*, 29 August 1930, 1.

97. "Al Smith, Rome, Liquor, Tammany Hall, Raskob on Democratic Mule Second Time," *Fundamentalist*, 6 March 1931, 1 and 4.

98. "Shall Rome and Liquor Capture the White House?" *Fundamentalist*, 20 March 1931, 6-7.

99. "Al Smith, Rome, Liquor, Tammany Hall, Raskob on Democratic Mule Second Time," 4; and "Will the Papacy Rule the Italian Government and Will Raskobism Capture the White House?" *Fundamentalist*, 12 June 1931, 6 (quote).

100. "A Trumpet Call to Prohibitionists," *Fundamentalist*, 8 July 1932, 3.

101. Ibid., 3-4; and Norris to M.A. Matthews, 30 June 1932, Norris Papers.

102. Norris to Tarrant County Medical Association, 15 June 1932, Norris Papers; and "A Trumpet Call to Prohibitionists," 4.

103. "Let All the Prohibitionists Vote July 23 against Liquor," *Fundamentalist*, 15 July 1932, 2.

104. Norris to Gerald Winrod, Wichita, Kansas, 27 August 1932, Norris Papers.

105. Norris to Mark Matthews, Seattle, 30 July 1932, Norris Papers.

106. "A Reply to the Liquor Stand of Bishop Moore," *Fundamentalist*, 2 December 1932, 2, 5-6.

107. "The Tragedy of American History—Doom of the Eighteenth Amendment," *Fundamentalist*, 6 January 1933, 8.

108. "The Fight against Liquor," *Fundamentalist*, 27 January 1933, 6; and "Lord How Long Shall the Wicked Triumph," *Fundamentalist*, 24 February 1933, 1.

109. "Greatest Mass Meeting in History of Fort Worth," *Fundamentalist*, 17 March 1933, 1.

110. "There Is Death in the Pot," *Fundamentalist,* 7 April 1933, 2; "Brewers Caught Buying Members of Legislature at Austin," *Fundamentalist,* 14 April 1933, 1; and "The Record of Brewery Money in Texas Politics," *Fundamentalist,* 21 April 1933, 1 and 6-7.

111. "Brewers Caught Buying Members of Legislature at Austin," 1.

112. *Fundamentalist,* 21 April 1933, 1; and "Coca-Cola Company Paying Norris Fifty Thousand to Make Anti Beer Campaign," *Fundamentalist,* 14 July 1933, 3.

113. "The Lobby Investigation at the Texas Legislature," *Fundamentalist,* 14 July 1933, 1; "Sunday Historic Day for Righteousness," *Fundamentalist,* 25 August 1933, 1; "Majority of Counties of Texas Remain Dry," *Fundamentalist,* 1 September 1933, 1; and "'Ye Are Cursed with a Curse': The Curse of Liquor," *Fundamentalist,* 22 September 1933, 2, 4, and 7.

114. "Will Liquor and Gambling Forces Succeed in Shutting Norris Off the Radio?" *Fundamentalist,* 25 May 1934, 2; "'There Is More Drinking since Repeal,'" *Fundamentalist,* 12 January 1934, 1. Here Norris cited the Dallas *Evening Journal* as condemning the adverse effects of the repeal of prohibition. For another "I told you so," see "'A Gluttonous Whisky Trust Worse than Prohibition,'" *Fundamentalist,* 5 January 1934, 1. In this article he quoted a man who had favored repeal but who came to believe that liquor companies had too much influence in politics. For Norris's recognition that there will be no prohibition until Christ returns see "The NRA and the Mark of the Beast," *Fundamentalist,* 18 October 1935, 2, 6, and 8.

115. "Editorial on Dr. J. Frank Norris in Austin Tribune," *Fundamentalist,* 1 March 1940, 1.

116. See chapter 7 for a discussion of Norris's alignment with the Roman Catholic Church against communism.

117. Norris to Connally, 10 September 1951; and Connally to Norris, 1 October 1951. See also Norris to Connally, 9 October 1951; and Connally to Norris, 13 October 1951. For Norris's statement to MacArthur, see Norris to MacArthur, 19 June 1951, Norris Papers. Why Norris changed his mind is not readily apparent. He may have realized by the fall that Shivers had little chance of defeating Connally anyway, so he moved to bolster his good standing with the incumbent with whom he had enjoyed a long-standing relationship. Had he backed Shivers publicly and lost, Norris would have forfeited his influence with Connally.

118. W.W. McGinty, Keller, Tex., to Norris, 18 March 1951; and Norris to McGinty, 20 March 1951, Norris Papers.

4. Dispensational Prophet

1. Weber, "The Two-Edged Sword," 114.

2. See Timothy Weber, *Living in the Shadow of the Second Coming: American Premillennialism, 1875–1925* (New York: Oxford Univ. Press, 1979), 13-42. For a brief discussion of Augustine's division of history see David Bebbington, *Patterns in History: A Christian Perspective on Historical Thought* (Grand Rapids: Baker Book House, 1990), 57. For an excellent recent analysis of end-times prophecy, see Paul Boyer, *When Time Shall Be No More: Prophecy Belief in Modern American Culture* (Cambridge: Harvard University Press, 1992).

3. Danny Howe, "An Analysis of Dispensationalism and Its Implications for the Theologies of James Robinson Graves, John Franklyn Norris, and Wallie Amos Criswell," 161-65; Norris, "Shots on the Wing," *Searchlight*, 28 August 1925, 1. It was in this second source that Norris cited Haldeman's influence. His reference here should be viewed with caution. He was in New York at the time, writing some impressions, one of which was about Haldeman, who pastored First Baptist New York for forty-five years. Whether Haldeman's writings were solely responsible for Norris's conversion to dispensationalism remains highly doubtful.

4. "Where the Scofield Bible Is in Gross Error," *Fundamentalist*, 26 February 1943, 7; and "Where Scofield Missed It," *Fundamentalist*, 16 November 1945, 1. In the first article the specific error had to do with Isaiah 21. Norris charged that the Scofield Bible notes claimed that the passage referred to the invasion of Jerusalem by Sennacherib when it really is about the invasion of Babylon by the Medes and Persians. It perhaps should be noted that when Norris cited Scofield's errors, he was advertising his own pamphlet on the Book of Isaiah. In this respect, he was classing himself with probably the best-known Bible scholar in the history of fundamentalism to that time.

5. "A Message from Ezekiel," *Fundamentalist*, 10 August 1951, 2.

6. "First Baptist Church Will Remain Forever Anchored to the Fundamentals of the Faith and Will Never Go Back into the Baptist General Convention of Texas, Southern Baptist Convention, World Baptist Alliance or Any Other Modernistic, Ecclesiastical Machine," *Fundamentalist*, 8 December 1944, 1.

7. "The Second Coming," *Fundamentalist*, 29 September 1939, 6, and "Why Millions Living Will Not See Death," *Fundamentalist*, 23 February 1945, 3, 6-7. In the second sermon Norris implied clearly in the title that the second coming of Christ was going to take place very soon. In the sermon itself, however, he backed off somewhat, saying only that this might be the case—yet another example of his sensationalism.

8. "Is This the Last Generation?" *Fundamentalist*, 20 April 1945, 3-5.

9. For an extended discussion of the importance of World War I for the development of fundamentalism see George Marsden, *Fundamentalism and American Culture*, 141-53. For a brief outline of this argument see Marsden's 1991 book, *Understanding Fundamentalism and Evangelicalism*, 174. Marsden uses Bryan and Sunday to show the divergence of views among evangelicals.

10. Paolo Coletta, *William Jennings Bryan*, 3 vols. (Lincoln: Univ. of Nebraska Press, 1964-1969), 2:335-36.

11. Quoted in William G. McLoughlin Jr., *Billy Sunday Was His Real Name* (Chicago: Univ. of Chicago Press, 1955), 257-58.

12. Ray H. Abrams, *Preachers Present Arms: The Role of the American Churches and Clergy in World Wars I and II with Some Observations on the War in Vietnam* (Scottdale, Penn.: Herald Press, 1969), 66-68. To be sure, Abrams has selected the most belligerent statements for presentation and all but ignored more moderate ones. However, his book does illustrate that some pastors, perhaps most, who spoke on the war gave it their enthusiastic support. Indeed, one commentator has gone so far as to call the churches' attitude toward the war the "fall of Christianity." Quoted in Guy Franklin Hershberger, *War,*

Peace and Non-Resistance (Scottsdale, Penn.: Herald Press, 1969) , 79. For a balance to Abrams see John F. Piper Jr., *The American Churches in World War I* (Athens: Ohio Univ. Press, 1985).

13. Weber, *Living in the Shadow of the Second Coming*, 120-25.

14. *Searchlight*, 13 April 1917, 1; *Searchlight*, 23 April 1917, 1; *Searchlight*, 1 June 1917 , 1; and *Searchlight*, 15 June 1917, 1.

15. *Searchlight*, 22 June 1917, 1 and 4.

16. See Marsden, *Fundamentalism and American Culture*, 141-53; and Weber, *Living in the Shadow of the Second Coming*, 128-31.

17. "WWI Needed to Fulfill the Word of the Bible," *Searchlight*, 3 July 1919, 3.

18. "Palestine Restored to the Jews," *Searchlight*, 21 October 1920, 1.

19. "Jerusalem," *Searchlight*, 28 October 1920, 3 (quotation); continued in *Searchlight*, 2 December 1920, 1-2. See also "Palestine Restored to the Jews," *Searchlight*, 21 October 1920, 2.

20. "Jerusalem," *Searchlight*, 2 December 1920, 1-2.

21. "The Persecution of the Jews in Germany," *Fundamentalist*, 7 April 1933, 3.

22. "Protocols of the Wise Men of Zion," *Fundamentalist*, 22 October 1937, 5-7.

23. *Fundamentalist*, 18 March 1938, 3.

24. "Protocols of the Wise Men of Zion," 1.

25. For a discussion of Norris and Smith see chapter 6.

26. See "Did the Jews Write the Protocols?—The Upheaval in Palestine and What It Means," *Fundamentalist*, 18 February 1938, 1; "Dr. W.B. Riley Goes Back to Texas Baptist Machine and Apologizes to the Machine for the Many Years He Was with Norris," *Fundamentalist*, 4 March 1938, 1-3; and "The Norris-Riley Discussion of the Jews, One Hundred Thousand Copies Published," *Fundamentalist*, 1 April 1938, 1. Whether in fact Norris published 100,000 copies of the discussion with Riley is anyone's guess. He often claimed to have published 100,000 copies of various addresses. The 4 March 1938 article was a reprint of Riley's address to Texas Baptists in which he said he was sorry he had ever aligned with Norris.

27. Trollinger believes that Riley's anti-Semitism stemmed from his frustrations at having lost nearly every theological battle in which he had been involved. See Trollinger, *God's Empire*, 62-82.

28. Photostatic copies of these and articles from other newspapers appeared in the *Fundamentalist*, 10 October 1947, 3.

29. "Halt Loans to Britain, Pastor Urges," Fort Worth *Star Telegram*, 6 October 1947, 2. A photostatic copy of this article appeared in the *Fundamentalist*, 17 October 1947, 6. Norris published his letter to Truman in "Who Owns or Has the Title to Palestine?" *Fundamentalist*, 10 October 1947, 1 and 3.

30. "Norris Hits Embargo of Arms for Israel," Memphis *Commercial Appeal*, 18 May 1948. A photostatic copy of this article appeared in the *Fundamentalist*, 28 May 1948, 3. For the report of Norris's meeting with the Grand Mufti see *Fundamentalist*, 9 January 1948, 8. Included was a photograph of Norris and the Muslim leader.

31. *Searchlight*, 11 September 1919, 3.

32. "League of Nations," *Searchlight*, 18 November 1920, 1-2; "The Conspiracy of Rum and Romanism to Rule This Government," *Searchlight*, 6 February 1926, 6.

33. *Searchlight*, 9 September 1920, 2.

34. "The Folly of the Anti-British Feeling," *Fundamentalist*, 23 February 1940, 3.

35. "Can the Leopard Change His Spots or the Ethiopian His Skin?" *Fundamentalist*, 7 August 1941, 5.

36. "The Coming Red Hot United States Senatorial Race in Texas," *Fundamentalist*, 22 May 1942, 6.

37. *Searchlight*, 9 September 1920, 2.

38. *Searchlight*, 16 September 1920, 1.

39. "Brewers Caught Buying Members of Legislature at Austin," *Fundamentalist*, 14 April 1933, 1.

40. *Searchlight*, 16 September 1920, 4.

41. "Mussolini—The Earmarks of the Beast of Prophecy," *Searchlight*, 22 October 1926, 5. While there may be some who would make a distinction between the "beast of prophecy" and the Antichrist, Norris seems to have used the two terms loosely and nearly interchangeably when writing for a popular audience. Whenever one speaks of apocalyptic literature, difficulties abound. For example, the Book of Revelation speaks not only of the Antichrist but of several Antichrists. The Book of Daniel, meanwhile, does not use the term *Antichrist* at all, but his "beast" seems very similar to the references in Revelation.

42. "Mussolini a Type of the Beast of Prophecy," *Fundamentalist*, 6 April 1928, 2 (emphasis mine). Premillennial dispensationalists believed that the ten nations that emerged from the Roman Empire would be reconstituted by the Antichrist just before the Jews returned to Palestine. See Weber, *Living in the Shadow of the Second Coming*, 109-12.

43. See "'But Christ'—The Unholy Alliance of the Papacy and Mussolini," *Fundamentalist*, 3 May 1929, 1 and 6-8; "The Sound of Their Wings Running to Battle," *Fundamentalist*, 7 June 1929, 1-2; and "Will the Papacy Rule the Italian Government and Will Raskobism Capture the White House?" *Fundamentalist*, 12 June 1931, 1, 3, and 6-7.

44. "Joseph Stalin of Russia and the Earmarks of the Beast," *Fundamentalist*, 2 October 1931, 2, 4, and 6.

45. "The Prophesied Worldwide Dictatorship," *Fundamentalist*, 9 June 1933, 1-2; and "The Mark of the Beast and the Duty of the Christian in This Present Hour," *Fundamentalist*, 21 July 1933, 3. See chapter 5 for more on Norris's view of FDR.

46. "Second Sermon on the Mark of the Beast or Why We Should Support the President's Program and Put the Sign of the Blue Eagle on the Front Door," *Fundamentalist*, 28 July 1933, 1-3.

47. "Secretary of Agriculture Member of the President's Cabinet Advocates 'Totalitarian' or Communistic State; Also Declares People Have Lost 'Faith in God,' 'And The Future Life,'" *Fundamentalist*, 31 July 1936, 6.

48. "The Mark of the Beast and the Duty of a Christian in This Present Hour," 1-3; and "Second Sermon on the Mark of the Beast, 1-3.

49. "Another Little Horn," *Fundamentalist*, 21 April 1933, 4.

50. "The Prophesied Worldwide Dictatorship," 1; and "The Revolution in America—Are We Passing under Dictatorship?" *Fundamentalist*, 2 February 1934, 3-4 and 6.

51. "The Persecution of the Jews in Germany," *Fundamentalist*, 7 April 1933, 5. In this sermon Norris talked about the Jews a lot and about Germany hardly at all.

52. "Are the Days of Mass Evangelism Over?" *Fundamentalist*, 17 July 1936, 5; and "The League of Nations Will Go to Pieces over Ethiopia," *Fundamentalist*, 7 February 1936, 1. See chapter 7 for a discussion of Norris's anticommunism.

53. "President Roosevelt Calls America to Revival," *Fundamentalist*, 13 March 1936, 1. Norris was always heartened when any American president said anything about religion. FDR's statement here is clearly of the civil religion variety, calling people to a vague sort of "religion" that will undergird the nation in time of distress. For a discussion of FDR's civil religion see Richard V. Pierard and Robert D. Linder, *Civil Religion and the Presidency* (Grand Rapids: Zondervan, 1988), 161-83.

54. "Seventeen Years Ago in Germany and Now," *Fundamentalist*, 6 August 1937, 5.

55. "Can Anything Good Come Out of Germany?" *Fundamentalist*, 13 August 1937, 7.

56. Coyus Fabricius, "Germany in the Religious World Situation," *Fundamentalist*, 20 August 1937, 7.

57. "Get Closer to Germany," *Fundamentalist*, 27 August 1937, 7.

58. "Notes on Vienna," *Fundamentalist*, 13 August 1937, 8.

59. "Hitler and the Earmarks of the Beast," *Fundamentalist*, 7 October 1938, 3. While Norris sometimes classed FDR with the three dictators, he does not appear to have ever believed that the American president was the Antichrist.

60. "Protocols of the Wise Men of Zion," 1. The leading anti-Semites of the 1930s were Gerald Winrod, Gerald L.K. Smith, William D. Pelley, and Father Charles Coughlin. See Leo P. Ribuffo, *The Old Christian Right: The Protestant Far Right from the Great Depression to the Cold War* (Philadelphia: Temple Univ. Press, 1983) for an extended discussion of Pelley, Winrod, and Smith. See Ahlstrom, *A Religious History of the American People*, Garden City, N.Y.: Image Books, 1975), 2:418-21, for a discussion of these three plus Coughlin. See also Alan Brinkley, *Voices of Protest: Huey Long, Father Coughlin, and the Great Depression* (New York: Knopf, 1982).

61. "U.S. Liberty Threatened, Pastor Says," Toledo *Blade*, 31 March 1938; photostatic copy in the *Fundamentalist*, 8 April 1938, 7.

62. See "Can Anything Good Come Out of Germany? How Adolph Hitler Has Set an Example for the Whole World on Liquor and Tobacco," *Fundamentalist*, 31 March 1939, 2-3.

63. G.B. Vick, interview, tape recording, Baylor University Institute for Oral History, 26 July 1973.

5. Motor City Man

1. G.B. Vick, interview, Baylor University Institute for Oral History, 26 July 1973, tape 1; Morris, "He Changed Things" (Ph.D. diss., Texas Tech Uni-

versity, 1973), 369-71. Vick was Norris's first lieutenant at Temple for nearly the entire time Norris pastored Temple. Norris brought Vick to Detroit almost immediately after accepting the congregation's call. Vick settled in Detroit overseeing the day-to-day affairs of the church while Norris was in Fort Worth or traveling across America holding revivals. In 1950, when the congregation dismissed Norris, Vick became head pastor of the church.

2. Vick, interview, tape 1.

3. Morris, "He Changed Things," 371-75. Without extant church rolls, it is impossible to verify with assurance the membership of the two churches. Norris's claim of twenty-five thousand, however, does seem plausible. In discussing Norris with those who remember him, I've encountered no one who seems to believe that he wildly exaggerated the size of First Baptist and Temple.

4. See Barry Hankins, "The Ambivalent Fundamentalist: Luther Peak's Sojourn with J. Frank Norris," *Fides et Historia* 27:2 (summer 1995). See also Luther Peak oral memoir, Baylor University, Institute for Oral History, and Peak to Norris, 31 May 1932, Norris Papers.

5. Fort Worth *Star Telegram*, 1 November 1937 (morning edition only), 12. Norris placed this in his history of First Baptist and Temple as "Sinclair Lewis Attends First Baptist Church Oct. 31, 1937," in *Inside History of First Baptist Church Fort Worth and Temple Baptist Church Detroit*, 5.

6. "Spiritual Lessons from the Twenty-five Billion Dollar Crash," *Fundamentalist*, 8 November 1929, 1.

7. "The Bank Failure in Ft. Worth and the Bank That Never Fails," *Fundamentalist*, 14 February 1930, 1-2.

8. "The Whole Nation Cursed with a Curse," *Fundamentalist*, 8 August 1930, 1-2.

9. "Dark Underground Conspiracy of Raskobism, Romanism, and Liquor Exposed—Raskob Gives $250,000 a Year to Malign Hoover," *Fundamentalist*, 29 August 1930, 1, 5, and 8; "Al Smith, Rome, Liquor, Tammany Hall, Raskob on Democratic Mule Second Time," *Fundamentalist*, 6 March 1931, 4; "Moratorium of President Hoover Has Brought New Hope," *Fundamentalist*, 10 July 1931, 1, 2, and 6; "President Hoover Puts Al Capone behind Bars," *Fundamentalist*, 10 July 1931, 1; "'A Time of Peace'—Will a Hoover Arise among Texas Baptists?" *Fundamentalist*, 24 July 1931, 1; and "The New York Times on President Hoover's Moratorium," *Fundamentalist*, 24 July 1931, 1.

10. "Joseph Stalin of Russia and the Earmarks of the Beast," *Fundamentalist*, 25 September 1931, 4. The title of this sermon was an error. See *Fundamentalist*, 1 October 1931, 2, for a statement saying that the title had been placed on the sermon by mistake. For the announcement of the relief effort of First Baptist see "'For I Was an Hungered, and Ye Gave Me Meat; Naked and Ye Clothed Me,'" *Fundamentalist*, 23 December 1932, 1.

11. "Another Little Horn—The United States Passing under Dictatorship," *Fundamentalist*, 21 April 1933, 2.

12. "The Prophesied Worldwide Dictatorship," *Fundamentalist*, 9 June 1933, 2.

13. "The Mark of the Beast and the Duty of a Christian in This Present Hour," *Fundamentalist*, 21 July 1933, 3.

14. "The Revolution in America—Are We Passing under Dictatorship?" *Fundamentalist*, 2 February 1934, 4 and 6.

15. "The Jews Rule the U.S. and the World," *Fundamentalist*, 16 February 1934, 2. The point Norris was trying to make was that a German Jew—Marx—had influenced even the present government of the United States. The significance is that he could believe this at a time when he was in support of the New Deal. After 1935, as will be shown, he will use the allegation of communism to condemn the New Deal.

16. "Fifteen Bible Reasons Why I Support Roosevelt's Recovery," *Fundamentalist*, 23 March 1934, 2.

17. Ibid., 5.

18. Ibid., 5-6.

19. Ibid., 6.

20. The term *Great Reversal* comes from David Moberg, *The Great Reversal: Evangelism versus Social Concern* (Philadelphia: Lippincott, 1972). Moberg documents how evangelicals moved away from social Christianity toward a more exclusively evangelistic emphasis. Norris's shift away from the New Deal does not fit this paradigm exactly because he certainly did not forego politics. Norris's marriage to anti–New Deal efforts and anticommunism more nearly approximates what Richard Pierard has called *The Unequal Yoke* (Philadelphia: Lippincott, 1970).

21. This point has been argued by Clovis Gwin Morris in "He Changed Things."

22. Ahlstrom, *A Religious History of the American People*, 2:412. See also Paul A. Carter, *Decline and Revival of the Social Gospel: Social and Political Liberalism in American Protestant Churches, 1920–1940* (Ithaca, N.Y.: Cornell Univ. Press,1956).

23. "There Can Be No Economic Recovery without First a Spiritual Recovery," *Fundamentalist*, 7 September 1934, 4.

24. "Will the New Dealers Put Norris Off the Air?" *Fundamentalist*, 3 January 1935, 3.

25. "Gambling a Boy for an Harlot and a Girl for Wine," *Fundamentalist*, 23 August 1935, 6.

26. "What Will Survive the Present World Conflict?" *Fundamentalist*, 9 August 1935, 6-7.

27. *New Dealism (Russian Communism) Exposed* (n.p., n.d.), 34-35. This booklet appears to have been published in the fall of 1935 or early in 1936.

28. "Dr. J.B. Cranfill Delivers Body Blows to Poteatism," *Fundamentalist*, 30 August 1935, 1.

29. "W.B. Riley and Chief Justice Charles Evans Hughes Give Double Knock Out to the Report of Social Action Commission of Northern Baptist Convention," *Fundamentalist*, 26 July 1935, 1.

30. "Scriptural Teaching on Share-the-Wealth Plan," *Fundamentalist*, 11 October 1935, 6-7; and "The NRA and the Mark of the Beast," *Fundamentalist*, 18 October 1935, 6. Norris later came to believe that Christians should resist Hitler even if he was the prophesied Antichrist.

31. *New Dealism (Russian Communism) Exposed*, 35.

32. Ibid., 42.

33. Ibid., 6-7. Though this radio broadcast is recorded in one of Norris's own publications, there is little doubt in my mind that it is authentic. The verbatim presentation of the broadcast, covering almost two pages in print, makes it very unlikely that the words could have been fabricated by Norris or his associates.

34. "Ethiopia Stretches Forth Her Hands to God," *Fundamentalist*, 4 October 1935, 7.

35. "The NRA and the Mark of the Beast," *Fundamentalist*, 18 October 1935, 6 and 2. Civil religion refers to the combination of religious traits and concepts with national ones, the result being a common national faith that exists alongside particular expressions of religion. Civil religion mixes religion and nationalism until it is hard to separate the two. Sociologist Robert Bellah touched off a debate on the subject with the publication of "Civil Religion in America," *Daedalus* 96 (winter 1967): 1-21. Since that article, many books and articles have come forth dealing with the topic. See Robert D. Linder and Richard V. Pierard, *Twilight of the Saints: Biblical Christianity and Civil Religion in America* (Downers Grove, Ill.: InterVarsity Press, 1976); and Bellah and Phillip E. Hammond, *Varieties of Civil Religion* (San Francisco: Harper and Row, 1980). As this last book would imply, scholars have identified many types of civil religion. While most agree that civil religion does exist, there is no consensus as to its exact nature.

36. "Secretary of Agriculture Member of President's Cabinet Advocates 'Totalitarian' or Communistic State; Also Declares People Have Lost 'Faith in God,' 'And the Future Life,'" *Fundamentalist*, 31 July 1936, 6 and 8.

37. "Roosevelt Leaves God Out," *Fundamentalist*, 7 August 1936, 5.

38. "Statement of Dr. J. Frank Norris, Concerning General Motors Corporation over WJR 9 A.M., Sunday Nov. 3, 1935," *Fundamentalist*, 8 November 1935, 5. The donation was announced on the first page. It is not clear whether General Motors gave the property to Temple Baptist outright or simply allowed Temple to erect a temporary building on the land for evangelistic meetings.

39. "Secretary of Agriculture Member of the President's Cabinet Advocates 'Totalitarian' or Communistic State," 4.

40. "The Second American Revolution," *Fundamentalist*, 6 November 1936, 1 and 7.

41. "Shall America Remain under the Present Dictatorship?" *Fundamentalist*, 8 April 1938, 1-3.

42. "The G.P.U. National Labor Relations Board," *Fundamentalist*, 7 January 1938, 2.

43. "Al Smith, Rome, Liquor, Tammany Hall, Raskob On Democratic Mule Second Time," *Fundamentalist*, 6 March 1931, 4.

44. "Preparation for One Hundred Thousand at Evangelistic Meeting on Belle Isle June Fifth," *Fundamentalist*, 29 April 1938, 1.

45. Cecil Dye, "Rev. Charles E. Coughlin," *Fundamentalist*, 6 May 1938, 1.

46. "Shall America Remain under the Present Dictatorship?" *Fundamentalist*, 8 April 1938, 2.

47. "Evangelist Assails Lewis as 'Most Dangerous Man,'" Pittsburgh *Sun-Telegraph*, 21 October 1938; photostatic copy in *Fundamentalist*, 28 October 1938, 4.

48. "New Deal Sovietizing U.S., Fundamentalist Declares," Buffalo *Evening News*, 28 October 1938; photostatic copy in *Fundamentalist*, 4 November 1938, 5.

49. "Rich Must Meet Labor Issues," *Searchlight*, 5 June 1919, 1 and 4.

50. *Searchlight*, 7 October 1920, 3; and "Prophesied Conflict between Capital and Labor Sign of Approaching End of Age," *Searchlight*, 21 September 1923, 1.

51. For a brief discussion of the strike see Mary Beth Norton et al., *A People and a Nation: A History of the United States*, 2d ed. (Boston: Houghton Mifflin, 1986), 2:750-51.

52. "The Sit-Down Strike and Its Effects on Labor and Christianity," *Fundamentalist*, 2 April 1937, 4.

53. Richard Hofstadter, *Anti-Intellectualism in American Life* (New York: Knopf, 1963), 135. For a discussion of the revivalist tradition in fundamentalism see Marsden, *Fundamentalism and American Culture*, 223-25.

54. See "Conspiracy of John L. Lewis," *Fundamentalist*, 22 January 1937, 1 and 5-6; and "American Civil Liberties Union and Federal Church Council," *Fundamentalist*, 29 January 1937, 1. In the sermon published 29 January he announced that the booklets on Lewis would be made available.

55. "Conspiracy of John L. Lewis, 6-7.

56. Ibid., 5-6.

57. Henry Ford, "Will John L. Lewis Rake Off $1,200,000 Fees from Ford Employees?" *Fundamentalist*, 11 June 1937, 3. The title was by Norris.

58. "Clergyman Flays Church Council for 'Sympathy' with Sit-Downers," *Fundamentalist*, 16 April 1937, 4; "'You Haven't Got the Intestinal Fortitude to File Suit,'" *Fundamentalist*, 18 June 1937, 1; "UAW Officials on Warpath and Going after J. Frank Norris," *Fundamentalist*, 2 July 1937, 1; and "The UAW Makes Attack on Henry Ford and J. Frank Norris," *Fundamentalist*, 16 July 1937, 1.

59. "The UAW Makes Attack on Henry Ford and J. Frank Norris," 2.

60. "The G.P.U. National Labor Relations Board," *Fundamentalist*, 7 January 1938, 2.

61. "The Need of the Right Kind of Labor Board," *Fundamentalist*, 14 January 1938, 2.

62. "UAW Makes Attack on Henry Ford and J. Frank Norris," 2.

63. "Historic Victory in Detroit for Honest Labor, Law, Free Speech and Freedom of Worship," *Fundamentalist*, 5 November 1937, 1.

64. "Communistic CIO Broke Its Own Neck," *Fundamentalist*, 6 August 1937, 4.

65. "Evangelist Assails Lewis as 'Most Dangerous Man,'" Pittsburgh *Sun-Telegraph*, 21 October 1938; photostatic copy in *Fundamentalist*, 28 October 1938, 4. See also "Most Crushing Defeat to the Reds and Their Subversive Alienisms," *Fundamentalist*, 10 February 1939, 1, for Norris's praise of the Dies committee.

66. Roy K. Lawrence, "Boo Preacher at Talk Here," Flint *Journal*, 24 October 1938, 1; and "A Revival: The Greatest Need of America," *Fundamentalist*, 4 November 1938, 2. The Flint reporter made it clear that Norris had dropped the topic of politics after he encountered the resistance.

67. "UAW Makes Attack on Henry Ford and J. Frank Norris," 2. G.B. Vick estimated that during the Norris years at Temple Baptist there were more transplants from Kentucky and Tennessee than there were Michigan natives. Vick, tape 1.

68. "Calling American to Christian Patriotism and to God—Elliot Roosevelt, Convention Hall Detroit, June 9, 7:30 P.M.," *Fundamentalist*, 7 June 1940, 1, and 14 June 1940, 1-2.

69. *Fundamentalist*, 7 June 1940, 7; and "Southern Baptist Convention Should Pray for and not Criticize the President," *Fundamentalist*, 28 June 1940, 2.

70. "Difference between Franklin Roosevelt and Woodrow Wilson," *Fundamentalist*, 28 June 1940, 4.

71. William Allen White, "The Right Attitude of Patriotic Anti-Roosevelt People," *Fundamentalist*, 30 August 1940, 6. Norris appears to have given White's article this title.

72. "Excerpts from Message of Dr. J. Frank Norris on the Draft Law at First Baptist Church and Broadcast over Radio Network," *Fundamentalist*, 25 October 1940, 8.

73. *Fundamentalist*, 15 November 1940, 1.

74. "Will President Roosevelt Turn Conservative?" *Fundamentalist*, 22 November 1940, 1.

75. "Have Faith in God," *Fundamentalist*, 24 May 1940, 4.

76. Norris's need to portray FDR as at least partly conservative and somewhat religious foreshadowed the same sort of attitude evangelist Billy Graham would exhibit toward presidents Eisenhower, Johnson, and Nixon. Graham depicted all three as far more committed to Christianity than other observers believed they were. See Richard Pierard, "Billy Graham and the U.S. Presidency," *Journal of Church and State* 22 (winter 1980): 119; see also Barry Hankins, "Billy Graham and American Nationalism" (M.A. thesis, Baylor University, 1983).

77. "Address of Dr. J. Frank Norris before Texas Legislature," *Fundamentalist*, 28 February 1941, 1-2 and 6; "Georgia Legislature Is Turned into Revival by 'Flying Parson,'" *Atlanta Journal*, n.d., photostatic copy in *Fundamentalist* 7 March 1941, 2.

78. "Newspapers Give Large Heading," *Fundamentalist*, 11 July 1941, 4.

79. "Dr. J. Frank Norris on Radio Every Sunday at Detroit and Every Sunday in Fort Worth," *Fundamentalist*, 14 March 1941, 1.

80. Cordell Hull to Winston Churchill, 28 August 1941; a photostatic copy of this letter appeared in the *Fundamentalist*, 5 September 1941, 1.

81. Sumner Welles to John G. Winant, 22 August 1941, photostatic copy in *Fundamentalist*, 5 September 1941.

82. Frank Knox to A.V. Alexander, 29 August 1941, photostatic copy in *Fundamentalist*, 5 September 1941.

83. Wendell Willkie to Winston Churchill, 18 August 1941, photostatic copy in *Fundamentalist*, 5 September 1941.

84. J.M. North to press of Great Britain, 22 August 1941, photostatic copy in *Fundamentalist*, 5 September 1941.

85. "'Declare War' He Cables to Roosevelt," *Evening Standard Reporter*, 16 September 1941, n.d.; a photostatic copy of this article appeared in the *Fundamentalist*, 3 October 1941, 5. The city in which this paper was published

was not visible. See also "U.S. Expected to Be in War in 30 Days," *China Press,* 28 September 1941, photostatic copy in the *Fundamentalist,* 7 November 1941, 2. While Norris's September prediction was in error by about sixty days from the time he made it, it was almost exactly correct from the time he reprinted it in the *Fundamentalist.*

86. "'I Have the Same Faith I Received from My Mother,'" *Fundamentalist,* 26 September 1941, 1 and 7. See page 3 of this issue for the pictures of Churchill. For articles on Norris's preaching after his return from England, see photostatic copies of newspaper articles in *Fundamentalist,* 21 November 1941, 2 and 6, and 28 November 1941, 6.

87. For example, Norris would periodically include in the *Fundamentalist* pictures and brief stories about his sons' activities. See *Fundamentalist,* 2 April 1943, 7, and 3 Sept 1943, 3, for pictures of his sons J. Frank Jr., who was a lieutenant in the army and involved in recruiting, and Jim Gaddy Norris, who was in the navy.

88. "Army Evangelic Tour Planned by Dr. Norris," *Detroit News,* 13 December 1941, photostatic copy in *Fundamentalist,* 19 December 1941, 4; "67,602 Face Brick for Douglas MacArthur Temple," *Fundamentalist,* 27 February 1942, 1; "Auditorium at Camp Wolters under Direction of Rev. George Crittenden," *Fundamentalist,* 7 August 1942, 4; "Camp Wolters Tabernacle Finished and Paid For," *Fundamentalist,* 14 August 1942, 1; "The *Fundamentalist* Going to Army 10,000 Free Copies," *Fundamentalist,* 30 October 1942, 1; and "First Baptist and Temple Baptist in Fifty Thousand Dollar U.S. Bond Campaign," *Fundamentalist,* 13 November 1942, 1.

6. Sphinx

1. Norris, "The Meacham-Carr Graft on Taxpayers of Fort Worth," *Searchlight,* 9 July 1926, 15.

2. *Searchlight,* 16 July 1926, 1-2 and 5.

3. Entzminger, *Norris I Have Known,* 109; Russell, *Voices of American Fundamentalism,* 35.

4. "*Searchlight,* 23 July 1926, 1 and 5.

5. "Norris Weeps, Then Cool under Grilling, Fort Worth *Record-Telegram,* 22 January 1927, 1; "Norris Found Not Guilty, Weeps Aloud," Fort Worth *Record-Telegram,* 26 January 1927, 1. For the celebration following the trial see *Fundamentalist,* 15 July 1927, 1.

6. Luther Peak, oral memoir, transcript, Baylor University Institute for Oral History, 46-50, 197.

7. Ibid., 99.

8. Ibid., 193-196, 198, 71-72.

9. "Dr. Norris Admits He Plotted Disturbance at Baptist Convention," Fort Worth *Press,* 13 November 1947; photostatic copy in *Fundamentalist,* 21 November 1947, 3. This event was also covered in the Chicago *Tribune,* 13 November and the Dallas *News,* 12 November. See photostatic copies of these articles in *Fundamentalist,* 21 November 1947, 4 and 8. For Peak's recollection of this event see his oral memoir, 77-79. For more on Norris's attacks on Newton see chapter 7.

10. Peak to Whom It May Concern, 29 May 1950, Norris Papers; and "Tes-

timony of Dr. Luther C. Peak, Pastor of Central Baptist Church, Dallas," Norris Papers.

11. Norris to Peak, 17 May 1947; Peak to Norris, 28 October 1947; Norris to Peak, 30 March 1949; and Peak to Norris, 12 May 1949, Norris Papers.

12. Norris to Peak, 12 March 1951, Norris Papers.

13. "Peak Inauguration a Historical Week," *Fundamentalist*, 10 August 1951, 1.

14. Peak, oral memoir, 209-12. I cannot be sure if this event took place while Peak was president of the seminary or prior to this when Peak was merely teaching there. Although Peak did not indicate the year, however, it seems plausible that it was while he was president in that he felt he had the authority to put Lakin before the entire student body without Norris's permission. Lakin lived into the 1980s and was always considered a leading preacher in the Baptist Bible Fellowship, which split off from Norris's movement. Jerry Falwell counted Lakin as a major influence on his own ministry and in the early 1980s had Lakin preach occasionally on the *Old-Time Gospel Hour*.

15. Norris to Peak, 25 October 1951, Norris Papers; "Luther Peak Accepts First Church, *Fundamentalist*, 30 November 1951, 1. "Dr. Peak Takes Dr. Norris Post," Fort Worth *Star Telegram*, 19 November 1951, 1; and "Norris Turns First Baptist Over to Peak," Fort Worth *Star Telegram*, 19 November 1951, 1. There are clippings of these articles in Norris Papers. See also Peak, oral memoir, 79-80; and, Peak to Norris, 15 December 1951, Norris Papers. In this lengthy letter to Norris, Peak lays everything out in the open. Even though Peak was to be head pastor officially, he was hesitant to even assume that title, writing, "For the public, and for the psychological value, it is alright to call me the pastor. Actually I recognize that you are the guiding genius and director of the church and this is as it should be."

16. Peak, oral memoir, 80-82.

17. Peak to the Membership of First Baptist Church, 8 June 1952, Norris Papers.

18. Peak, oral memoir, 81-82

19. "Why We Left Fundamentalism to Work with Southern Baptists," *Baptist Standard*, 7 April 1956, 6-7.

20. Peak, oral memoir, 259 and 255.

21. Ibid.,, 225-26, 224.

22. Ibid., 315-24, 215.

23. Luther Peak to author, 2 February 1993.

24. G.B. Vick to Norris, 17 May 1950, Norris Papers, Texas Collection, Baylor University.

25. G.B. Vick and D.E. Dowell, interview by Royce Measures, 27 July 1973, Baylor University Institute for Oral History, tape BP79Z10D-1; G.B. Vick and Billy Bartlett, interview by Royce Measures, 28 February 1974, Baylor University Institute for Oral History, tape BP79Z10B-1; and G.B. Vick and John Rawlings, interview, 26 September 1973, Baylor University Institute for Oral History. Vick's charges of fiscal mismanagement are in the third source. When I used these tapes, they had not yet been transcribed.

26. G.B. Vick, interview, 26 July 1973, tape 1; G.B. Vick and D.E. Dowell, interview by Royce Measures, 27 July 1973, Baylor University Institute for Oral History, tape 1; G.B. Vick and Billy Bartlett, interview, 28 February 1974, tape 1;

and Vick to Norris, 17 May 1950, Norris Papers. For Norris's accusation that Vick was trying to cover up his daughter's marital infidelity see Norris to Vick, 23 June 1950, Norris Papers. For the cartoon of the sex case see "Crime against Nature," *Fundamentalist*, 11 August 1950, 3. On the same page was a photostatic copy of a court document from *State of Arizona v Charles Dyer*. The Phoenix document included a sworn statement from the arresting police officer saying that on 23 May 1949 Dyer "attempted to commit the act of sodomy on a young negro boy, John P. McGhee, the age of 13."

27. Both the forged letter and Vick's letter to William H. Crofts of Huntington, West Virginia, appear in a folder entitled simply "Vick, G.B., 1951." This folder appears in the microfilmed set of Norris's papers. As to how Norris got hold of Vick's letter to Crofts, one can only speculate. It is doubtful that Vick sent a copy to Norris because he claims in the letter that he has not written to Norris since May 1950. In keeping with this, Vick really washed his hands of Norris after the schism and seems to have ceased contact. If Vick wanted to challenge Norris on the forged letter, it seems that he would have written directly to Norris rather than sending him a copy of a letter to Crofts. It is possible that Crofts himself forwarded Vick's letter to Norris, perhaps seeking an explanation. As to the form letter that Vick sent out from Temple Baptist, it begins "Inasmuch as you have always seemed interested in our work, I am enclosing [a] copy of our Annual Report from which you can readily see that last year was the greatest in the history of our church." When I first read this letter, I thought that perhaps Vick had sent it to Norris either to show Norris that Temple was doing fine without him or in an honest effort to inform Norris about the progress of his old church. The fact that Norris kept his own forgery and the intercepted letter exposing it makes this whole affair especially curious.

28. George Norris to "Dear Friend," 26 January 1945, Norris File, Roberts Library, Southwestern Baptist Theological Seminary, Fort Worth. This letter details George's experience at First Baptist including his resignation. It appears to have been intended for the members of the church. See also item in file, October 1944, Norris Papers. This document is a transcript of some church proceeding having to do with George's departure. It reads like a trial transcript in which George is the defendant.

29. Norris to George Norris, 22 March 1940, Norris Papers.

30. Norris to George Norris, 23 March 1940, Norris Papers.

31. Norris to George, 9 January 1945, Norris Papers.

32. Norris to George, 24 January, 1945, Norris Papers.

33. Norris to George, 25 January 1945, Norris Papers.

34. Norris to George, 5 June 1945, Norris Papers.

35. Norris to George, 27 June 1940, Norris Papers.

36. G.B. Vick and John Rawlings, interview, 26 September 1973, Baylor University Institute for Oral History, tape BP79Z10C.

37. Ibid.

38. Quoted in Mark G. Toulouse, "A Case Study in Schism: J. Frank Norris and the Southern Baptist Convention," *Foundations* 24 (January-March 1981): 50.

39. W.A. Criswell, oral memoir, no. 1, 21, Texas Collection, Baylor University Institute for Oral History. Norris pumped Criswell in the *Fundamentalist*, portraying the young paster as a courageous fundamentalist who was taking up the battle against modernism. Norris was pleased that the premillennial

Criswell had replaced the postmillennial Truett. (Norris believed that anyone who was not a premillennialist was a postmillennialist.) See "Dr. W.A. Criswell a Man of Conviction and Courage," *Fundamentalist*, 24 September 1948, 1-2.

40. Norris to George Truett, 9 March 1940, Truett File, Roberts Library, Southwestern Baptist Theological Library, Fort Worth. The assistant who intercepted the letter was Robert H. Coleman. The Coleman family kept the letter for more than forty years before Coleman's grandson donated it to Southwestern Seminary.

41. Rufus Spain, interview by author, Waco, Texas, 20 September 1989.

42. The school is called the Norris Bible Baptist Institute and is advertised as "a preacher training institute dedicated to the memory of J. Frank Norris." The 1992 graduating class comprised ten students. See *Searchlight*, May 1992, 6 and 11.

43. Clovis Gwin Morris, who wrote a doctoral dissertation on Norris in the early seventies, once asked descendants of Norris's father-in-law about this story. It appears that J.M. Gaddy was not murdered by Norris or anyone else. Morris told me this in his office at Baylor University in 1990 or 1991.

44. James E. Wood Jr. of the J. M. Dawson Institute of Church-State Studies at Baylor told me this story. Wood did not claim to have heard such a broadcast, and he told the story in passing. While it may in fact be true, it has the ring of apocrypha to it as do many other such stories about Norris that float around Texas even today.

45. Norris to Coyle, 27 February 1947, Norris Papers. See also Smith to Norris, 19 January 1947; Smith to Norris, 18 January 1947; Smith to Norris, 22 January 1947, Norris Papers. As was often the case when Norris wrote to Coyle on religious matters, the businessman responded that he had no real opinion on the matter. At times he seemed puzzled as to why Norris even told him these things. See Coyle to Norris, 5 March 1947, Norris Papers.

46. *Fundamentalist*, 14 February 1947, 8.

47. Norris to Smith, 20 May 1947, Norris Papers.

48. See Smith to Norris, 21 February 1947; Norris to Smith, 27 February 1947; and Smith to Norris, 5 March 1947, Norris Papers.

49. For the criticism of Norris see Carl F. Page, Abilene, Texas, to Norris, 23 March 1947; S.A. Tyler, Baton Rouge, Louisiana, to Norris, 23 March 1947; and Mrs. Thomas M. Hutchins, Fort Worth, Texas, to Norris, 26 March 1947, Norris Papers. Smith's suggestions to Norris were in Smith to Norris, 25 March 1947, Norris Papers.

50. Norris to Smith, 3 June 1947, Norris Papers.

51. Smith to Norris, 7 June 1947; Smith to Norris, 11 June 1947, Norris Papers.

52. "'Jesus Christ Was Not a Jew'—Gerald L.K. Smith," *Fundamentalist*, 31 October 1947, 1.

53. Smith to Norris, 3 December 1947, Norris Papers.

54. *The Cross and the Flag*, January 1948, 5–6, 19.

55. Norris to Smith, 7 June 1948; Smith to Norris, 25 June 1948, Norris Papers.

56. Norris to Mrs. R.K. Campbell, 25 January 1947; Norris to Helen Gahagan Douglas, 1 February 1947, Norris Papers.

57. C.E. Overturf, Bird City, Kansas, to Norris, 18 June 1948, Norris

Papers. Overturf was a self-styled layman prophet who had written to Norris on at least one other occasion. Overturf recounted to Norris how he had traveled to California several years earlier to warn evangelist Aimee Semple MacPherson about her pending second marriage, and he claimed that had she listened to him, she would still be alive. Overturf was warning Norris to listen to his criticism concerning Congresswoman Douglas.

7. Anticommunist

1. For a discussion of anticommunism within fundamentalism see Pierard, *The Unequal Yoke*, 74-105; Erling Jorstad, *The Politics of Doomsday: Fundamentalists of the Far Right* (Nashville: Abingdon Press, 1970); and Ralph Lord Roy, *Apostles of Discord: A Study of Organized Bigotry and Disruption on the Fringes of Protestantism* (Boston: Beacon Press, 1953), 228-84.

2. "The Best Way to Fight Russia," *Searchlight*, 16 September 1920, 1 and 4.

3. *Searchlight*, 9 October 1920, 3. Palmer's raids had been based largely on the premise that Russian immigrants were anarchists or Bolshevik revolutionaries.

4. "Notes from Jacksonville on the Southern Baptist Convention," *Searchlight*, 2 June 1922, 1.

5. "Three to One Victory for Bone-Dry Prohibition," *Fundamentalist*, 1 August 1930, 1.

6. "The World-Wide Sweep of Russian Bolshevism and Its Relation to the Second Coming of Christ," *Fundamentalist*, 24 April 1931, 1.

7. "The Red Menace of Communism," *Fundamentalist*, 10 June 1932, 1 and 6.

8. Norris to Dr. W.S. Allen, Baylor University, 20 May 1932, Norris Papers.

9. "Why Temple Baptist Church Withdraws from Northern Baptist Convention," *Fundamentalist*, 12 July 1935, 2-4.

10. Ibid., 4 and 6.

11. Ibid., 2 and 4.

12. "What Shall Survive the Present World Conflict—For What Is a Man Profited If He Shall Gain the Whole World, and Lose His Own Soul," *Fundamentalist*, 9 August 1935, 2 and 6.

13. "Fundamentalist Baptists Start Nation-Wide Communistic Crusade," *Fundamentalist*, 19 July 1935, 1.

14. Dr. J. Frank Norris On 50,000-Watt Radio Station WJR, 750 Kilocycles," *Fundamentalist*, 4 October 1935, 1. For more on civil religion see Robert N. Bellah, *The Broken Covenant: American Civil Religion in Time of Trial* (New York: Seabury Press, 1975); and Bellah and Hammond, eds., *Varieties of Civil Religion*. Dealing specifically with evangelical Christianity and civil religion see Linder and Pierard, *Twilight of the Saints*.

15. "Why Temple Baptist Withdraws from the Northern Baptist Convention," 7.

16. "Ethiopia Stretches Forth Her Hands to God," *Fundamentalist*, 4 October 1935, 7.

17. "Sovietizing America through Churches, Colleges, and Consumers' Co-Operatives," *Fundamentalist*, 8 May 1936, 2.

18. *Fundamentalist*, 3 April 1936, 1.

19. "Sovietizing America through Churches, Colleges, and Consumers' Co-Operatives," 2 and 7.

20. "'While Men Slept the Enemy Sowed Tares'—Sovietizing Public Schools," *Fundamentalist*, 10 April 1936, 3; See *Fundamentalist*, 22 May 1936, 4, for Norris's attack on Kagawa; and *Fundamentalist*, 22 May 1936, 3, for a report on his competition with the Southern Baptist Convention. In the *Fundamentalist*, 27 May 1938, 3, Norris produced correspondence between himself and the superintendent of the Fort Worth schools in which the superintendent acknowledged that the book on communism had been removed.

21. *Fundamentalist*, 12 June 1936, 5.

22. "Why a Communist Cannot Take Oath of Office and Should Not Be Permitted to Testify in Court," *Fundamentalist*, 14 August 1936, 2-3.

23. This and other articles in the Buffalo newspapers were photostated and published in the *Fundamentalist*, 16 April 1937, 4.

24. Norris to Dr. Samuel McCrea Cavert, 24 October 1936; and Norris to Cavert, 2 January 1937, Norris Papers.

25. "The Conspiracy of John L. Lewis to Destroy Present Economic System and Become the Joseph Stalin of U.S.A.," *Fundamentalist*, 5 February 1937, 1.

26. *The Federal Council of Churches Unmasked* (n.p., n.d.), 5-8 and 12-13. The address that made up much of this booklet was given in February 1939 at Temple Baptist.

27. "American Civil Liberties Union and Federal Church Council," *Fundamentalist*, 29 January 1937, 1 and 4-5.

28. See *Fundamentalist*, 10 January 1947, 1; and Ralph Lord Roy, *Communism and the Churches* (New York: Harcourt, Brace, and World, 1960), 176-77.

29. "Is Louie Newton Stalin's Front Man in United States?" *Fundamentalist*, 18 April 1947, 1 and 3.

30. Norris to M.E. Coyle, Detroit, 9 April 1947; Norris to Coyle, 19 April 1947, Norris Papers. Quote in second letter. Coyle, a Roman Catholic, responded that it was difficult for him to appraise the situation in the SBC. See Coyle to Norris, 16 April 1947, Norris Papers.

31. See "Baptist Meeting Thrown in Disorder as Rev. Frank Norris Makes Query," Atlanta *Journal Constitution*, 7 May 1947, 1-2; photostatic copy in *Fundamentalist*, 16 May 1947, 3.

32. "Dr. Norris Admits He Plotted Disturbance at Baptist Convention," Fort Worth *Press*, 13 November 1947, 1; photostatic copy in *Fundamentalist*, 21 November 1947, 3. This event was also covered in the Chicago *Tribune*, 13 November and in the Dallas *News* 12 November. See *Fundamentalist*, 21 November 1947, 4 and 8, for photostatic copies of those articles.

33. Norris to Coyle, 12 May 1947, Norris Papers.

34. Norris to Rayburn, 29 May 1947; and Norris to Rev. W. Clay Wilson, Elizabethton, Tenn., 29 May 1947, Norris Papers. In the letter to Rayburn he did not mention that he wished to expose the SBC, but rather said he wished to expose prominent clergymen who were attempting to smear Truman on the issue of an ambassador to the Vatican.

35. Norris to Coyle, 29 May 1947, Norris Papers.

36. Norris to John Rankin, Washington D.C., 9 June 1947, Norris Papers.

37. "Dr. Newton to Be Investigated," *Fundamentalist*, 2 May 1947, 1; and "Worse and More of It—Louie Newton Now Confirms His Sympathetic Attitude toward Sovietism," *Fundamentalist*, 18 July 1947, 1.

38. "They Are All Out for Aid to Russia, Even Large Loans," *Fundamentalist*, 23 August 1946, 1; "Differences between Southern Baptists and Fundamental Baptists," *Fundamentalist*, 30 July 1948, 1 and 5; and "Open Letter To Southwestern Seminary, Dr. E.D. Head and Baptist Pastors," *Fundamentalist*, 27 August 1948, 1.

39. "Norris Flays Education Groups, Some Clerics as Red-Tinged," Abilene *Reporter News*, n.d.; photostatic copy in *Fundamentalist*, 15 April 1949, 2; and "'Texas Legislature Recognizes the Public Services Rendered by Dr. Norris,'" *Fundamentalist*, 6 May 1949, 10.

40. Fort Worth *Star Telegram*, 24 October 1948, sec. 2, 16; photostatic copy in *Fundamentalist*, 29 October 1948, 4-5.

41. " 'He That Sitteth in the Heavens Shall Laugh,'" *Fundamentalist*, 23 November 1945, 5.

42. Norris to Coyle, 27 February 1947; Norris to Coyle, 1 April 1947; Norris to Coyle, 2 July 1947; Norris to Coyle, 10 December 1947, Norris Papers. The quotation is in the 10 December letter.

43. "The Pitiful and Discredited Leaders of the Once Powerful Southern Baptist Machine Have Failed to Divert Attention of the People by Dragging Red Herring of Roman Catholicism across Trail," *Fundamentalist*, 4 July 1947, 1; "Pope Meets Baptist Ministers," New York *Sun*, 5 September 1947; photostatic copy in *Fundamentalist*, 19 September 1947, 4.

44. *Fundamentalist*, 17 October 1947, 1.

45. See "Dr. T.T. Shields Makes Bitter Attack on Dr. J. Frank Norris—the Real, Long Standing, Hidden Motive Will Be Given at a Later Date," *Fundamentalist*, 10 October 1947, 1 and 6.

46. "Halt Loans to British, Pastor Urges," Fort Worth *Star Telegram*, 6 October 1947, 2; photostatic copy in *Fundamentalist*, 17 October 1947, 6.

47. "Pope Meets Baptist Ministers," New York *Sun*, 5 September 1947; photostatic copy in *Fundamentalist*, 19 September 1947, 4.

48. Norris to Truman, 23 January 1950, Norris Papers.

49. See Carl McIntire, "Truman Violates Constitution and Appoints Ambassador to Rome," *Fundamentalist*, 2 November 1951, 1; and "Shall the United States Have an Ambassador to the Vatican?" *Fundamentalist*, 15 February 1952, 4. Although these articles are by McIntire, it is safe to say that Norris approved of their content. He had been praising McIntire in print consistently at the time these articles appeared. Also, Norris never printed an argument with which he disagreed unless he was setting it up for an attack of his own.

50. Jimmy Caston, "Most Triumphant Meeting in Texas Legislature," *Fundamentalist*, 29 April 1949, 1.

51. "Texas Legislature Recognizes the Public Services Rendered by Dr. Norris," 2.

52. Ibid., 6 and 12.

53. "The Coming Conflagration and Why Russia Is Doomed," *Fundamentalist*, 29 September 1950, 1.

54. See Noel Smith, "Hiss Is Not the Guiltiest of the Traitors," *Fundamentalist*, 10 February 1950, 2.

55. Norris to Connally, 3 May 1950, Norris Papers.

56. Connally to Norris, 8 May 1950, Norris Papers.

57. Norris to Joseph McCarthy, 18 July 1952, Norris Papers.

58. "'The New Deal Must Be Salvaged,'" *Fundamentalist,* 19 January 1940, 5.

59. See chapter 5 for Norris's support for FDR's war preparedness campaign and wartime policies.

60. See Herbert Brownell Jr. to Norris, 24 August 1944; and Brownell to Norris, 25 August 1944, Norris Papers. Brownell was chairman of the Republican National Committee. He wrote to thank Norris for his offer of support for Dewey.

61. Norris to Sam Rayburn, 29 May 1947, Norris Papers.

62. "Frank Norris Resolves to Back President Truman, v., Henry Wallace and Louie Newton," Fort Worth *Commercial Signal,* 18 April 1947, 1; photostatic copy in *Fundamentalist,* 2 May 1947, 5.

63. Norris to M.E. Coyle, 3 April 1948, Norris Papers.

64. Norris to Dewey, 28 June 1948, Norris Papers.

65. Norris to Dewey, 15 October 1948, Norris Papers.

66. Norris to Dewey, 25 October 1948, Norris Papers.

67. Norris to Truman, 22 January 1947, Norris Papers.

68. Norris to Truman, 22 June 1948, Norris Papers.

69. Norris to Truman, 15 July 1948, Norris Papers.

70. Norris to Truman, 15 September 1948, Norris Papers.

71. Norris to Coyle, 1 November 1948, Norris Papers.

72. On Norris's loss of memory, my source is Bill Carden of Waco, Texas, interview by author, 10 September 1989. Carden was a child in the 1940s when his parents left First Baptist Fort Worth to become charter members of George Norris's church, Gideon Baptist in Fort Worth. Years later when Carden had grown to adulthood, George Norris told him that his father had suffered memory loss and even hallucinations in his later years. Homer Ritchie recalls that Norris's health problems and irrational behavior began in the late 1940s. Homer Ritchie, interview by author, tape recording, Fort Worth, 26 May 1992.

73. Norris to Connally, 2 December 1948, Norris Papers.

74. Norris to Coyle, 7 March 1949, Norris Papers.

75. Norris to Truman, 27 March 1950, Norris Papers.

76. Norris to James M. Byrnes (governor of South Carolina), 30 November 1951, Norris Papers.

77. Norris to Bruce Cogle, Dixon Mills, Alabama, 17 December 1951, Norris Papers.

78. Norris to Connally, 20 December 1951, Norris Papers. Earlier Norris had defended Truman against criticism from Baptist leaders on the Vatican ambassador issue.

79. Norris to Wingate Lucas, 15 January 1952, Norris Papers. Lucas was a supporter of Norris, having written a week earlier to Norris, "You are to be commended for the forthright attitude you are taking in an effort to preserve our people's liberties. You make me proud to be your representative."

80. Norris to Rayburn, 15 January 1952; Norris to Kefauver, 24 January 1952; and Norris to Harriman, 1 June 1952, Norris Papers.

81. Norris to Truman, 14 May 1952, Norris Papers.

82. Norris to Truman, 2 July 1952; and William D. Bassett to Norris, 12 July 1952, Norris Papers.

83. Norris to Bruce Cogle, 17 December 1951; Norris to Senator Richard Byrd, 23 July 1952; Norris to Congressman Judd, 10 July 1952; and Norris to Senator John Lodge, 10 July 1952, Norris Papers.

84. Norris to Eisenhower, 10 July 1952; Norris to Eisenhower, 11 July 1952; Norris to Eisenhower, 13 July 1952; Norris to Eisenhower, 16 July 1952; Norris to Richard Nixon, 12 July 1952; and Norris to Nixon, 5 August 1952, Norris Papers.

85. "Eisenhower for President," *Fundamentalist*, 18 July 1952, 1-2; "Landslide Texas Election for Dwight D. Eisenhower," *Fundamentalist*, 1 August 1952, 1-2

86. "Eisenhower to Enlarge Social Security Program," *Fundamentalist*, 15 August 1952, 3.

87. "Eisenhower's Platform—God, Home and Mother," *Fundamentalist*, 8 August 1952, 1-4; and William Fraser, "Dr. Norris' Visit with General Eisenhower," *Fundamentalist*, 8 August 1952, 1.

8. The Race Card

1. *Baptist Message*, 29 June 1995, 11. The text of the resolution can be found in many state Baptist newspapers. For a discussion of the founding of the SBC and the issue of slavery see H. Leon McBeth, *The Baptist Heritage: Four Centuries of Baptist Witness* (Nashville: Broadman Press, 1987), 382-83. McBeth wrote, "Slavery is the main issue that led to the 1845 schism [between Northern and Southern Baptists]; that is a blunt historical fact" (382).

2. John Lee Eighmy, *Churches in Cultural Captivity* (Knoxville: Univ. of Tennessee Press, 1972), 115.

3. Quoted in Andrew Michael Manis, *Southern Civil Religions in Conflict* (Athens: Univ. of Georgia Press, 1987), 30.

4. "Shots on the Wing," *Searchlight*, 28 August 1925, 1.

5. "The Earmarks of the Beast," *Searchlight*, 2 October 1925, 4.

6. "All Hail Senator Simmons of North Carolina," *Fundamentalist*, 1 June 1928, 1.

7. "Six Thousand Dallasites Enthusiastically Cheer," *Fundamentalist*, 24 August 1924, 2.

8. "Al Smith and the Negro," *Fundamentalist*, 19 October, 1928, 6.

9. Ibid.

10. *Fundamentalist*, 19 October 1928, 1; and *Fundamentalist*, 26 October 1928, 1 and 6. See also Norris to Senator Pat Harrison, New York, 14 October 1928, Norris Papers.

11. "When the Wicked Beareth Rule The People Mourn," *Fundamentalist*, 28 June 1929, 2.

12. "Judge Wilson, K.C.'s Ku Klux Klan and Bootleggers," *Searchlight*, May 12, 1922, 1.

13. John Boles, *The South through Time: A History of an American Region* (Englewood Cliffs, N.J.: Prentice Hall, 1995), 425.

14. H.W. Evans, "Tammany—Model Political Graft Machine," *Fundamentalist*, 4 May 1928, 5. For Norris's criticism and praise for the Klan see "Sermon Delivered Sunday Night to Audience of Ten Thousand," *Searchlight*, 1 August 1924, 3; editorial, *Searchlight*, 29 August 1924, 2; and "Should the Ku Klux Klan Be Issue among Texas Baptists?" *Searchlight*, 26 September 1924, 3-4.

15. "Should the Ku Klux Klan Be Issue among Texas Baptists?"

16. "Sermon Delivered Sunday Night to Audience of Ten Thousand."

17. Norris to Dr. W.S. Allen, Baylor University, 20 May 1932, Norris Papers.

18. "Why a Communist Cannot Take Oath of Office and Should Not Be Permitted to Testify in Court," *Fundamentalist*, 14 August 1936, 2-3.

19. "'Texas Legislature Recognizes the Public Services Rendered by Dr. Norris," 10.

20. *Fundamentalist*, 26 May 1950, 1.

21. *Fundamentalist*, 14 February 1947, 8.

22. *Searchlight*, 29 April 1920, 2.

23. "Landslide in Texas Election for Dwight D. Eisenhower," *Fundamentalist*, 1 August 1952, 2.

24. Luther Peak, oral memoir, transcript, Baylor University Institute for Oral History, 315-24.

25. Samuel S. Hill Jr., *Southern Churches in Crisis* (New York: Holt, Rinehart, and Winston, 1966), 173.

26. Trollinger, *God's Empire*, 62-82.

27. Timothy Weber, *Living in the Shadow of the Second Coming*, 185-203.

28. See William Martin, *A Prophet with Honor: The Billy Graham Story* (New York: William Morrow, 1991), 172.

Conclusion

1. "Every Hand That's Been Lifted against the First Baptist Church Has Failed to Prosper," *Fundamentalist*, 9 February 1945, 3 and 6.

2. Some political commentators have applied this parade imagery to contemporary politicians. It also seems apt for a figure like Norris.

3. See Alan Brinkley, *Voices of Protest*, xi. For other examples of right-wing extremists see Ribuffo, *The Old Christian Right*.

4. George Marsden, *Understanding Fundamentalism and Evangelicalism*, 178.

5. The observation that fundamentalism is essentially Manichaean is usually attributed to Richard Hofstadter, *Anti-Intellectualism in American Life*, 135. Neo-evangelical theologican Edward G. Carnell identified what he considered the cultic tendencies in fundamentalism in his book *The Case for Orthodox Theology* (Philadelphia: Westminster Press, 1959), 113-26. For Marsden's discussion of Machen see *Understanding Fundamentalism and Evangelicalism*, 183.

6. See Marsden, *Reforming Fundamentalism*.

7. Without reference to particular fundamentalist leaders, Marsden observes the southward shift of fundamentalism in "From Fundamentalism to Evangelicalism," in *The Evangelicals*, 147.

Index

DATE DUE

APR 1 4 2001		
MAR 0 4 2005		
APR 3 0 2009		

Demco, Inc. 38-293

The
Oratorio Anthology

Soprano

Compiled and Edited by Richard Walters

Assistant Editors: Elaine Schmidt, Laura Ward
Historical Consultant: Virginia Saya

On the cover: André Derain, French, *The Last Supper*, oil on canvas, 1911, 226.7 x 288.3 cm,
Gift of Mrs. Frank R. Lillie, 1946.339. © 1993, The Art Institute of Chicago, All Rights Reserved.

ISBN 0-7935-2505-5

HAL•LEONARD
CORPORATION
7777 W. BLUEMOUND RD. P.O. BOX 13819 MILWAUKEE, WI 53213

Contents

Notes and Translations

Johann Sebastian Bach
1685-1750

CANTATA No. 21
Ich hatte viel Bekümmernis
(I had a great affliction)
BWV 21
c1714 (or before; the date of composition is uncertain)
text attributed to Salomo Franck (1659-1715), based on I Peter 5:6-11, and Luke 15:1-10 (the Luther German Bible)

Possibly first performed June 17, 1714, the third Sunday of Trinity in the church year. The aria describes the pain of an anguished heart which can only be comforted by the peace of God.

Seufzer, Thränen, Kummer, Noth   *[Sighing, weeping, sorrow, need]*

Seufzer, Thränen, Kummer, Noth,	*Sighs, tears, grief, distress,*
ängstlich Sehnen,	*nervously watching,*
Furcht und Tod	*fear and death*
nagen mein beklemmtes Herz,	*gnaw at my anguished heart,*
ich empfinde Jammer, Schmerz.	*I feel misery, pain.*

CANTATA No. 68
Also hat Gott die Welt geliebt
(Thus has God loved the world)
BWV 68
1725
text possibly by M. von Ziegler (to whom the cantata is dedicated), based on Acts 10:42-48, and John 3:16-21 (the Luther German Bible)

The church cantata was first performed on Whit Monday, May 21, 1725, in Leipzig. The music for "Mein gläubiges Herze" is an enlarged arrangement of "Weil die wollenreichen Herden" from Bach's secular cantata *Was mir behagt, ist nur die muntre Jagd* (lost).

Mein gläubiges Herze   *[My heart ever faithful]*

Mein gläubiges Herze,	*My faithful heart,*
frohlokke, sing', scherze,	*rejoice, sing, make merry,*
dein Jesus ist nah!	*your Jesus is near!*
Weg Jammer,	*Away misery,*
weg Klagen,	*away complaining,*
ich will euch nur sagen	*to you I will say only*
mein Jesus ist da.	*my Jesus is here.*

Dates throughout are for first performances unless otherwise noted. The bracketed aria titles are those used when performing the singing English translation found in the musical score. The notes in this section are by the editor.

MAGNIFICAT

BWV 243a and 243

1723

text taken from Luke 1:46-55, from the Vulgate (the 4th century, authorized Roman Catholic Latin translation of Bible); besides these verses a Magnificat (the canticle of the Virgin) traditionally includes two additional verses of the Lesser Doxology "Gloria Patri et Filio"

Composed for Bach's first Christmas in Leipzig. It was later revised (c1728-1731) and transposed from E-flat to D. The revision replaces recorders with flutes and omits 4 interpolated hymns (laudes), which had previously rendered the text appropriate to the Christmas season. The revised Magnificat was possibly first performed July 2, 1733 for the Feast of the Visitation of Mary. The Magnificat was sung in German for Sunday vespers, and in Latin on Christmas Day.

Quia respexit

This is the third movement of the revised Magnificat (fourth movement of the original version). The text is based on Luke 1:48. Scored for oboe and continuo.

Quia respexit humilitatem	*For he has regarded the low estate*
ancillæ suæ:	*of his handmaiden:*
ecce enim ex hoc beatam me	*behold, for from this time,*
dicent .	*may I be called blessed.*

PASSIO SECUNDUM JOANNEM

(Johannes-Passion/St. John Passion)

BWV 245

1724

libretto based primarily on *Der für die Sünden der Welt gemarterte und sterbende Jesus* (Jesus tortured and dying for the sins of the world) by Barthold Heinrich Brockes (1712), with some additional free texts from a 1704 Passion libretto by Christian Heinrich Postel (free text refers to poetry that is not an adaptation or paraphrase of Scripture), with adaptations and additional material by the composer

Composed in 1723, the Passion was first performed on Good Friday, April 7, 1724 at Thomaskirche, Leipzig. The piece was revised, with additions, deletions and substitutions, for performances in 1725, but basically restored to the original version for performances in c1730 and 1740. A Passion is a musical setting of Jesus' sufferings and death as related by one of the four Gospel writers. Brockes' libretto, cited above, was the most often set of Passion librettos by composers in the 18th century.

Ich Folge dir gleichfalls   *[I follow Thee also]*

From Part I (no. 13), the aria is scored for flute (or flutes) and continuo; a free text, largely unaltered from Brockes' libretto. The aria relates Simon Peter's feelings as he follows the bound Jesus, being led away to the high priest, Annas.

Ich folge dir gleichfalls	*I follow you also*
mit freudigen Schritten	*with joyful steps*
und lasse dich nicht,	*and leave you not,*
mein Leben, mein Licht.	*my life, my light.*
Befördre den Lauf	*Hasten the flow*
und höre nicht auf,	*and stop not*
selbst an mir zu ziehen,	*to draw me to yourself*
zu schieben, zu bitten.	*to lead, to intercede.*

Zerfliesse, mein Herze   *[My heart breaks in anguish]*

From Part II (no. 63), scored for flutes, oboes da caccia, and continuo. The free text is from Brocke's libretto. A song of sorrow following the death of Jesus. Bach borrowed from the Gospels of Matthew and Mark, quoting their mention of the temple veil tearing and the earth quaking. This aria follows, at the point where both Gospels mention Mary Magdalene and Mary the mother of Jesus looking on from afar.

Zerfliesse, mein Herze,	*Dissolve, my heart,*
in Fluten der Zähren	*in floods of tears*
dem Höchsten zu Ehren!	*the Highest to honor!*
Erzähle der Welt	*Tell the world*
und dem Himmel die Not:	*and heaven the sorrow:*
Dein Jesus ist tot!	*Your Jesus is dead!*

5

PASSIO SECUNDUM MATTHÆUM

(Matthäus-Passion/St. Matthew Passion)

BWV 244

1727 or 1729

libretto by Picander, a pseudonym for Christian Friedrich Henrici (1700-1764); it is probable that the free text poems only were by Henrici (free text refers to poetry that is not a paraphrase or adaptation directly from Scripture), with biblical narrative from the Gospel of Matthew and some chorale texts by the composer

The date of first performance of the Passion is in dispute, occuring at Thomaskirche, Leipzig, on either April 11, 1727 or April 15, 1729. A revised version was performed March 30, 1736. A Passion is a musical setting of Jesus' sufferings and death as related by one of the four Gospel writers

Blute nur du liebes Herz   *[Bleed and break, thou loving heart]*

From Part I (no. 12), scored for flues, strings and continuo. A lament for the mother of Judas Iscariot, following the announcement of his intent to betray Jesus.

Blute nur,	*Only bleed,*
du liebes Herz!	*you beloved heart!*
Ach! ein Kind,	*Oh, a child*
das du erzogen,	*that you brought up,*
das an deiner Brust gesogen,	*that nursed at your breast,*
droht den Pfleger zu ermorden,	*threatens to murder the guardian*
denn es ist zur	*for (the child) has*
Schlange worden.	*become the serpent.*

Ich will dir mein Herze schenken   *[Lord, to Thee my heart is given]*

From Part I (no. 19), scored for 2 oboes d'amore and continue. An expression of eternal love between Christ and his disciples, following the institution of the Eucharist.

Wiewohl mein Herz in Tränen schwimmt,	*Although my heart swims in tears,*
dass Jesus von mir Abschied nimmt,	*that Jesus departs from me,*
so macht mich doch sein Testament erfreut:	*I am still delighted by His Testament:*
Sein Fleisch und Blut,	*His flesh and blood,*
o Kostbarkeit,	*O precious gift,*
vermacht er mir in meine Hände.	*He bequeaths into my hands.*
Wie er es auf der Welt	*As he was in the world*
mit denen Seinen nicht böse können meinen,	*with those He could never intend to harm,*
so liebt er sie bis an das Ende.	*so He loves them until the end.*
Ich will dir mein Herze schenken,	*I will give you my heart,*
senke dich,	*lower yourself,*
mein Heil, hinein!	*my salvation, there in!*
Ich will mich in dir versenken;	*I lose myself in you;*
ist dir gleich die Welt zu klein,	*as for you the world is too small*
ei so sollst du mir allein	*so, to me, are you alone*
mehr als Welt und Himmel sein.	*more than earth and heaven.*

WEIHNACHTS-ORATORIUM

(Christmas Oratorio)
BWV 248
1734-1735
text attributed to Picander, a pseudonym for Christian Friedrich Henrici (1700-1764); based on Luke 2:1, 3-12, and Matthew 1:1-12 (the Luther German Bible)

The Weihnachts-Oratorium is actually a collection of six individual church cantatas, designed to be performed at each of the six church events between Christmas and Epiphany. The piece contains newly composed music and adaptations from three secular cantatas (BWV 213-215). The first cantata was first performed on Christmas Day, 1734 at Thomaskirche, Leipzig. The remaining cantatas followed in order on the second and third days following Christmas, on New Year's Day (Feast of the Circumcision), on the Sunday after New Year, and on the Feast of the Epiphany. Performances took place at both Thomaskirche and Nikolaikirche, Leipzig.

Nur ein Wink von seinem Händen   *[Naught against the pow'r]*

From Part 6 (the sixth cantata), Feast of the Epiphany, based on Matthew 2;7-12. A warning to King Herod, who has sent wise men to search for the baby Jesus. He has hidden his intention to kill the child, professing a desire to worship the baby king.

Du Falscher, suche nur den Herrn zu fällen,
nimm alle falsche List, dem Heiland nachzustellen;
der, desen Kraft kein Mensch ermisst,
bleibt doch in sichrer Hand.
Dein Herz, dein falsches Herz ist schon,
nebst aller seiner List, des Höchsten Sohn,
den du zu stürzen suchst, sehr wohl bekannt.

You false one, who seeks only the Lord to fell,
take all false cunning to waylay the Savior;
He whose strength no one can measure
remains after all in safe hand.
Your heart, your false heart is already,
together with all your cunning, to the Highest's Son,
whom you seek to fell, very well known.

Nur ein Wink von seinen Händen
stürzt ohnmächtger Menschen Macht,
Hier wird alle Kraft verlacht!
Spricht der Höchste nur ein Wort,
seiner Feinde Stolz zu enden,
o, so müssen sich sofort
Sterblicher Gedanken wenden.

Only a wave from His hands
dashes powerless humanity's might,
here will all strengh be derided!
Speaks the hightest only a word,
his enemy's pride to end,
oh, thus must mortals immediately
change their thoughts.

Ludwig van Beethoven
1770-1827

CHRISTUS AM ÖLBERGE

(Christ on the Mount of Olives)
Opus 85
1803
libretto by Franz Xaver Huber, based on the Gospel accounts of Jesus in the Garden of Gethsemane

First performed April 5, 1803 at the Theater am Wien (Vienna). Revised 1804-1811. The aria is presented in the final form.

Preist des Erlösers Güte

The soprano sings the role of a Seraph who appears to Christ in the Garden of Gethsemane, revealing to him his fate.

Erzittre Erde,	*Tremble, earth,*
Jehova's Sohn liegt hier!	*God's Son lies here!*
sein Antlitz tief in Staub gedrückt,	*his face deep in dust depressed,*
vom Vater ganz verlassen,	*by the Father entirely abandoned,*
und leidet unnennbare Qual.	*and suffers unutterable torment.*
Der Gütige!	*The benevolent one!*
er ist bereit,	*He is willing,*
den martervollsten Tod	*a martyr's death*
zu sterben, damit die Menschen,	*to die, so that the people,*
die er liebt,	*that he loves,*
vom Tode auferstehen	*from death arise*
und ewig leben!	*and eternally live.*

Preist des Erlösers Güte,	*Praise the Redeemer's kindness,*
preist Menschen preist seine Huld!	*People praise thy favor!*
Er stirbt für euch aus Liebe,	*He dies for you out of love,*
sein Blut tilgt eure Schuld.	*His blood wipes out your guilt.*
O Heil euch! ihr Erlösten,	*O rejoice! you redeemed,*
euch winket Seeligkeit,	*you receive bliss,*
Wenn ihr getreu in Liebe,	*when you constant in love,*
in Glaub' und Hoffnung seid.	*in faith and hope remain.*
Doch weh! die frech entehren	*But woe the impudent, dishonoring*
sas Blut, das für sie floss,	*the blood that for them flowed,*
sie trifft der Fluch des Richters,	*they meet with the curse of the judge,*
Verdammung ist ihr Loos.	*damnation is their lot.*

Gabriel Fauré

1845-1924

REQUIEM

Opus 48

1888

text is from the traditional Latin Requiem Mass of the Roman Catholic liturgy; Requiem ("rest") is a Mass for the dead

The manuscript is dated 1887. First performance at the Church of the Madeleine, Paris, January 16, 1888. Revisions and additions made 1887-1890 and in 1893. The first version (scored for violas, cellos, basses, harp, timpani, organ, and violin solo) included a boy choir and boy soloist, and consisted of five movements: Introit et Kyrie, Sanctus, Pie Jesu, Agnus Dei, and In Paradisum. The 1893 version adds the Offertoire and Libera me and includes adult soloists and brass. The 1900 revision and orchestration expands to full orchestra, adding more strings as well as woodwinds. Fauré's Requiem does not conform to the liturgical requirements of the Roman Catholic Church. The Dies Irae is omitted, except for the last two lines, which appear as the Pie Jesu.

Pie Jesu

Pie Jesu Domine,	*Holy Jesus Lord,*
Dona eis requiem,	*Give them rest,*
sempiternam requiem.	*eternal rest.*

George Frideric Handel

1685-1759

JEPHTHA

1752

libretto by Thomas Morell (1703-1784), quoting and paraphrasing Judges 11, *Jephthes Sive Votum* (1554) by G. Buchanan, Milton's "Nativing Ode," Addison's "The Campaign," and John Pope's "Essay on Man"

First performance at the Theatre Royal at Covent Garden, London, February 26, 1752. *Jephtha* was revived in 1758 "with new additions and alterations." The oratorio is based on the story of the Jews' defeat of the Ammonites.

Tune the soft melodious flute

From Act II. In praying for victory, Jephtha has made a vow to sacrifice whoever comes through the doors of his house upon his return if God allows him to win the battle. He returns victorious. Iphis, his daughter, is the first to appear from his house, singing "Tune the soft melodious flute." The aria was one of the additions made for the 1758 Covent Garden revival.

JOSHUA

1748

libretto by Thomas Morell (1703-1784), based on the book of Joshua

Composed July and August, 1747. First performance took place March 9, 1748 at Theatre Royal at Covent Garden, London. The oratorio tells the story of the Jewish conquest of Canaan under the leadership of Joshua.

Oh! had I Jubal's lyre

The aria is sung in Act III by Achsas, Caleb's daughter, declaring her love for her fiancé Othaniel, a young chieftan. Handel originally composed the melody in his teens, and it was first used in *Psalm Laudate Pueri* of 1702.

JUDAS MACCABÆUS

1747

libretto by Thomas Morell (1703-1784), based on the book of the Maccabees and the twelfth book of Josephus' *Antiquities of the Jews*

Commissioned by Frederic, Prince of Wales. First performed at the Theatre Royal at Covent Garden, April 1, 1747. Revisions and additions were made for frequent new productions, in 1748, then annually from 1750 through 1759. The oratorio relates the restoration of liberty to the Jews under leader Judas Maccabæus.

O liberty, thou choicest treasure

This aria is found in the conductor's score in the composer's handwriting, and the music had first appeared in Handel's *Occasional Oratorio* (1746). As Judas appeals to the patriotism of the Jews to rouse them in battle, an Israelite woman extols the virtues of liberty.

MESSIAH

1742

text by Charles Jennens (1700-1773), drawn from various biblical sources and the Prayer Book Psalter

Composed between August 22 and September 12, 1741. First performed April 13, 1742 at the Music Hall on Fishamble Street, Dublin. The performance was a benefit for several of the city's charities. The libretto is drawn from the Prophets, the Gospels, the Pauline Epistles, and Revelation, detailing the prophecy of Christ's coming, his life, death resurrection, promise of second coming, and the response of believers. *Messiah* is theological in nature, not the more common dramatic Handelian oratorio. The soloists are impersonal, and the chorus assumes an expanded role as commentators. Many changes and additions were made in the oratorio, with 13 revisions of the score in the years 1743-1759. Many of the solo movements were sometimes sung by different voice types in different versions and keys, a practice the composer directed.

Rejoice greatly, O daughter of Zion

From Part I. The text is based on Zechariah 9:9-10. The aria was originally written in 12/8 meter, and was re-composed in 4/4, probably in 1750. The 4/4 version was used exclusively from that time forward by Handel.

I know that my Redeemer liveth

From Part III. The text is based on Job 19:25-26, the words of Job, who is in the depths of despair when sunlight breaks through the clouds, and on I Corinthians 15:20. Though the aria was never fully recomposed, text underlay was variously altered.

If God be for us

From Part III. The text is based on Romans 8:31, 33-34. Though originally composed for soprano, the aria was actually transposed for alto for the first performance in 1742. It was first sung in the original soprano version in 1749.

SAMSON
1743
libretto adapted by Newburgh Hamilton from Milton's *Samson Agonistes* and other poems

Composed 1741. First performed February 18, 1743, at the Theatre Royal at Covent Garden, London. Additions and revisions were made for performances in 1745 and 1754. The oratorio relates the story from Judges, with the addition of the character of Micah.

Let the bright Seraphim

From Act III. Samson has just pulled down the Philistine temple, and has perished with his enemies in the rubble. Samson's father asks the Israelites to stop mourning and rejoice in his son's heroism. An Israelite woman sings joyfully of the angels united in their praise of Samson. In the context of the complete oratorio the aria has no *da capo*, but an excerpted performance requires one to complete the form of the music. There is a prominent solo trumpet obbligato in the orchestra part (provided in this edition).

Franz Joseph Haydn
1732-1809

DIE JAHRESZEITEN
(The Seasons)
1801
libretto by Baron Gottfried van Swieten after "The Seasons," a lengthy pastoral poem by James Thomson, translated into German by Barthold Heinrich Brockes

Begun in 1799, the oratorio was first performed May 20, 1801. Under Haydn's direction and consent, a singing English translation by Swieten (adapting the original poem by Thomson) was included in the first edition of the oratorio, published in 1802 by Breikopf & Härtel. (A German-French edition was also released at the same time.) The aria below is from Summer.

Welche Labung für die Sinne   *[Oh how pleasing]*

Wilkommen jetzt, o dunkler Hain,   *Welcome now, o shady grove,*
wo der bejahrten Eiche Dach   *where the aged oak dome*
den kühlenden Schirm gewährt,   *which cooling shelter has been,*
und wo der schlanken Espe Laub   *and where the slim Aspen leaves*
mit leisem Gelispel rauscht!   *with faint whisper rustle!*

Am weichen Moose rieselt da   *On the soft moss trickles here*
in heller Flut der Bach,   *in clear flood the brook,*
und frölich summend irrt und wirrt   *and cheerful hum, confused and jumbled,*
die bunte Sonnenbrut.   *the bright colored sun-brood.*
Der Kräuter reinen Balsam-duft   *The herbs clean balmy-scent*
verbreitet Zephirs Hauch,   *spread Zephyr's breath,*
und aus dem nahen Busche tönt   *and from the nearby thicket sounds*
des jungen Schäfers Rohr.   *the young shepherds reed-flute.*

Welche Labung für die Sinne!	*What refreshment for the senses!*
Welch' Erholung für das Herz!	*What recovery for the heart!*
Jeden Aderzweig durchströmet,	*Through each vein streams,*
und in jeder Nerve bebt	*and in each nerve shakes*
erquikkendes, erquikkendes Gefühl.	*revived, revived feeling.*
Die Seele wachet auf	*The soul awakes*
zum reizenden Genuss,	*to the enticing pleasure,*
und neue Kraft erhebt	*and new strength uplifts*
durch milden Drang die Brust.	*by gentle pressure, the breast.*

DIE SCHÖPFUNG
Ein Oratorium für jeden Geschmack und jede Zeit

THE CREATION

An Oratorio for All Tastes and Times

1798

libretto attributed to T. Linley or Lidley (sources are unclear about his name), translated from the original English to German and abridged by Baron Gottfried van Swieten, based on chapters from Genesis, selected Psalms, and paraphrases of Milton's *Paradise Lost*

Composition began in 1796. A first, private performance of the oratorio was given April 30, 1798 at the Schwartzenberg Palais (preceded by an open rehearsal April 29). First public performance given March 19, 1799. Haydn composed the piece in German, but the English version followed quickly, being basically the original libretto adapted by Swieten. (One of the primary manuscript scores used by Haydn to conduct has both German and English.) English was included in the first published edition, 1800. Since it was the composer's intention that the piece be heard in English in English-speaking countries, in the editor's opinion that is the appropriate language in those locales.

In 1801 Haydn composed a Mass in B-flat that is known as *Schöpfungmesse* (Creation Mass), but this piece is entirely different from the oratorio *Die Schöpfung*. (In the "qui tollis" of the mass Haydn quotes from the oratorio *Die Schöpfung*.)

Nun beut die Flur   *[With verdure clad]*

From Part I. In the recitative Gabriel, the soprano role, quotes Genesis 1:11. In the aria Gabriel breaks into song over the beauty that has just been created.

Und Gott sprach:	*And God spoke:*
Es bringe die Erde Gras hervor,	*Let the earth bring forth grass,*
Kräuter, die Samen geben,	*herbs, which yiled seeds,*
und Obstbäume, die Früchte bringen	*and fruit trees, whose harvests yield*
ihrer Art gemäss,	*according to their species,*
die ihren Samen in sich selbst haben	*which have their seeds inside themselves*
auf der Erde,	*on the earth,*
und es ward so.	*and it was so.*
Nun beut die Flur das frische Grün	*Now the fresh green meadow*
dem Auge zur Ergötzung dar;	*which delights the eye;*
den anmuthsvollen Blick	*the charming appearance*
erhöht der Blumen sanfter Schmuck.	*is enhanced by flower's tender ornament.*
Hier duften Kräuter Balsam aus;	*Here the balsam herbs are fragrant;*
hier sprosst den Wunden Heil.	*here sprouts the healing plant.*
Der Zweige krümmt der goldnen Früchte Last;	*the branch bends with golden fruit's weight*
hier wölbt der Hain zum kühlen	*here arches the grove in cool*
Schirme sich; den steilen Berg	*protective cover; the steep mountain*
bekrönt ein dichter Wald.	*is crowned with a thick forest.*

Auf starkem Fittige *[On mighty pens]*

From Part II. Gabriel quotes Genesis 1:20 in the recitative. The aria is about the beauty and grace of birds in response to the verse of the recitative. "Pens," meaning wings, is a poetic reference to quill feathers of birds.

Und Gott sprach:	*And God spoke:*
Es bringe das Wasser	*Let the water bring forth*
in der Fülle hervor webende Geschöpfe,	*in abundance the moving creatures,*
die Leben haben, und Vögel,	*that have life, and birds,*
die über der Erde fliegen mögen	*which over the earth may fly*
in dem offenen Firmamente des Himmels.	*in the open firmament of the heavens.*
Auf starkem Fittige schwinget sich	*On strong wings soars*
der Adler stolz,	*the proud eagle,*
und teilet die Luft,	*and through the air,*
im schnellesten Fluge zu Sonne hin.	*in the swiftest flying up to the sun.*
Den Morgen grüsst der Lerche frohes Lied,	*The lark greets the morning with happy song,*
und Liebe, girrt das zarte Taubenpaar.	*and love, the tender pair of doves coo.*
Aus jedem Busch und Hain erschallt	*From every bush and grove resounds*
der Nachtigallen süsse Kehle,	*the nightingale's sweet fluting,*
noch drückte Gram nicht ihre Brust,	*no grief yet pressures his breast,*
noch war zur Klage nicht gestimmt	*still no lamentation tunes*
ihr reizender Gesang.	*his charming song.*

STABAT MATER
1767
text is traditional Latin from the Roman Catholic liturgy, a 13th century sequence attributed to the Franciscan Jacopone da Todi

Composed 1767, Eszterháza. No record of a performance exists from around that time, but the work was performed in the 1770s at Piaristenkirche in Vienna, conducted by the composer. Stabat Mater (literally translated as "mother standing") refers to Mary standing at the base of the cross. The text of the Stabat Mater is still used in the Roman Catholic Church for the Feast of the Seven Sorrows (September 15).

Quis non posset

Quis non posset contristari,	*Who would not be saddened,*
piam Matrem contemplari,	*contemplating Christ's mother,*
dolentem cum filio?	*sharing her Son's grief?*

Felix Mendelssohn
1809-1847

ELIJAH
(Elias)
Opus 70
1846
libretto by Julius Schubring, after I Kings 17-19, II Kings 2, and other biblical passages; English libretto by William Bartholomew

Composed summer of 1846. First performed August 26, 1846, at the Birmingham Festival, England. William Bartholomew was given the *Elijah* libretto in the middle of May, 1846, and was engaged to translate it into English for the August premiere, receiving sections as they were completed. Mendelssohn and Schubring had used Luther's translation of the Bible, interpolating and paraphrasing liberally. Bartholomew's task was not only to translate, but also to make the text agree with the King James Bible. He added the following disclaimer to the libretto of *Elijah*: "The author of this English version has endeavored to render it as nearly in accordance with the Scriptural Texts as the Music to which it is adapted will admit: the references are therefore to be considered rather as authorities than quotations."

The aria is presented in both English, the language of the premiere, and German, the working language of Mendelssohn's composition. It may be assumed that the composer intended for English speaking audiences to hear the piece in the vernacular.

Hear ye, Israel! (Höre, Israel)

The text for the aria, which opens Part II of the oratorio, is based on Isaiah 41:10, 48:1,18, 51:12-13, 53:1. Originally written for the voice of soprano Jenny Lind; expanded and reconstructed for performances in 1847.

Wolfgang Amadeus Mozart
1756-1791

MASS IN C MINOR
K. 427 (417a)
1783
text is the traditional Latin Mass from the Roman Catholic liturgy

The "Grand" (or "Great") Mass in C minor was first performed October 26, 1783 at St. Peter's Abbey, Salzburg. Left incomplete at the time of the premiere, Mozart perhaps filled in the missing sections with parts of earlier mass settings, or perhaps they were sung as chant in the performance. The composer never completed the work. There is no Agnus Dei. Only the "Et incarnatus est" exists of the Credo section. The Sanctus section is fragmentary.

Laudamus te

The edition of "Laudamus te" that appears in this volume may not be familiar to some. The Breitkopf & Härtel edition that was published in 1901, edited by Alois Schmitt, often reprinted (it is the G. Schirmer edition in use in the U.S.), contains an abridged version of the movement. The Schmitt edition was the only edition available for several decades. The edition in this anthology is based on the autograph full score. The role is for a second soprano, but may be sung by a mezzo-soprano. (This number has also been included in the alto volume of this anthology.)

Laudamus te	*We praise Thee,*
Benediciums te,	*we bless thee,*
Adoramus te,	*we adore Thee,*
Glorificamus te.	*we glorify Thee.*

VESPERAE SOLENNES DE CONFESSORE
(Solemn Vespers)
K. 339
1780
text is traditional Latin, from the Vulgate (the 4th century, authorized Roman Catholic Latin translation of the Bible), from the Roman Catholic liturgy

Composed 1780 for the Salzburg Cathedral, probably intended for a Festum Pallii (an important feast day), although there is no record of a performance there. Vespers is the seventh canonical office in the Roman Catholic liturgy, celebrated at sunset. Its principle elements are Psalms, the canticle Magnificat, and their antiphons. "Laudate Dominum" is the fifth section of this Vespers, based on Psalm 117 in the Vulgate (Psalm 118 in the Protestant Bible).

Laudate Dominum

Laudate Dominum omnes gentes,	*Praise the Lord all nations,*
laudate eum omnes populi	*praise Him all ye people*
Quoniam confirmata est supernos misericordia ejus,	*For his merciful kindness is great toward us,*
et veritas Domini manet in æternum.	*and the truth of the Lord endureth forever.*

Giovanni Battista Pergolesi
1710-1736

STABAT MATER
1736
text is traditional Latin from the Roman Catholic liturgy, a 13th century sequence attributed to the Franciscan Jacopone da Todi

First performed March 17, 1736, Naples. Traditionally believed to have been commissioned by the Confraternity of San Luigi di Palazzo, Naples, although there is evidence that shows Duke Marzio Domenico IV Carafa Maddaloni as the patron. Stabat Mater (literally translated as "mother standing") refers to Mary standing at the base of the cross. The text of the Stabat Mater is still used in the Roman Catholic Church for the Feast of the Seven Sorrows (September 15).

Cujus animam gementem

Cujus animam gementem,	*Whose soul laments*
contristantem et dolentem	*sorrowful and anguished*
pertransivit gladius.	*pierced by a sword.*

Vidit suum dulcem natum

Vidit suum dulcem natum	*[She] saw her sweet child*
moriendo desolatum,	*dying forsaken,*
dum emisit spiritum.	*until he sent forth his spirit.*

Henry Purcell
1659-1695

COME YE SONS OF ART
1694
libretto attributed to Nahum Tate (1652-1715)

A secular ode written for the birthday celebration of Queen Mary II, this is the sixth and final birthday ode by Purcell, first performed April 30, 1694. The piece is scored for flutes, oboes, trumpets, drums, strings, and continuo.

Bid the Virtues, bid the Graces

Gioachino Rossini
1792-1868

STABAT MATER
1832; 1842
text is traditional Latin from the Roman Catholic liturgy, a 13th century sequence attributed to the Franciscan Jacopone da Todi

First performed on Good Friday, 1833 at Cappella di San Filippo El Real, Madrid. Due to illness, Rossini requested that Giovanni Tadolini compose six of the twelve sections in order to complete the work for the premiere. In 1841 Rossini replaced the six Tadolini movements with new composition. The revised Stabat Mater was first performed January 7, 1842 at the Théâtre Italien, Paris. Stabat Mater (literally translated as "mother standing") refers to Mary standing at the base of the cross. The text of the Stabat Mater is still used in the Roman Catholic Church for the Feast of the Seven Sorrows (September 15).

Inflammatus et accensus

The aria prominently features the chorus.

Inflammatus et accensus
per te, Virgo, sim defensus
in die judicii.
Fac me cruce custodiri,
morte Christi præmuniri,
confoveri gratia.

Inflamed and in flames
through the Virgin I am defended
in the day of judgement.
May I by the cross be guarded
by the death of Christ made safe,
by Thy eternal grace.

Antonio Vivaldi
1669-1741

GLORIA
RV 589
text is the traditional Gloria section from the Latin Mass of the Roman Catholic liturgy

This is the second of two D major Glorias composed by Vivaldi. No exact chronology of Vivaldi's sacred works exists, but both Glorias are believed to have been written after 1708. The first modern performance of this Gloria took place in Siena, Italy, in 1939.

Domine Deus

Domine Deus,
Rex cœlestis,
Deus Pater omnipotens.

Lord God,
heavenly king,
God the Father Almighty.

Seufzer, Thränen, Kummer, Noth
(Sighing, Weeping, Sorrow, Need)
from
CANTATA No. 21

Johann Sebastian Bach

21

Schmerz;   Seuf - zer,   Thrä - nen,   Kum - mer,   Kum-mer,
pain;   *Sigh - ing,*   *weep - ing,*   *sor - row,*   *sor - row,*

23

Noth!
need.

[*mf*]

26

28

Mein gläubiges Herze
(My Heart Ever Faithful)
from
CANTATA No. 68

Johann Sebastian Bach

Mein gläu - bi - ges Her - ze, froh -
My heart ev - er faith - ful, sing

lok - ke, — sing', scher - ze,
prais - es, be joy - ful,

mein
My

24

gläu - bi - ges Her - ze, froh - lok - ke, _____ sing', scher - ze,
heart _____ ev - er faith - ful, sing prais - es, be joy - ful,

mein
My

gläu - bi - ges Her - ze, froh - lok - ke, _____ sing', scher - ze, froh -
heart _____ ev - er faith - ful, sing prais - es, be joy - ful, sing

gläu - bi - ges Her - ze, froh - lok - ke, ___ sing', scher - ze, froh -
heart ___ *ev - er faith - ful, sing prais - es, be joy - ful, sing*

lok - ke, ___ sing', scher - ze, dein Je - sus ___ ist nah!
prais - es, be joy - ful, thy Je - sus is near!

Quia respexit
from
MAGNIFICAT

Johann Sebastian Bach

*Small size notes are to be played in the absence of an oboe.

*Only play the lower third with the oboe, omit with piano alone.

Quia respexit
from
MAGNIFICAT

Johann Sebastian Bach

*The part was originally written for oboe d'amore.

The part may be carefully cut from the book.

Zerfliesse, mein Herze
(My Heart Breaks in Anguish)
from
PASSIO SECUNDUM JOANNEM
(St. John Passion)

Johann Sebastian Bach

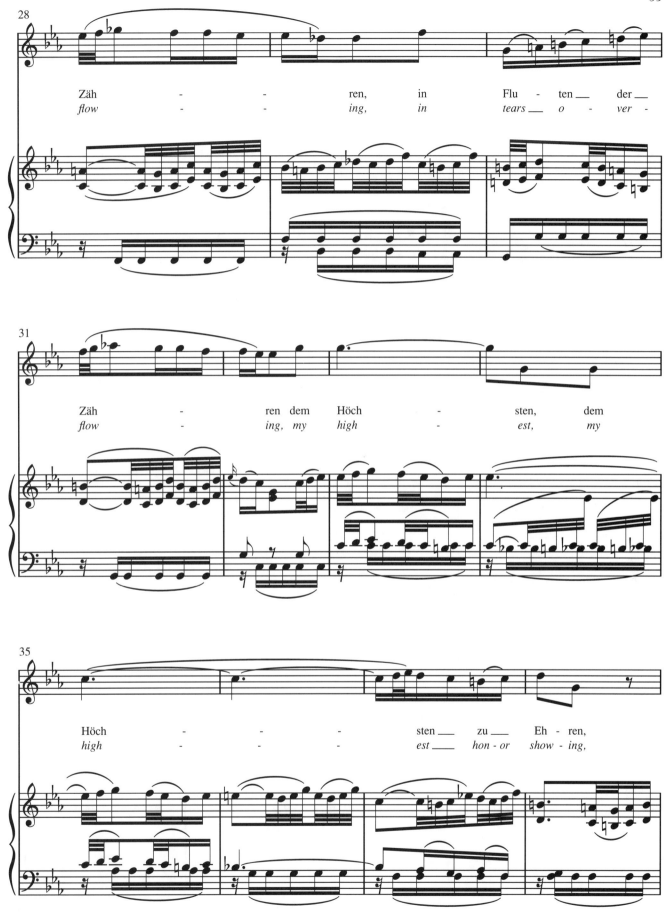

Er - zäh - le ___ der Welt und dem
Through Heav - en ___ and earth let the

Him - mel ___ die ___ Not, er - zäh - le ___ der
ti - dings ___ be ___ spread, er through Heav - en ___ and

Welt und dem Him - mel ___ die ___ Not: Dein Je - sus,
earth let the ti - dings ___ be ___ spread: Thy Je - sus,

dein Je - sus ___ ist ___ tot, ___
thy Je - sus ___ is ___ dead, ___

(L.H.)

dein Je - sus, dein Je - sus ___ ist ___ tot,
thy Je - sus, thy Je - sus ___ is ___ dead,

dein   Je - sus ____ ist ____ tot,   tot,
thy   Je - sus ____ is ____ dead,   dead,

tot, _____   dein Je - sus   ist   tot, _____
dead, _____   thy   Je - sus   is   dead, _____

tot, _____   dein _____ Je - sus ist ___ tot!
dead, ____   thy _____ Je - sus is ___ dead!

Zer - flies - se, __ mein Her - ze, in Flu - ten __ der __
My heart __ breaks __ in an - guish, in tears __ o - ver -

Zäh - ren, zer -
flow - ing, my

115

- sten ___ zu ___ Eh - ren;
- est ___ hon - or show - ing;

zer -
my

119

flies - se, ___ mein ___ Her - ze, ___ in ___ Flu - ten ___ der ___ Zäh - ren dem ___
heart ___ breaks ___ in ___ an - guish, ___ in ___ tears ___ o - ver - flow - ing, ___ my ___

123

*

Höch-sten zu ___ Eh - ren!
high - est hon-or show - ing!

*appoggiatura recommended

Ich folge dir gleichfalls
(I Follow Thee Also)
from
PASSIO SECUNDUM JOANNEM
(St. John Passion)

Johann Sebastian Bach

The part may be carefully cut from the book.

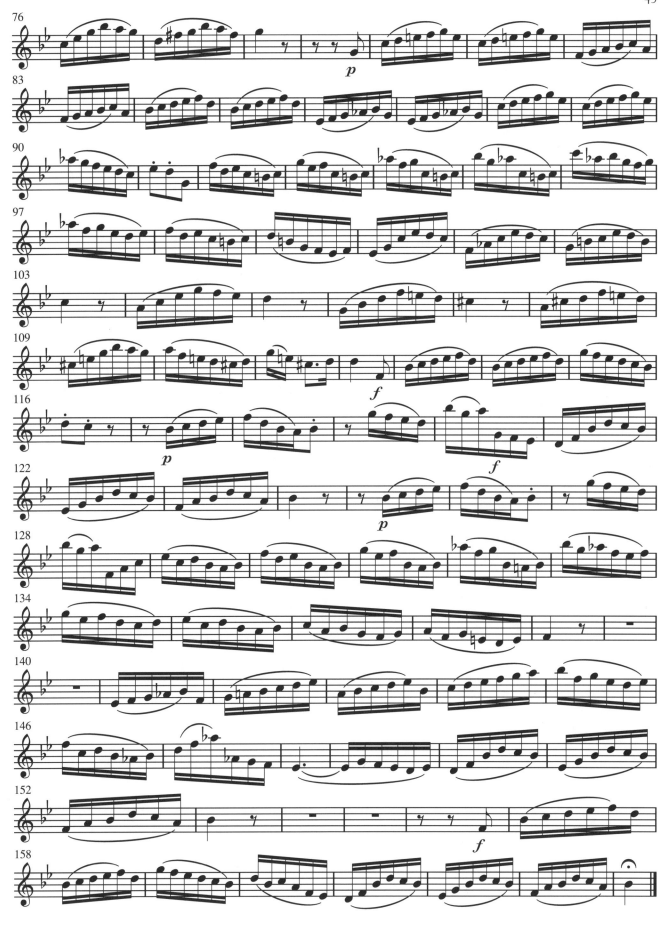

Ich folge dir gleichfalls
(I Follow Thee Also)
from
PASSIO SECUNDUM JOANNEM
(St. John Passion)

Johann Sebastian Bach

*Small size notes are to be played in the absence of a flute.

24

ich fol - ge _ dir _ gleich-falls mit freu - di - gen _ Schrit-ten und las - se _ dich
I fol - low _ Thee _ al - so with joy _ in _ my _ foot - steps, and leave not _ Thy

30

nicht, mein Le - ben, _ mein Licht, und las - se _ dich nicht, _ mein Le - ben, _ mein
sight, my life and _ my light, and leave not _ Thy sight, _ my life and _ my

36

Licht, und las - se dich nicht, mein _ Le - ben, _ mein _ Licht.
light, and leave not Thy sight, my _ life _____ and _ my _ light.

f

42

gleich-falls mit freu - di - gen _ Schrit - ten,
al - so with joy _ in _ my _ foot - steps,

ich fol - ge _ dir _ gleich-falls mit freu - di - gen Schrit - ten und las - se _ dich
I fol - low _ Thee _ al - so with joy _ in _ my _ foot - steps, and leave not _ Thy

nicht, mein Le - ben, _ mein Licht, ich fol -
sight, my life and _ my light, I fol -

- - ge dir gleich-falls mit freu - di - gen _ Schrit - ten und
low _ Thee al - so with joy _ in _ my _ foot - steps, and

Blute nur, du liebes Herz

(Bleed and Break, Thou Loving Heart)
from
PASSIO SECUNDUM MATTHÆUM
(St. Matthew Passion)

Johann Sebastian Bach

blu - te nur, du lie - bes Herz, blu - te nur, du lie - bes Herz, blu - te nur, du lie - bes
bleed _ and break, thou lov - ing heart, bleed _ and break, thou lov - ing heart, bleed _ and break, thou lov - ing

Herz, blu - te nur, du lie - bes Herz, _____ blu - te nur, du lie - bes
heart, bleed _ and break, thou lov - ing heart, _____ bleed _ and break, thou lov - ing

Herz, blu - te nur, du lie - bes Herz!
heart, bleed _ and break, thou lov - ing heart!

56

*Fermatas on Fine

Da Capo al Fine

Ich will dir mein Herze schenken

(Lord, to Thee My Heart is Given)

from

PASSIO SECUNDUM MATTHÆUM

(St. Matthew Passion)

Recit.

Johann Sebastian Bach

*appaggiatura possible

*appoggiatura possible

Aria

[Andante]

Ich will dir mein Her - ze schen - ken, sen - ke _ dich, sen en -
Lord, to thee my heart __ is giv - en, en - ter _ Thou, en -

- ke _ dich, sen - ke dich, _ mein _____ Heil, _ hin - ein,
- ter _ Thou, en - ter Thou _ and _____ dwell _ in _ me,

13

ich ___ will dir mein ___ Her - ze schen - ken, ___ sen - ke _ dich, ___
Lord, ___ to thee my ___ heart ___ is giv - en, ___ en - ter Thou

16

___mein Heil, _ hin - ein, ich will dir mein Her - ze, _ mein _ Her - ze schen -
___and dwell _ in _ me, to Thee is my heart, ____ my _ heart ___ is giv -

19

- - - - ken, sen - ke dich, _ mein _
- - - - en, en - ter Thou, _ and ___

22

_ Heil hin - ein, ___ sen - ke _ dich, _ mein Heil, _ hin - ein!
_ dwell in me, ___ en - ter _ Thou, _ and dwell _ in ___ me.

62

*Fermatas on Fine

Da capo al fine

Nur ein Wink von seinem Händen

(Naught Against the Pow'r)

from

WEINACHTS-ORATORIUM

(The Christmas Oratorio)

Johann Sebastian Bach

*appoggiatura recommended

List, des Höch-sten Sohn, den du zu stür-zen suchst, sehr wohl be-kannt.
craft, its trai-t'rous part Be-fore the Lord thou seek'st to kill dis-plays.

Aria

Largo

simile

*appoggiatura recommended

al - le Kraft _ ver - lacht!
all our might _ a - vail.

müs - sen_ sich_ so - fort, so - fort, so - fort, so - fort
once___ His_ haught-y foes, at once, at once, at once,

Sterb - li - cher_____ Ge - dan - ken_ wen - den;
Them no_ pride_____ from ru - in_ shield - eth.

70

fort, ___ Sterb - li - cher _ Ge - dan - ken _ wen - den.
foes; ___ Them ___ no _ pride _ from ru - in _ shield - eth.

Preist der Erlösers Güte

from

CHRISTUS AM ÖLBERGE

Ludwig van Beethoven

*appoggiatura possible

29

Preist, preist des Er - lö - sers___ Gü - te, preist,___ Men - schen,___
Praise, praise the Re - deem - er's___ good-ness. All on earth, pro -

35

sei - ne___ Huld! Er stirbt für euch aus Lie - be, für euch aus
claim His___ grace! He dies in lov-ing kind-ness, in lov - ing

41

Lie - be, sein___ Blut, sein___ Blut tilgt eu - re___ Schuld. Preist,
kind-ness to ___ save, to ___ save our sin - ful___ race,___ praise,

47

Allegro

Men - schen,___ preist _____ sei - ne Huld!
all on earth___ praise, _____ praise ____ His name!

69

Heil euch, ihr_____ Er - lö - sten, euch win - ket,
tri - umph, all_____ ye ran - somed, *O tri - umph,*

73

euch win - ket Se - lig - keit, euch
ye shall to bliss at - tain, *ye*

cresc. *tr*
ff *sf* *p*

77

win - ket Se - lig - keit, wenn ihr ge - treu_____ in__ Lie - be, in
shall to bliss at - tain, if ye in love_____ un - fail - ing, in

cresc. *p*

82

Glaub' und Hoff - nung__ seid, ge - treu__ in__ Lie - - -
*faith and hope re - main, ev - er in__ love,*_____

tr
fz *cresc.* *p*

- be, in Glaub' ___ und ___ Hoff - nung seid,
in faith ___ and ___ hope re - main,

wenn ihr ge - treu in ___ Lie - be,
If ye in ___ love un - fail - ing,

in ___ Lie - be, in Glaub' und ___ Hoff - nung ___ seid.
in ___ love and ___ faith and ___ hope re - main.

Doch weh!
But woe

Pie Jesu
from
REQUIEM

Gabriel Fauré

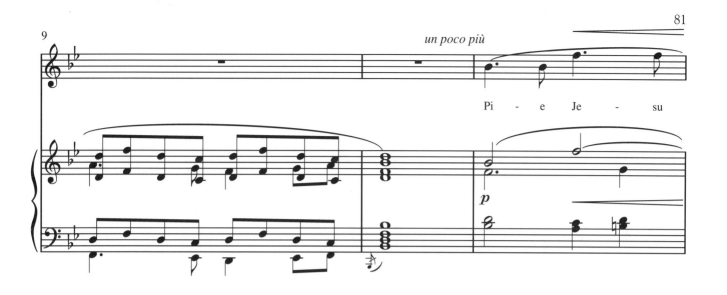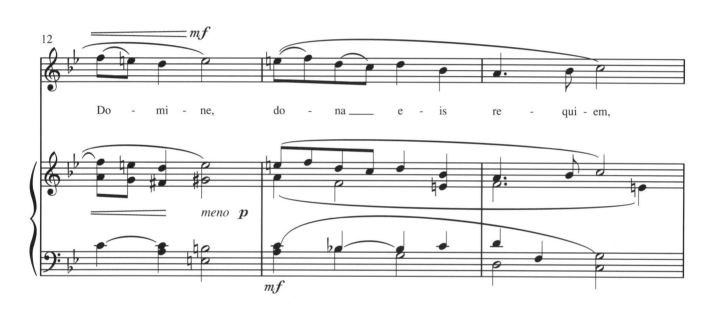

Do - mi - ne do - na___ e - is do - na___ e - is

sem - pi - ter - nam re - qui - em,

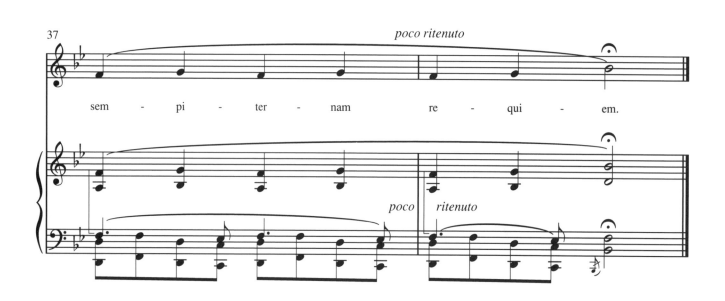

poco ritenuto

sem - pi - ter - nam re - qui - em.

poco ritenuto

Oh! had I Jubal's lyre

from
JOSHUA

George Frideric Handel

27

in songs ___ like hers ___ re-joice.

31

Oh! had I Ju-bal's lyre, or

34

Mi - riam's _ tune-ful _ voice, oh! had I Ju-bal's lyre, or Mi - riam's _ tune-ful _ voice! To

37

sounds like _ his I would ___ as-pire, In songs like _ hers, in songs like _ hers re-

hum - ble _ strains but faint - ly _ show, How _ much _ to _ heav'n _ and _ thee _ I owe, how _

much to heav'n and _ thee I owe.

Tune the soft melodious lute
from
JEPHTHA

George Frideric Handel

92

O liberty, thou choicest treasure

from
JUDAS MACCABAEUS

George Frideric Handel

Recit.

ISRAELITE WOMAN:

To Heav'n's al-might-y King we kneel, For bless-ings on this ex-em-pla-ry zeal. Bless him, Je-ho-vah, bless him and once more __ To Thy own Is-ra-el lib-er-ty re-store. __

Aria

Largo sostenuto

I know that my Redeemer liveth

from
MESSIAH

George Frideric Handel

*appoggiatura possible

98

**Though not found in historical sources, often sung in this manner.

upon the earth, I know that my Redeemer liveth, and that He shall stand at the latter day upon the earth, upon the earth.

**ossia: and He shall stand at the

ris - en   from ___ the   dead, ___   the

Adagio   **Tempo I**

first _____ fruits   of   them ___   that   sleep.

Rejoice greatly, O daughter of Zion

from
MESSIAH

George Frideric Handel

Zi - on! re - joice, _____ re - joice, _____

_____ re - joice! _____

_____ O

daugh-ter of Zi-on! Re - joice _____ great-ly, shout, O daugh-ter of Je-ru-sa-lem:

*Simplified in some editions to:

be - hold, _ thy _ King _ com-eth un - to _ thee, _ com-eth un-to thee;

Sav - iour, and he shall speak, he shall speak peace,

peace, _____ he shall speak peace _____ un - to the

hea - then.

Re-joice, re - joice, re-joice _____ great-ly,

If God be for us

from
MESSIAH

George Frideric Handel

*The original underlay of words

died, yea ra - ther, that is ris - en a - gain,

who is at the right hand of __ God, who

makes in - ter - ces - sion for us, who makes in - ter - ces - sion for us, in - ter -

ces - sion for us, who makes in - ter - ces - -

God, _ who makes in - ter - ces - sion for us.

Let the bright Seraphim

from
SAMSON

George Frideric Handel

AN ISRAELITE WOMAN:

Let the bright Se - ra-phim in burn - ing row, their

*Play the small size notes in the absence of a trumpet.

tune - ful choirs, touch their im - mor - tal harps _____ with gold - en wires,

let the Che - ru - bic host, in _____ tune - - ful choirs, touch

their im - mor - tal harps, touch their im - mor - tal harps _____

Da Capo al Fine

Let the bright Seraphim
from
SAMSON

George Frideric Handel

Welche Labung für die Sinne

(O how pleasing to the senses)

from

DIE JAHRESZEITEN

(The Seasons)

Franz Joseph Haydn

33
wei - chen Moo - se   rie - selt da
dow - ny moss the   purl - ing brook
in   hel - ler Flut der
Its   li - quid sil - ver

p

37
Bach,
rolls,

pp

39
und fröh-lich
And' neath the

41
sum - mend irrt und wirrt
shade, with sooth-ing hum,
die bun - te Son - nen - brut.
The sport-ive in - sects play.

pp

45

Der Kräu - ter rei - nen Bal - sam - duft
The balm - y scent of fra-grant herbs

p

50

ver - brei - tet Ze-phirs Hauch,
On ze - phyr's wing is borne,

p *pp*

54

und aus dem na - hen Bu - sche
and from the ev'n - ing bow'r is

58

tönt des jun-gen Schä - fers Rohr.
heard The shep-herd's tune - ful lay.

p *rall.* *f*

Aria

Und neu - e Kraft er - hebt durch
O'er na - ture bears the soul On

mil - den Drang, durch mil - den Drang die Brust und
sweet, on sweet, on sweet en - chant - ed wing; O'er

neu
na

Nun beut die Flur
(With Verdure Clad)
from
DIE SCHÖPFUNG
(The Creation)

Franz Joseph Haydn

Aria

Andante

Nun
With

beut — die Flur das fri - sche Grün dem Au - ge - zur — Er - göt - zung dar; — den an - muts-
ver - dure clad the fields ap - pear, De - light - ful to — the ra - vish'd sense; — By flow - ers

vol - len — Blick er - höht — der Blu - men sanf - ter Schmuck er -
sweet — and — gay En - han - ced is — the charm - ing sight, En -

höht _____ der Blu - men sanf - ter Schmuck.
han - ced — is — the charm - ing sight.

34

hier sprosst — den Wun — den Heil.
Here shoots — the heal - ing plant.

37

Die Zwei - ge krümmt der
With co - pious fruit th'ex -

40

gold — nen — Früch - te Last;
pand - ed — boughs — are hung;

hier
In

43

wölbt — der Hain zum küh - len Schir - me sich;
leaf - y arch - es twine the — sha - dy groves;

den stei - len Berg be -
O'er lof - ty hills ma -

Auf starkem Fittige
(On Mighty Pens)
from
DIE SCHÖPFUNG
(The Creation)

Franz Joseph Haydn

Aria

Moderato

Son - ne hin, zur _ Son - ne hin.
blaz - ing sun, to the blaz - ing sun.

Den
His

Mor - gen grüsst der Ler - che fro - hes Lied, den
wel - come bids to morn the mer - ry lark, *His*

Mor - gen grüsst der Ler - che fro - hes Lied, und
wel - come bids to morn the mer - ry lark; *and*

Aus je - dem Busch _____ und Hain er - schallt der Nach - ti -
From ev' - ry bush _____ and grove re - sound the night - in -

gal - len süs - se Keh - le,
gale's de - light - ful notes;

pp

fz   fz

156

135

Quis non posset
from
STABAT MATER

Franz Joseph Haydn

- tem _ cum _ fi - li - o?

Quis non pos - set con - tri - sta - ri,

pi - am Ma - trem con - tem - pla - ri,

quis non __ pos - set con - tri - sta - ri,

166

do - len - tem cum fi - li - o?

Hear ye, Israel!
from
ELIJAH

Felix Mendelssohn

the Lord, will strength-en thee, for
- che nicht, ich stär - ke dich, ich

I, thy God, _____ will strength-en thee. Say, who art thou?
bin dein Gott, _____ ich stär - ke dich! Wer bist du denn?

Say, who art thou, that thou art a - fraid of a man that shall
wer bist du denn, dass du dich vor Men - schen fürch-test, die doch

Laudamus te
from
MASS IN C MINOR

Wolfgang Amadeus Mozart

ra - mus te.

Glo - ri - fi - ca - - - - - - - -

- - - - mus te, glo -

ri - fi - ca - - - -

- - - - mus te.

Laudate Dominum
from
VESPERAE SOLENNES DE CONFESSORE

Wolfgang Amadeus Mozart

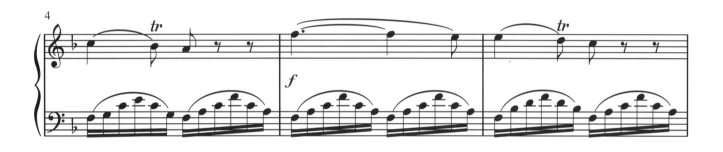

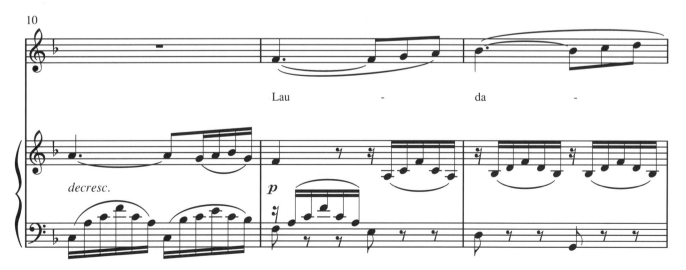

Lau - da -

*The chorus strophe has been abridged for this solo version.

Bid the Virtues, bid the Graces
from
COME YE SONS OF ART

Henry Purcell

Bid the Vir - tues, bid the Gra - - ces,

bid the Grac-es to the sa - - - -

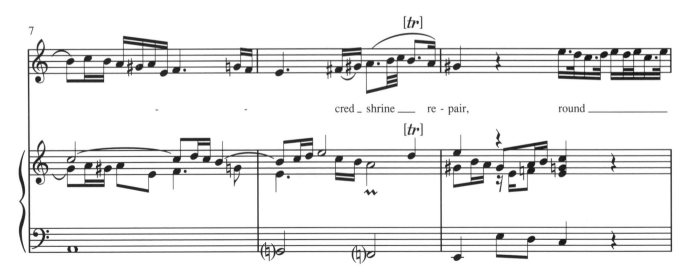

- - cred _ shrine _ re - pair, round _____

the al - tar take, _____ take _____ their pla - ces, round _____ the al - tar take, _____ take _____ their pla - ces, bless-ing with re - turns _____ of pray'r, bless-ing with re - turns _____ of pray'r their great _____ de - fend - er's

194

Cujus animam gementem
from
STABAT MATER

Giovanni Battista Pergolesi

Vidit suum dulcem natum
from
STABAT MATER

Giovanni Battista Pergolesi

en - do de - so - la - tum, dum e - mi - sit spi -

- ri - tum.

Vi - dit su - um dul - cem na - tum mo - ri - en - do

de - so - la - tum, de - so - la - tum, dum e - mi - sit spi - ri -

tum; vi - dit su - um dul - cem na - tem mo - ri - en - do de - so -

la __ tum, de - so - la - tum, dum e - mi - sit,

dum e - mi - sit spi - ri - tum.

f *dolce* *pp sempre*

Inflammatus et accensus
from
STABAT MATER

Gioachino Rossini

fen - sus in di - e ju -

di - - - - - - - ci -

i.

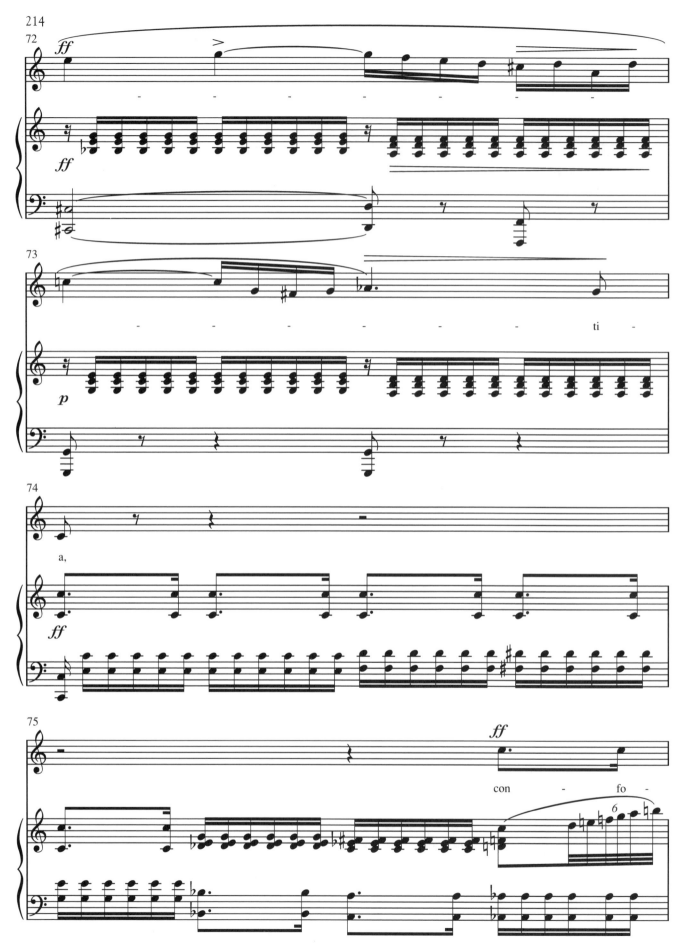

Optional cut to M. 80

*Measures 76-79 may be effectively cut in a solo presentation of this movement.

216

Domine Deus
from
GLORIA

Antonio Vivaldi

*The small notes in the keyboard part are to be played in the absence of a violin or oboe solo.

ter, Pa -

ter __ om-ni - po-tens.

Domine Deus

from
GLORIA

Antonio Vivaldi

The part may be carefully cut from the book.